3-00

no time to grow

By the same author
BROKEN BLOOD: THE RISE AND FALL OF THE TENNANT FAMILY

no time to grow

A SHATTERED CHILDHOOD

SIMON BLOW

JOHN MURRAY
Albemarle Street, London

Typeset in 11.5 pt Bembo by Servis Filmsetting Ltd, Manchester

Printed and bound in Great Britain by
The University Press, Cambridge

I dedicate these pages to all 'hurt' people who have fought to rise above it. Also I dedicate them to all who have shown me love from the moment when clouds first darkened my child's day. I hope, too, that there may be found here a warning for the indifferent and the callous. And finally, for my brother David who was often with me.

1

It's Saturday morning so Daddy won't be going into town today to do business. In fact it's ten o'clock and he's still wrapped up in his bath towel. We're all having breakfast in the kitchen with Daddy sitting at one end of the table, and Mummy at the other.

Once breakfast's over but before he's finished his coffee, Daddy goes to a cupboard in the kitchen dresser. Mummy's face looks fairly pained as she sees him do it; she knows it's wiser to say nothing. The cupboard door makes a ping when he opens it. Ping, and then ping again as he shuts it. Then to the cupboard where the glasses are, and another ping. He pours some liquid from a green bottle and mixes it in the glass with a Schweppes tonic and knocks it back fast. I might have wondered if it was medicine, but somehow I never have. I've always known what it was.

'Why don't you go upstairs,' Mummy says, 'and play with your animals.'

So I go upstairs because I know my mother does not want me to see. In bed I clutch Fuzziepeg hard against my stomach as if his fur against my skin will quieten this churning. When you're small – I mean a child – you like to know what's likely to happen next. If you're going to go for a walk, say, then have lunch, followed by an afternoon rest. Now that's not something I ever know at home. Because when my father takes the green bottle from the cupboard shelf I can be sure the day won't have that calm which stops the churning and the tight clutching of Fuzziepeg.

Who is Fuzziepeg? He's my koala bear and every night he sleeps in my arms. He's my security, too, and although he's only a stuffed animal I make him talk to me and hug me otherwise I'm hopelessly exposed to the noise that's coming from downstairs. After three of his mixtures my father usually starts to raise his voice, telling us all that he knows best and that he's going to make us all this money if my mother will just stop interfering.

'How dare you! How dare you!' he shouts. 'I'll never be a smalltimer.' He's always throwing out this word as if we're trying to turn him into a lower form of life – like the ants and the worms that I find in the garden. And he doesn't listen to my mother soothing him but imagines that everybody is out to put him down. Of course it's the mixture exciting him and I have to tell myself that he isn't really like this – that he really is my father with that tenderness that I believe a father can have. But I don't see this ideal Daddy very much, although I have constructed an image of what he could be like.

I know there's hitting now because I can hear noise – the noise of things flying. It's a pity this Saturday has to be so horrid because Michael is coming to see me this afternoon. I don't want my friends to know what is happening; I want them to share this image that I've made of how my home life ought to be. For a long time now, I've lived in two places – the real and the imagined. The stomach-churning only stops when I dream. But it's difficult to put across dreams to others.

My mother is so patient when my father's like this. But I worry that he might hurt her. And I worry more being upstairs and not able to see what he is doing. He has hurt her quite a lot in the past. Once he emptied a hot-water bottle on her and she couldn't go out of the house for three weeks. Now I can hear the shouting and his pacing: he always paces, going backwards

and forwards and drawing hard on a cigarette. I am frightened –
there's no use pretending I'm not, and I am going downstairs
because . . . well, what if he killed Mummy?

My father's pacing and turning and pacing like an animal
trapped. His eyes shoot everywhere, but rest nowhere. The scene
has erupted out of nothing, as these scenes will, and now my
father's carrying on some kind of argument as if we're all against
him. But nobody is; it's just the green bottle stuff has tripped off
a bit of his brain that can't handle reason.

Suddenly he's giving my mother this whack across the face,
which sends her sideways. Whack! and then Whack! again.

'Don't ever tell me what to do!' he shouts, leaning over my
mother, who's fallen across a chair.

'Where's your control? Not in front of Simon, please,' she says,
her beautiful face twisted upwards and discoloured from the
whack.

Then it's more pacing and more arguing. My father does this
repeated pacing when rage and drink are inside him. I'm standing at the door watching. He goes past me as if I'm not there.
He goes half-way down the hall, then swings back on the polished wooden floor. He's back in our sitting-room again. There's
a lot of light in this room which comes from the french
windows. But the bright garden light doesn't lighten anything
just now because I'm cowed by this fierce look on my father's
face. He puts one lip over the other, and the eyes glare as if
murder's on his mind.

My mother's pulled herself up but he's going over to set on
her again.

Bang! he goes with his fist now and he's knocked my mother
off her feet. She falls against the wall and a table rattles and as she
hits the wall with a thud a mirror crashes to the ground. I've got
this retching now. I'm sick without being sick. It can't be normal
what he's doing, I know it isn't normal, otherwise I wouldn't
have this shaking inside.

'Go away. Go away, at once!' my father shouts at me.

'You're killing my mother,' I say. 'Why do you want to kill my mother?' And in spite of the inside shaking, I say this quite calmly, like I might say 'Can I have a Kit-Kat?'

This is not breaking down. You learn it early when home is really bad. The breaking happens inside.

'It's all right, darling,' my mother says. But I can see that it isn't because she's got this huge swollen bulge coming up on her arm. There's a line of red across her face, and I always remember that line; it's as though she'd been scratched by barbed wire, but of course it's been done by his hand.

She doesn't cry. She's starting to pick up the bits of broken glass. My father's out of the room again. He's standing in the hall looking as if he doesn't know why he's there or what he's been doing. He's wearing a white shirt and corduroy trousers, which means he's after his cigarettes. Usually they're in his jacket pocket, but not on Saturdays because he's at home. I watch him grappling for one out of the packet of one hundred that's open on the hall table. I don't want to look at him any more. How can I look at him when he's done this to my mother? I go into the sitting-room and help my mother with the bits of glass. 'Why don't you go upstairs,' she says. 'I didn't want you to see this.'

'No, I want to stay with you.'

I follow her through to the kitchen. I see my father standing in the same place in the hall drawing hard on a cigarette. My mother says nothing because she knows that whatever she says he will take as another attack. I don't understand my father, and that's frightening.

Eventually she sits down at our big scrubbed kitchen table. I sit there, too, my legs twitching, moving under the chair.

'We've got to make him quiet again,' my mother says.

I'm thinking what a waste of this lovely day when I could have taken my boat to the pond at Kew Gardens and let the light wind ripple her over the water. But there's no time for dreaming about what isn't going to happen because at the moment all that matters is that we get my father to calm down and relax.

I have these blinding flashes that I'm outdoors in the sunlight holding my mother's hand and that David, my brother, is walking beside us reciting a poem. He's already at his prep school and they're making him learn a lot of heroic verse. There's a story about an English ship fighting the Spanish and my brother's quite carried away with it. It's full of lines like, 'We be all good English men./ Let us bang those dogs of Seville, the children of the devil.' It's a story that really exalts the English because one English ship takes on fifty-three Spanish ships. I suppose the whole point of the poem is to make you stand up well to adversity. It gets more and more tragic as it goes on because finally the little *Revenge,* having sunk single-handed half the Spanish fleet, has to surrender to the 'mountain-like San Philip . . . of fifteen hundred tons,/ And up-shadowing high above us with her yawning tiers of guns . . .' My mother is really impressed as my brother goes on, both of them almost getting tearful with heroism as he comes to those lines:

'I have fought for Queen and Faith like a valiant man and
    true;
I have only done my duty as a man is bound to do:
With a joyful spirit I Sir Richard Grenville die!'
And he fell upon her decks and he died.

At his prep school my brother's being turned into this resilient English boy so that if another war happens they'll all stand – tough as Winston Churchill – at the ready.

Then the flashes end and I'm in the kitchen again and my father's come in and gone to the cupboard where the green bottle mixture is. Nobody speaks, just silence, silence, then the squelching sound of my father swallowing.

Now he's at the kitchen drawer where the knives and things are kept. He takes out a knife and my mother, sitting bolt upright at the end of the table, stares at him.

'I wouldn't, Purcell, I wouldn't.'

But he's got his one-lip-over-the-other act on, and the knife races through the air at my mother. She ducks, he misses. But she needn't have ducked because the knife was yards out anyway. The miss makes nothing better. Daddy's mad, I say to myself, except I don't know anything about madness. I keep sitting there, watching, with the inside shaking going on, my hands tight over the sides of the chair. Nobody says a word.

Now my mother gets up from the table, leaves the room, and I hear her crossing the hall and going upstairs. And my father's looking at me now but not responding to my being there. It's that look which says 'I don't know any more what's happening'. I jump from my chair and, not looking behind me, run from the kitchen, glancing at the knife that lies, like a killed bird, on the floor.

'Your father overworks,' Mummy says to me upstairs, and she's saying this because she wants to protect him and to protect me too. She begs me to forget what I've seen and says, 'I think the war still affects him sometimes.' She talks about 'shell-shock', but I don't understand. I know she can't accept yet that Daddy's not quite right. I don't think I do either because it's too terrible a thought to have to live with.

I can hear my father coming unsteadily up the stairs. I've seen him doing this – swinging from one side of the staircase to the other like a man clinging to the deck of a lurching boat. But now I can hear him reach the landing and cross to my parents' bedroom. There's a thud as he hits the bed while I lie here in silence with my mother, silent too and sitting on my bed, like those who wait for a thunderstorm to pass. It's over when we hear his drawn-out funnelled snores: it's then we know my father has struck oblivion.

My mother's sitting with me on my bed and the whole house has gone hushed suddenly. I've got Fuzziepeg held hard against my stomach and my mother says I must stay in bed and rest for a while. She seems to have pulled herself around from my father's awfulness, although her eyes are brimful of water. I wonder if she will cry.

★

I'm wondering all the time why things aren't as they should be. Why isn't our life like this hamper of put-away clothes in the attic? Yesterday, when the house was silent, I climbed up to the attic and pulled the hamper open. So many dresses made of so many expensive materials are packed inside it. These are Mummy's clothes – I guessed that quickly – but she never puts them on. I shook several of the dresses open and held them up and I had this vision of how life must have been for her once.

'Mummy, what did you do with all those clothes?' I said to her today. She laughed and held my head against her waist and said, 'That's all so long ago, darling.'

I wonder if she's missing those dresses put away in the hamper. I want to ask more about them because I've got this idea that once she floated across ballrooms in them. And there must have been men in tail coats and white ties who floated with her. The trouble is she hardly goes out now, and she's really pretty. Dark hair, and that face you see on films and go, wow just look at that! If you could see her now, as I can see her, you'd understand.

Already I'm in love with this world she left behind. I keep arranging and rearranging it in my mind. I've made it my escape from the days – the nearly-every-days here. I'm in houses where nothing crashes and there's no hitting and a band plays songs I've heard my mother singing. There's one called 'Blue Moon' that I hum myself to sleep on. Or sometimes I switch in mid-hum to 'Night and Day' – that's another – and then slip back to 'Blue Moon'. She'll sway a little as she sings, imitating the singer, and as if she's got all this choice again. At least that's what I see, but I suppose it's all tied up in dreams, like my humming.

Why did my mother marry my father?

She was born Diana Bethell, the only daughter of a foxhunt-ing landowner who had ten thousand acres of good East Yorkshire land. Adrian Bethell, her father, didn't farm this land – his tenants did, while he lived off the income. The Bethells had settled at their seat, Rise Park, in the late sixteenth century. They had moved north from Herefordshire, bought land, and continued to buy, until in the nineteenth century it stood at nearly fourteen thousand acres. The Bethells were solid and, in the tradition of landed families, intermarried with other Yorkshire grandees. Adrian Bethell's mother – Marie-Myrtle – was a Willoughby, and a daughter of the immensely land-rich Lord Middleton.

'Marry land,' Adrian Bethell told his daughter, my mother. 'You must marry land. I can't provide for you.'

'I must marry for love,' said my mother. She was thinking of all the fairy stories she had read, in her bedroom at Rise, getting up from time to time to look from her window at the park filled with deer, silhouetted by a moon.

Adrian Bethell worried because a daughter has no inheritance rights. Although my mother was his firstborn, she must come after her three brothers by his second marriage. He could leave her only a silly amount – a few thousand pounds by comparison with all that he had. So, as a débutante, my mother went on to the society marriage market. The magazines snapped her up, putting her on their covers with headlines like 'Hunting beauty and chic' or introducing her as 'one of the prettiest girls in society'.

'It's Lord Granard for Miss Diana,' announced the butler at Rise Park. Sitting opposite Diana on the sofa, Adrian Bethell put down his Racing Calendar and waited. 'Well?' he said to Diana as she re-entered the room. 'I've put him off,' Diana said. 'He's getting too keen.'

Adrian Bethell's face fell. He fingered the white carnation in his buttonhole. 'You're going to starve if you don't marry properly,' he said.

Diana did the rounds of the country houses, dances and race meetings. There was only one attachment for her among myriad admirers: Valerian Wellesley – a blond, blue-eyed undergraduate and soldier and a descendant of the Iron Duke, though at the time not an heir, simply the nephew of the then Duke and inheritor.

But suddenly the attachment ended and the blue-eyed, blond-haired Wellesley was a stranger again. Diana rejected all further suitors until she met my father, Richard Purcell Blow.

My father had grown up in a house high on romance, a mansion dramatically perched on the edge of the Cotswold escarpment in Gloucestershire, where the winds echoed and storms could play. It had been built by his father, the architect Detmar Blow, as a country house but full of fantasy, with bold projecting bays and mullioned windows, like the ruin of a great house. Below was nothing but the misty spread of the Severn Valley until, in the far distance, you glimpsed the Malvern Hills.

'What do you want to be when you grow up?' a family friend had asked my father when he was nine.

'An architect,' he replied simply.

But his mother had decided that, after Stowe and Trinity College Cambridge, her artistic son was to shine in the drawing-rooms. She wanted him to have social recognition, and to double this with that wonderful career he so wanted.

So my father learnt extravagance. The ground had already been laid at Trinity, where he had bought horses he could not afford and mixed with a sporting élite whose means were far greater than his. His mother pushed him out there to be star but gave him a pittance of an allowance, when she could have given more. Winifred Blow was a dominating, imperious woman and she confused my father.

'You cad. You utter cad,' she said, as she stood in a voluminous nightdress at the top of the stone stairs at Carlos Place, the family home in town. Coming up them was her eldest son – my father – swinging from one side to the other in an excess of alcohol and high spirits, white tie askew and his knees knocking with fatigue. It was a quarter to four in the morning.

Winifred thought she was exerting discipline, but by pushing Purcell on to the social map she had only encouraged his *folie de grandeur.* From then on, my father never did anything in small measures.

'I've found it,' Diana said to her father, after meeting Purcell Blow.

'What?'

'Love,' she said. 'I've found it.'

'But the Blows haven't any land. Nine hundred acres – that's not nearly enough. You're going to starve.'

'I can't,' Diana insisted. 'He loves me.'

So there was marriage and after that, immediately, the war. For three years Richard Purcell Blow was in the desert. For his regiment there was almost no action. The days and weeks went slowly; party-going and drinking became *de rigueur.* Meanwhile, Diana waited for him in England, a baby in her arms, living with her father's sister, Aunt Phyllie.

Soon there was only Aunt Phyllie, because in 1941, at the age of fifty, Diana's father died. A sudden outbreak of cancer in the lung through wounds sustained in the First World War had killed him. The happy hunting squire would hunt no more. Diana followed the coffin through the park at Rise, her half-brothers at her side. But there was no mother there for her. Diana hardly knew her mother. She remained a mystery and a painful loss to her. All she had was a frozen-faced stepmother, Cicely, whose attentions towards Diana were never affectionate. Diana held to one dream: that Purcell would return from the war and show her the love he assured her of every week in his letters.

Then the war is over. In the years following, Purcell is there fulfilling his promise. Two small boys now walk by Diana's side, and one of them is me. My father is studying architecture and then he has done his exams, and he is in practice. But we are not always in London. We go to Hilles where Granny Blow lives, and to Aunt Phyllie who lives in a castellated 'seat' in the Midlands, to Rise Park, and to stay with the Tennants in Scotland – the family of Diana's absent mother. My father rarely comes with us.

He stays in London. He has architectural schemes. My mother tells the family that 'Purcell is terribly busy.'

And my father *is* busy, working late into the night at drawings. He has bought dilapidated houses in Chelsea, and the scheme is that he will do them up and sell them at a good profit.

'I'm going to make our fortune,' Daddy says. 'I'll make a million.' Mummy believed him totally for a while – and she still tries to – but the fortune hasn't come yet, and instead on the table downstairs are two cheques that have been bounced by the bank.

It's half-past two and the door knocker bangs. That'll be Michael, I know. He's my friend from round the corner. All around us in Roehampton Lane, SW15 – that's the name of our street – are these lines of red-brick houses. Our house is joined on one side with only a few yards separating it from the next house on the other. We're living here because we should be in the country, but my father says he can't make a million unless we're in London. So my mother said 'All right but I want to bring my children up close to a park that's filled with fresh air.' And if you walk up Roehampton Lane towards Wimbledon, and take a turn on your right, a shaded lane takes you to Richmond Park. It's an enormous place, with planets of grass, and deer rising out of the bracken and everywhere these vast trees. It's because of Richmond Park that we're living in Roehampton.

But if we lived somewhere else I wouldn't know Michael. He's quite different from the cousins we go to stay with. He's pretty outspoken and he keeps telling me all the time not to be so shy. At Sunday school he asks these leading questions which the rather prim lady in horn-rimmed spectacles can't handle. It's odd how people look like their job, and Mrs McAlistair really does. Michael calls her the Virgin Mary, which is a bit disrespectful, but she will put on this fake holy act. Michael asked her one day what Jesus did for sex and she sent him straight out of the room for the rest of the class. 'Michael Ivens, punishment enough will come to you for what you've said,' and she pointed a withered finger at the door.

I don't tell Michael that my father's sleeping it off, but immediately he asks me why the house is so silent. He's only been to our house twice before, and both times my father was out. Michael's met my mother and he asked her straight away why she married my father.

'He drew beautifully,' she said, 'and he read to me.' Michael didn't think that was enough and later he asked me what they did in bed.

I couldn't answer that one – although I could now – but I know Michael's never satisfied until he's shaken everything inside out. 'My dad's not well,' I say to Michael. But he looks at me suspiciously because of the very healthy snores coming from my parents' bedroom. 'He's been seen walking zigzag down our avenue,' Michael says, not prepared to let the subject drop. 'He's always had a funny walk,' I say; 'he was born that way.'

Today Michael leaves the matter there. But I know I'll have to tell him the whole truth soon. He's going to think I'm an idiot if I don't come clean. I know I have these dreams about how our life ought to be, but maybe that's only for myself. He wants this deep friendship and I'm making him feel cut off. I should have realised that it's wonderful to have this offered, as apart from cousins I don't have that much opportunity for closeness. My cousins are quite different from me, and if they don't think about it, I do.

'Michael, there's some weird stuff in the attic, shall we go there?' I say.

'You mean really sinister?' he says. I tell Michael that it's not scary in the way that ghost trains and dark passages are but it's like coming across a life that's been discarded. That spooks Michael immediately and he says, 'Let's go.'

The attic is a large area made up of wooden rafters and floorboards which my father says will soon be extra rooms. But the rooms have never happened and what's there are odds and ends, and in one corner about forty jars of bottled pears. The bottled pears are lodged for ever in my mind because we never get through them. There's this ancient pear tree in the garden – ancient like an oak – that produces pears to feed a regiment. My father insists that every pear be bottled, and so the bottled jars never seem to grow any less.

I take Michael towards the hamper. It sits there hiding secrets. We open the lid and sequinned and shimmering dresses, bejewelled shoes, gold and silver belts, and wafts of incense from long-ago parties carry us into a land remote from the suburbs of Roehampton and Wimbledon. 'A society girl,' Michael announces, holding up one of the dresses to the light. We pull the dresses out and spread them over the floor as if a hundred parties are taking place at the same time. I explain that I know nothing of this distant universe except that I have been told that Mummy was a débutante and went to the Palace to curtsy to the King and Queen.

I am aware, but also unaware, of class. I am aware that life is not the same for everybody. I realise, too, that not every girl does this curtsying. Looking at the spread-out clothes I wonder what my mother gained, or experienced, or felt from being exhibited at the top. It occurs to me that this might not have happened to Michael's mother because he says nothing as he holds up the dresses. And yet I have no more contact with those vanished days than he does, and by looking into the hamper with him I am making his life a part of mine. I don't want to be separated from him by different experiences. My father's shouting is isolating us, and already I know about that loneliness inside which should only come to people later. And it lessens that loneliness to be with Michael now, in our attic in Roehampton Lane, staring at a mystery that neither of us can answer.

My father does not wake up that day. He goes on sleeping while my mother makes tea for us in the kitchen. We don't tell my mother where we have been, although I'm sure she has guessed. She looks at me as if she can tell I've been poking about. The trouble is I'm confined to this house. And if something is wrong I want to know why. Because there are no answers I can't stop opening drawers when no one is looking. Suddenly Michael says to her, 'You must have had a good time once.' And she answers him, raising her eyelids and fixing on him her hazel brown eyes, 'Yes, it was fun, but none of it was real.'

Well, in that case, I'd rather have the unreal. I don't see the point of the real if it makes you churn and clutch at Fuzziepeg. But next week I'm going off to Granny Blow because my brother is back from school and in the school holidays we're not in London so much. Granny Blow lives in this big house in the country and we go visiting farms with her. My father doesn't come with us as he says he has far too much work to do. It's funny he doesn't want to see his mother. He talks a lot to my mother about the importance of being independent. But he can't be that independent because of the green bottle stuff.

'You've a scratch on your face,' Michael says. 'Who did it?'

'Nobody did it,' says my mother, faltering, not expecting Michael to notice it. 'I was tying back a rose bush in the garden.'

'I fell over too,' she adds, pointing to the bruise.

Michael is about to go. I don't want to think about the evening ahead because the arguing could start. 'I'll walk with you,' I say to Michael and he is pleased. My mother says it's all right but I mustn't stay out too long. She's still bringing me up as if everything is normal, because she wants to convince herself that it is – that one day there will be no more bounced cheques, that my father will make that million, and that he will give her the love she needs.

I like to think that if my mother and father had come from decent straightforward backgrounds none of the awfulness would have happened. Of course I could be wrong, except that as I was to discover, both of them had come from childhoods that only the upper classes are capable of arranging. I'm sorry to use that term 'upper class', because it indicates superiority, but

I've often sensed a kind of silent superiority – you can't miss it when you're with them. The upper classes, for example, don't believe that their actions can ever be questioned; they don't believe for a moment that they should look inwards at themselves. They believe they are golden.

I am determined to be on the level with Michael. How can I have a friend and not let him into what's happening? I want always to be his friend and to be able to escape down the streets to his home. There aren't any big differences just now because I never mention the sort of places we go to when we go away from Roehampton. But I had to show him that hamper. The thing is he's got this imagination that soars way above the front-room parlours of the neighbourhood. I think Michael's hungry for experiences and there are times he says to me, 'I want thrills! I want something to happen! Mum and Dad have tea at the same time – to the minute – every Saturday.'

He'll have to know what's going on soon but I'm worried he'll start asking my mother questions. Plenty of times I've been round to his house and his mother says to me, 'Your father seems very overworked. How are the houses doing?'

It's these houses of my father's that are meant to make us rich. But why aren't we rich already? This is what I don't understand. My father's family live on an estate, a 'land' estate with masses of fields, woods, farms and all that. In fact Granny Blow's family, when she married my grandfather, virtually owned counties. These aren't things I can say now, though, so I tell Mrs Ivens, 'It's a worrying time. Daddy keeps putting out all this money.'

'Your mother's so young and so lovely, I'm sure one day you'll have a car,' says Michael's mum. Suddenly I feel I've slipped downwards somewhere, and I can only think, thank goodness she doesn't know for certain about the green bottle mixture.

'My mother doesn't drive. And my father hasn't driven for years – not since he drove a tank in the desert.'

People watch you here. It's not like staying at Granny Blow's where there's a long private drive before you reach the house.

Here they can see you coming out of the front door and walking to the bus stop. Do they think it odd that we take the 74 bus – or go on the underground from Hammersmith – to the centre of London? Do they think because of my parents' posh talk that we shouldn't be doing this? Or because Michael's dad has a car that we should have one too? But it's second nature for my mother to hop on a bus, taking us with her. I can't explain to Mrs Ivens that my mother doesn't think of appearances.

'You see the bomb sites from the top of a bus – and sometimes I see my grandmother,' I say.

'What?' says Michael's mother. 'Her ghost, you mean? Was she killed in a raid?'

'No. We see her walking down the street – down Sloane Street. When we go into London on the bus. My mother says, "Look, there's my mother." And we look down, and there she is.'

This is the grandmother who married my grandfather, Adrian Bethell. Clare Tennant was eighteen when she married Adrian. It was the First World War and Adrian was a lieutenant in the Life Guards. Clare was the daughter of the first Baron Glenconner and the granddaughter of Sir Charles Tennant, one of the great entrepreneurs of Victorian industry. Clare's mother, Pamela, had been painted by Sargent: *The Wyndham Sisters* was his most perfect statement on aristocratic beauty and poise. It hangs, today, alone on one wall in the Metropolitan Museum of Art in New York. But Pamela Wyndham trampled the Tennant industrial genes underfoot and presented her children to the world in the image of herself – as superb, unique aristocrats.

Clare announced to her many cousins that she wanted to marry a cavalry officer who hunted. Adrian did just that. Within two years, at twenty, Clare decided that she didn't want Adrian – who, anyway, was in the trenches – and she ran off with another man. She had this daughter, my mother, but she didn't want the daughter now that she didn't love Adrian. So Diana Hermione Bethell was shared by Clare's mother, Pamela, and by Adrian. As for Clare, she was snuggled up with the Honourable Lionel Tennyson, grandson and ultimate heir of Lord Alfred's title and estate. Lionel was both a remarkable cricketer and a remarkable bounder – and entirely lacked his grandfather's poetic sensibility. The divorce from Adrian came through and Clare married Lionel, the spendthrift bounder.

Clare was the youngest woman ever to be divorced. 'What a mess for a woman of twenty to have got herself into,' wrote the young Edward, Prince of Wales. But the scandal never touched Clare, whose fame as a beauty was for the remarkable freshness and innocence in her face. She side-stepped the issue, as if none of it had ever happened to her.

'I think we must adopt Diana,' said Clare's father and Diana's grandfather, Lord Glenconner.

This would have been wonderful as Eddy Glenconner was enormously rich and Diana would have grown up surrounded by trusts and settlements and all those arrangements which make upper-class children so safe. But it didn't happen.

'I can't permit that,' said Adrian. 'Diana is my daughter. It would be beneath my dignity.'

But at least Diana went often to stay with her grandmother, Pamela. Diana loved her grandmother. Meanwhile Clare made no attempt to see her discarded daughter. Her time was spent being photographed as a beauty and staying in country house after country house. She showed no conscience whatsoever about Diana. When friends of Clare's asked about Diana, Clare, raising that innocent face, would reply, 'I don't really know her.'

'The face of an angel, but the soul of a devil,' was how Pamela spoke of her daughter. And this was the face that I saw from the tops of buses. I knew nothing at eight of the devil behind the face. Clare was a mystery. I could only imagine what it was all about.

So I give my performance to the Ivenses.

Something snaps and, my shyness going, I find myself imitating this grandmother's controlled little walk. She's really neatly dressed, as if she's a model, and she walks as if everyone is looking at her. She has eyelashes which flicker upwards like in those love bits in a film, and there she is like she's on show, waiting to receive all the claps. Michael giggles and says, 'Let's find her.' But Mrs Ivens seems confused; she's not sure whether a small boy should mimic his grandmother.

'What would she say if she saw you?'

'Oh, she won't,' I say. 'We only see her from the tops of buses.'

'Oh,' she answers, not understanding. And I know I should explain more, but I don't. The Ivenses' house is not meant for stories of this sort; I look at Mr Ivens's black attaché case placed carefully by a chair in the hall. Things happen as they should happen here. There's nothing that can't be explained and I don't think the house could manage mad grandmothers. Michael's keen, but I ignore his quivering eyes because I am here to sink myself in their safety. Mrs Ivens changes the subject and asks how I like soccer. We've just started this game at the day school I go to with Michael. I say the older boys take advantage of the beginners, kicking the ball I can't control yet swiftly away from my feet. Mrs Ivens says it's odd to mix the boys up like that, and Michael interrupts saying that's to make us learn it faster. But now I'm thinking soon I must leave the Ivenses cosiness and return to my father's ranting. Or if that hasn't started up again, to his over-the-top 'I'm sorrys', or else to more of that unending snoring.

'Ask your mother to visit soon,' says Mrs Ivens. But often, like now, my mother can't go out because there's a bruise on her arm that she doesn't want to be seen. I say of course I will bring her but I know there's no certainty.

That night I clutch Fuzziepeg hard. My father's up again and ranting. Tomorrow there will be the apologies, always the apologies. I twist around my bed waiting for him to wear himself out, and for a second collapse to happen. This day has been one of the worst. Even humming those songs won't work to get me to sleep. The sickness stays in my stomach. I don't sleep until long after I hear silence. My mother comes into my room when all is quiet and I feel her wipe away some tears from my cheeks and from the head of Fuzziepeg.

It's a situation to cry over. Anyone would, I say to myself. Anyone.

2

ESCAPING LONDON IS an excitement. The train chuffs and hisses out of the station and I know that we're off to Stroud to stay with Granny Blow. The train goes faster and faster, going clickety-clack, clickety-clack over the rails. My mother sits in a corner of the compartment, her eyes closed and a headscarf knotted under her chin. She is calm now, but sad too, as if she can't unburden what's happening. I stand in the corridor with my brother, our noses pressed against the window, waiting for the last of the streets and houses to disappear and then the long hours of clickety-clack until we see the first stone walls that mean we're close to Granny Blow land.

But the excitement dies once I'm sitting in Granny Blow's car. I'm not Granny's favourite, and I feel that. 'What are we to do with him?' I hear her say, and all I've done is sit in silence as huge Granny Blow tugs at the wheel of her black car. She's in black, too, like the car, but with a presence that can wither. She runs her stone mansion and all the fields that surround it. When we pass houses far, far smaller than hers people standing in gardens acknowledge her. She receives their greetings as if they are her due. I'm told that everybody respects and admires her, but I can't believe that's really true. It's just that they don't dare to see her any other way because they've been brought up to accept that she's better than them. Granny Blow also knows how to play class. Granny Blow comes from the aristocracy.

'Are we *nouveau riche*?' my brother asks Granny Blow. He's picked up this funny term at prep school, where class and where we all come from are made real for the first time.

'I wish we were,' answers Granny. But she means the opposite. She couldn't exist without the aristocratic blood. I've heard her pretend that none of it's important, yet she's given all of us this book on her family. She talks about her ancestors until we see them large as life before us. The Black Prince walks the rooms of the stone mansion. The blood of the Plantagenets is weighed against the blood of the Tudors. The blood of the Plantagenets comes highest, and she is turning the heads of my father and his Teutonic-faced brother, saying, 'And which one has the Plantagenet profile?'

Granny is as large as a tub, but once she was tall and slim with tresses of auburn hair. My grandfather married her because of her lovely straight legs: the Tollemaches throw their legs out properly when they walk, he said. My grandfather, Detmar the architect, thought and thought about architecture, and saw in his wife-to-be, Winifred Tollemache, the symmetry that he judged good in a building. Now Granny Blow is no longer a fine building, but a heaving tumbling ruin.

Oh, Granny, please don't push my face into your bosoms . . . but she does and I inhale the sick sweet sweat of her heavy flesh.

The story is that my grandfather enjoyed her. He dropped his sketch-pad when he first saw her and had her there and then on his caravan floor. He was beefy, with curly dark hair and a Romany face, and she submitted quickly. And through the caravan window could be seen her home. The great Tudor hall, protected by its moat – where the Tollemaches had lived for ever – ebbed to the horizon of her mind as she threw her legs in joy around the gypsy darling who had caught her.

'You are marrying a commoner with no land,' her cousin, Lord Dysart, told her.

The caravan journeys stopped when the caravan drew up at a

ledge of the Cotswolds where the land drops away into miles of idle valley. Here my grandfather, the curly-headed lover, offered to build her a mansion to suit her station. So the house where Winifred played with ancestors grew, and into the house her husband and lover introduced tapestries and ancestor portraits. She no longer missed the great Tudor hall in Suffolk and saw herself as chatelaine of this other fantasy where she believed she could equally dazzle by her nobility, by her bearing.

Her need for status was not compatible with the fiery love-making in the caravan. Except that the house had a heartbeat far away from social concerns and this because its builder, my grand-father, was quite free and not conditioned – as she was – by the 'But don't you know who I am?' haughtiness. 'We don't know anybody in Gloucestershire,' Winifred said to curly-headed, caravan-journeying Detmar. His baptismal name was so distinc-tive that everyone wondered where he could have come from.

'You must get to know the shepherd,' Detmar told his wife. But Winifred, with her armigerous outlook, finally overbore him. A clutter of escutcheons took the spontaneity from his wilful penetration of her – and her desire for it – and after she had borne him four children, somewhere that passion ceased which knows neither time nor class.

'Sex is overrated,' Winifred announced to her daughter-in-law as my mother was beginning her attachment to my father. By then Hilles, the stone mansion, was no longer just a mansion and one farm, but a mansion and many farms. Compensation for the end of physical pleasure had come with her medieval role of Lady of the Manor. A role she assumed on the death of her husband. For to thoroughly please her, Detmar had acquired for the family the manorship rights. Yet Winifred, aware of her now unshapely figure – an excellent caricature for the Brothers Grimm – remained hard towards those who possessed what time had taken from her.

So Winifred resented her new daughter-in-law, while Diana arrived shy and fragile as a sylph, transported by the magic the gypsy builder had wrought in the house. That idyll which was to diminish over the years as she gained the measure of Winifred.

'Jonathan is a genius,' says Winifred about her second son, my father's younger brother. For she has lost my father to my mother, and she is determined that she will never lose Jonathan. She feeds him with admiring words that make him scared when away from her. He follows her around the house and he is devoured by envy of any who take the spotlight for a second off him.

'Little children are not to be seen in the kitchen,' Uncle Jonathan spits out and he tears my hand from the kitchen table, where I am watching Granny Blow make scones. I am hurled into the hall and the vast wooden door with the latch I cannot reach is banged noisily. I tiptoe across the hall and find my brother snuggled into a leather armchair that could take two of him, busy with cardboard soldiers dressed in uniforms of the eighteenth century. He plays a game that Uncle Jonathan plays with him – one that gives Uncle Jonathan the opportunity to display his military prowess. Uncle Jonathan takes the side of the French and at every successful move cries out *'Tête d'Armée!'* – the dying words of Napoleon.

There is a lot of identification with Napoleon. Uncle Jonathan shares the day of his birth with the Emperor and believes the path he is to take will be the same – minus, of course, Waterloo. My brother is working out moves to outwit his uncle, but the uncle must win three games out of five otherwise the sulking is unbearable.

Granny Blow dislikes spending money and she says there is none. I do not notice this, but my mother does not hide her difficulties with Granny. I've started having my first riding lessons. There are stables at the bottom of the apple orchard that I can see from my window, but there is only one horse and it is for Uncle Jonathan. My father had horses there once, but they are gone now. Apart from this wild, bad-tempered horse of Uncle Jonathan's the stables are empty. There is plenty of room for more but Granny will buy no ponies for us and my mother takes us over the beacon to a riding school. My mother pays for the lessons, not Lady of the Manor Granny.

Granny drives a black Ford Eight car. I worry that the car will run backwards with the weight of her body as it climbs the steep hill out of Gloucester. It seems to splutter, and if it was human I suppose it would be groaning terribly. There is a tall thin woman dressed, like Granny, in black, but far more frail, walking up the hill. She is a servant at Hilles, and as the car slows down I prepare for her to join us. But Granny Blow says, 'Walk, Miss Martinsdyke, walk.'

Adults do realise how they can frighten a child, but the child does not know why it is being frightened. Adults instil fear into a child when it pleases them. Granny Blow knows the power she possesses, and she uses it. In the back of the black spluttering car I am unable to counter a single one of her verbal swipes; I am silenced by fear.

The car halts on the gravel courtyard and I tumble out and run away up the hillside to the woods. I am alone – cut off even from my brother because my granny makes a fuss of him. He has the same auburn hair that she had before her hair turned white as bedlinen, and he reminds her of her dead husband. I do not possess either of these pluses: I have the dark brown hair of the grandmother who walks like a mannequin, and I have her eyes and the set of her face.

'What can we do with him? He's not one of us,' Granny says, and she goes on saying it.

When my mother hears her say this, she draws herself in. Now Granny Blow has insulted my mother's family, and she has done this on purpose. There is a person – my mother's grandmother Pamela – who slept with her husband, and even though it happened years before she met the gypsy architect who caressed her in his caravan, she cannot forgive the betrayal. To remind her of this she has only to look at the face of my mother and myself.

Of course there has been no betrayal, but Winifred sees any attention diverted from her as a dishonest act. Her behaviour is caused by even earlier wrongs. Half sleeping in her bedroom as a child, she overheard her mother announce that she preferred Winifred's elder sister, and Winifred saw this as desertion. Her mother had betrayed her. Consumed by fury, she now insists there is deception everywhere – even in the face of a child. She forgives only Jonathan, the son whom she encourages to demand of her anything he wishes. Jon-Jon has not left her. Jon-Jon will, she assures herself, allowing her large body to breathe quietly once more, not let her down.

'What an enchanted house,' friends say when they come to stay. 'The rooms are filled with magic – it's a fairy tale,' they say, bestowing compliment upon compliment on damaged Winifred. They see her, too, as part of what they call 'a rural dream' and as blessed with saintliness as the house.

I'm safe now, on the garlic-covered hillside. I look back on the house and see only the sun-glinting windows and no people. They're all inside. Granny shuffling, but upright and stately, across the stone floor of the sunlight-stroked hall to the kitchen. I've been inside and seen all this so many times. Granny pausing at a kitchen table that equals her in size. Granny preparing the food while Miss Martinsdyke takes plates from a dresser to warm in the oven. Uncle Jonathan pacing the landing upstairs: his tread is heard throughout the house as Aunt Luty, Granny Blow's youngest daughter, hovers with small quantities of carrots and broad beans lost in large china dishes that she is to place on our table.

'There simply isn't enough for all of us,' Winifred announces, taking the shoulder of lamb from the oven and turning the eight potatoes that surround it.

'But Mummy, I don't need to eat,' says the youngest daughter for whom Winifred has carved a role of total self-sacrifice.

'Winifred, my two boys must be fed,' insists Diana.

'Wait,' says Winifred. 'This is not your house.'

The builder had set in stone Christ's lamb, placed it in the centre of the lintel above the welcoming arms of the mansion's main door. The little lamb, watching the sins of the world, is silent as the stone. Can he redeem or does the symbol hold no more weight than water? Because the happiness with which Detmar laid his magic stones has gone. If this house could have been for him alone – and no one else – the happiness might be there still. But too many people bore down on the house, insulting the fabric with their disturbed selves.

Winifred played with her children. She played with their emotions and drew circles round them. The children became her buttress against demanding realities she refused to see, and she never once spoke to her two boys, throughout their whole growing up, about a life they might have one day without her.

'I want to build houses, like Daddy,' her eldest son said to her.

'Make me a daisy chain for my neck, Purcell. Your father is a genius.'

That name, Purcell, is more fantasy. The gypsy lover, the architect and builder, in presenting his pedigree to satisfy his armigerous Tollemache wife-to-be, produced John Blow, composer of the first English opera. Blow was found in Newark, one of the young boys collected by King Charles II to strengthen the King's private choir after its disbandment by Cromwell. This Child of the Chapel Royal – as Blow, like his fellow choristers, was known – rose to be its master and to teach the young Henry Purcell. The two musicians remained on the closest of terms throughout the short life of Blow's pupil. They played their work freely at the Abbey, Whitehall, and St Paul's in a continual music-making exchange, until the names were joined as Blow and Purcell. The connection impressed Winifred. My father was to carry in his baptismal name this reminder of the great composers' friendship. And now, to Winifred, if there is embarrassment that the Blows were not aristocrats of the land, she can and she will fantasise them as aristocrats of music.

I am being looked at by Dr John Blow, Master of the Royal Choristers, Organist of Westminster Abbey, and Master of the Private Musik to King Charles II. I am in a room that you enter through a carved wooden screen. One wall of this room is hung entirely with tapestries full of figures dressed in Bible clothes. They wear robes, hold staffs, and have eyes that stare out prophecies. I think of the Bible days and the reign of King Charles I – because someone mentioned the tapestries as coming from his time – as joined and eternally running together. It's a room that makes you think you are centuries away from now.

There's a window at the far end that curves right round the wall like on the prow of a ship. From this window there's a fantastic view, which goes on and on and on. Green trees, fields, and silver rivers everywhere. Cows munching too. I've heard grown-ups talking about the 'sunset land' when they stand at this window. I wonder if they mean that this would be a good place to die – the sky is so immense from here that they'd have no problem in getting into Heaven.

The Doctor wears a wig of brown curls that falls to his shoulders and in one hand he holds a piece of parchment on which music is written. His face is behind me and I am sitting at this small wooden piano which has a mellow echo. The notes sing as they come out of it. Granny calls it a 'harpsichord', but I can't pronounce that word. She sits next to me, her fat fingers striking the notes that she wants me to learn. I am to watch and then to copy. But I hit two wrong notes and she shakes her head and looks as if she never wants to see me again. She pulls my hands away.

'You goose! You goose!' she cries. 'It's easy, it's very easy – you must follow. Follow!'

She starts again, slowly now, and I am to follow or she will do something terrible. But her voice raised in disgust is enough. I want to turn round and find the warm arm of the Doctor – because I know he is gentle and forgiving. Do I dare? I say to myself. Do I dare?

Suddenly I have turned round and I am staring at this portrait. I drink in his warm smile and dream he is walking towards me and that Granny Blow gives up her seat to my distinguished ancestor. Granny Blow, for the first time, is retiring – humbled. Now the Doctor puts his sheet of music on the stand, adjusts the pedals and plays without rancour, humming as he does so.

'Be careful with the boy,' he says when he has paused. 'No musician was ever made through scolding.'

The Doctor is with me now and Granny Blow has retreated to the back of the room. His hands run across the keys and the music bounces out of the golden chords that move like puppets under the open lid. Stopping for a moment, he puts an arm round me and says, 'I would like to teach you. With encouragement I believe you could flower. Don't listen to your grandmother. She is eaten up inside by some unhappiness – but that has nothing to do with you.'

Then he resumes playing, his hands going so fast that the lace from his cuffs dances too. The room is filled with the singing of the music – I hear it swell and swell until I imagine the whole court of King Charles II moving in and out of the tapestried room, controlled by the music. It is their music and they have come to hear it. Many of the rooms at Hilles have these tapestries from long ago, as if the house was never meant for a time of concrete sheds and petrol smells.

After that day I would pray for the Doctor to come back, to make a second, third, fourth or fifth visit. Or better, to come and live with us for ever. If he could keep chastising Granny Blow then perhaps she would change. But all there is now is silence – and that tolerant smile in the portrait which seems to say, 'What are you doing? Take me back to my Abbey.' Am I to see that afternoon's intervention as a true live visit from him – or was I dreaming?

All right, the Doctor is back in his portrait, but I still believe he is somewhere. He's the best person there is at Hilles. He doesn't care about Granny Blow.

My world is the whole world to me and the people in it are as large as giants. All the time I'm trying to tether them down like the Lilliputians did Gulliver, but it's no good. They'll never grow any smaller, and I'll never grow any bigger. So I'm inventing my own life, away from them. I don't want them to go on trampling me, which is what they do at Hilles. I know they want to trample down my mother too, but she's older: she's an adult, and she can handle them. That's what I tell myself. So I crouch behind the huge wooden doors where these long old weapons are clustered, avoiding the worrying footfalls of adults.

'You mustn't make favourites, Winifred,' my mother says to her, and I'm sitting at the dining table listening.

'I don't. You imagine it. Everyone's equal. "Suffer the little children to come unto me".'

And with that I see my mother lose control. Suddenly all the knives, forks and spoons are in Winifred's lap. Granny Blow just sits there, looking into nowhere, and Aunt Luty lets out a cry. Uncle Jonathan goes to the sideboard. He helps himself to all the food in sight, sets it on a tray and swaggers upstairs.

I'm four years old and David, my brother, is six. Granny Blow has us on either side of her in bed. She's reading us a story and she has my nose pushed against one of her huge, swinging bosoms. The story is about a camel and its hump. When she's finished she recites these lines, her bosom rising then tumbling again as her breath comes out.

> The camel's hump is an ugly lump
> Which well you may see at the Zoo;
> But uglier yet is the hump we get
> From having too little to do.

Kiddies and grown-ups too-oo-oo,
If we haven't enough to do-oo-oo. . .

Granny Blow dwells on the last two lines and gives each of us a
look from her watering eyes. But all that sticks in my mind is the
hump and the terror that someone will stick one on to me – suddenly. That one of the giants will come and do it. Uncle
Jonathan, yes – he pushed me into this bed of nettles. I don't
really take in the story because I'm trapped by Granny's large arm
and believe that I will die, my nose against her rolling bosom. Is
this Granny's way of showing love to me? I don't understand why
she's too close at one moment, cold the next. 'Where am I?
Where am I?' I say, so nobody knows I'm saying it. I move my
nose out of Granny's bosom. I breathe.

Mummy tells me that Granny Blow puts on an act.

'Why doesn't Purcell come and see us more often?' Winifred
asks.

'He has to earn money for us, Winifred.'

Winifred sits on the steps of the house and she wears a grey
dress with flowers patterned over it. Her white hair is circled by
a band. She often sits on these steps looking out across the flag-
stoned terrace that is guarded on one side by the tall yew hedge
that divides the drive from the garden. No houses can be seen
from here, only in the distance some thatched stables and then
land falling away to the long stretch of valley. Christ's lamb stares
down at her from the stone lintel.

'All this may be his one day, I want him to appreciate it in my
lifetime.'

'It has to be his – he is the elder of your two sons,' says Diana
looking down at her mother-in-law.

Winifred says nothing. She knows that everything should go
to Purcell, but other plans are in her mind. Even her handmaiden
daughter, Lucilla – who I know as Aunt Luty – is considered as

a custodian of the place on her demise. She nods and continues to play with David, the grandson who resembles her late husband.

David races away in his pedal car, which trips on a flagstone and turns over. 'Oh Diana, you weren't watching,' says Winifred. But Diana isn't there any more. Winifred pulls herself up from the low step, her hands reaching out as if for the family she had thought to control. She moves the few yards to gather David, who lies crying on a flagstone, his face half covered by white daisies, and puts her two large arms around him. She makes clucking noises with her tongue which means that David is now quite safe with her.

I am on the hillside again where garlic is mixed with those other nodding white bells whose sweet smell says to me, alone, alone. And I think that flowers do know because it's true. There aren't many boys around to make friends with – there's no one like Michael. It's really all adults, Hilles. I can't believe in Granny Blow when she tries to be a child. Just an old person acting out a part she's trying to believe in. I can tell she doesn't really believe in it because she puts on this special puckered-up face and makes those dreadful clucking noises. Well, she doesn't do that when she's talking to adults. In fact, I've heard her be quite sharp. And I'm scared stiff of those breasts of hers. They're so huge, like those mountains of blancmange that wobble dangerously on the table. Some mornings I think I'm about to pass out; faint, I mean.

But there is one friend I've got – that is, apart from Fuzziepeg. He's called Gubbleydix and he's always waiting for me when I run up this hillside. I'm talking to him quite freely now. He knows everybody in the house, but they don't know him. He's a flesh and blood person; he's someone who exists out there in the air.

'Now where's Simon?' Granny Blow says, putting the bit of lamb down on the table.

'I'll find him,' Jonathan spits out in his clipped way, biting on every word he speaks.

'Perhaps it's best if I go,' Diana interrupts, in that voice of hers that's all gentle, so different from Jonathan's swagger voice.

'The food will get cold if we wait for him. And it's so expensive these days,' moans Aunt Luty. Aunt Luty has been taught by her mother to count the cost of everything.

I see my mother, her dark brown nearly black hair, climbing the garlic and the lily of the valley hillside. Behind her is the stone mansion getting smaller as she comes nearer. The thatch which covers the mansion's entire roof floats like an upturned barge under the blue sky. 'You must come in for lunch, darling,' she cries. But they're all there, in that room, being stared at by these enormous pictures of men in fancy dress. Uncle Jonathan, Granny Blow and Aunt Luty. I want my family to go back into the men-in-fancy-dress frames and for the monarchs in their fancy dress to come out and talk with me. What are pictures for if they won't come to life?

I'm discussing these monarchs with Gubbleydix now. As Gubbleydix doesn't belong in any time, he's explaining to me about kings being Divine and that kind of thing. I ask him if all these monarchs are ancestors, too. He says some, but not all. They're really in the house because Granny Blow's husband wanted to make Granny Blow secure. And yet they never do seem to make her quite secure enough. Gubbleydix says that's a failing in her, but I can't ask Granny Blow about it. I can't ask her about anything. I have to accept everything as it is.

My very pretty mummy is taking my hand now. 'Goodbye Gubbleydix. Goodbye,' I say. He never comes with me into the house. That's adults' country, and I don't want Gubbleydix upset by it. Mind you, he's strong and really he can cope with anything. I suppose I want him for myself. Yes, I've got to have him by me like a secret and then all his knowledge and gentleness will calm me. Because I am frightened by the people in this house. They're so powerful.

★

'You must never, ever be late again,' Jonathan says to his nephew. He takes my hand and squeezes it hard. He has a cold smile on his face. Winifred nods her approval, but Diana intercedes.

'He is my child,' she affirms, staring at Winifred. The table is silent and from above the fireplace the vast plasterwork coat of arms of the Stuarts, shining with gold and silver leaf, looks down. The unicorn prances and the lion growls, and that motto in gold, encircling the arms on the white Garter strap, surely needs some heeding. For, Winifred assures herself, there can be no evil anywhere in this house – and no whited sepulchres. She and her children must – surely, surely – be double blessed because of the words of that motto. So may evil indeed come to those who evil think.

'Don't give Simon so many carrots. There'll be none left for second helpings,' Winifred instructs Aunt Luty, ignoring Diana's remark. Soon Jonathan, going to the side table, takes huge helpings. Winifred glances with admiration. He sits down and, his mouth filled, talks about the terrible deprivations of the war. With that he gets up again and finishes off the shoulder of lamb.

Uncle Jonathan, during the war an officer in the Coldstream Guards, says that there is no better regiment. He begins a lot of his talk with, 'When I was an officer in the Coldstream . . .' Apparently, he was wounded, though nothing near fatal – however much is made of the wounded bit. Granny Blow glows with pride. They don't mention my father, and I don't think they know anything about the green bottle mixture, so it must be because he is simply not here. My mother does not mention him either. Or is it because there is always something wrong? I don't believe that . . . Now suddenly I want to go home.

'Can we go back tomorrow?' I say to my mother.

'What gratitude,' says Granny Blow.

She looks adoringly at David with a 'why is your brother so difficult' sigh. David's on to a winner with his chestnut hair and face like the gypsy lover. He can't do a thing wrong and he plays up to it. If only the house were filled with people, I could slip off. How horribly uncomfortable I feel when it's just the family. I wish they'd all stop staring at me. Uncle Jonathan, about to fill himself with Granny Blow's gooseberry fool, relents.

'We're going to call you Little Bear that Runs by Night,' he announces. When he's not Napoleon or the Black Prince, he's an Indian chief.

The train back to London goes slowly, so slowly. This always happens when you want to be somewhere fast. My brother, feeling grown up now he's at prep school, reads a book. I kick my legs, lie flat on the carriage seat, sit up again, lie down again, and pull at my white Aertex.

I don't know why it is but my mother is crying. She's dabbing her lower eyelids with the back of one hand. There's some make-up running too – that black stuff. David hasn't noticed because he's in his book. But I say, 'What's wrong, Mummy? What is it?'

'It's nothing at all – nothing.' And she puts her arm around me.

David looks up now. He seems alarmed, a little embarrassed. That's going to school, I suppose. Schoolboys aren't meant to cry, so a parent crying is pretty awful.

'What is it, Mummy?' he says. It's all we can do – just ask this same question.

We sit there watching her. The train is making those urgent clickety-clacks. Then it's dark for a few moments because we're in a tunnel. The lights spark on and it's all too bright. She tries to smile, but it doesn't come off. The tears are still running down her face.

Now it's daylight and I sit there crumpled and sad. I'm leaning against her body and I'm thinking I must be safe there. She has this soft, soft skin that I fold up in. David looks out of the window. Fields, churches, inns, houses, villages rush past as if they're running but they don't know where. Soon the allotments will begin and London with all those houses thick as armies will crush us.

'You must tell us what's wrong,' David says, looking at Mummy.

I push my head against my mother's stomach and say, 'If it's difficult, we can keep a secret.'

She puts one finger to her cheek and cups her head slightly in her hand. With the other she dabs her tears. It's like something in a film, I say to myself. She's a beautiful actress playing a part.

'I've had a baby removed. I've just lost a child,' and that's it – that's all. And now Mummy looks out of the window as if the flashing-by scenery will stop us asking more. But I know it's to do with Daddy and the scenes and the bounced cheques. I can see David can't take in what's happened, and I can't take it in either.

The slow chuffing starts and the train is at Paddington. Everywhere are people leaving platforms or reaching them. Porters in blue caps wheel piled-up cases. Smoke hisses and drifts, blinding all sight until past the ticket man. Mummy walks serenely, her red headscarf with white dots knotted once more under her chin. Looking up at her it's hard again to take in that we've got these troubles. It's harder because my mother's got that face of someone coming from where troubles aren't meant to be.

The porter walks ahead. My mother puts an arm round each of us. She says, as if half to herself and as if half for us to hear, 'I won't think about it today. I'll think about it tomorrow.'

Now she has a hand in each of ours. And she says, walking on, her head held high, 'There is always tomorrow.'

3

IF DADDY WILL stop drinking then everything is going to be all right. 'You don't need to do it,' is what Mummy keeps telling him. 'You're absolutely right, my darling girl,' he always replies.

For three or four days he stops, and takes us to a cricket match at Lord's because he's a member of the MCC. Middlesex County Cricket, I say over and over as I sit on the wooden benches watching the slow and then sudden fast movements of men in white flannels on this big piece of grass with the tall buildings all around. Sometimes I slide to one side and watch half lying down. It makes it go faster and I keep saying Middlesex County Cricket, like it's stuck in my head and won't get out. My father likes this cricket. It's a sort of holiday for him. He meets lots of friends and all at once he's not overdoing it.

Or else we go to see the houses my father's building – and he's so enthusiastic about these houses. He tells us why he's designed the windows in that way or why the railings are going to keep their old-fashioned look. But these normal days never last. The tomato juice he promises to keep swallowing is replaced by the green bottle stuff. I don't understand how he can keep building the houses at the same time. He's got this head builder, George, who tells the clients that Mr Blow is very very clever when my father darts off without explaining – in the middle of talking –

leaving the clients with their mouths hanging open. And then he darts back again.

'I'm six foot four. I could knock you down,' says my father. He's holding up the big black telephone receiver. There's someone on the other end asking my father to pay his bill. I'm standing at the top of the staircase listening. My father can't pay the bills because when he does have the money he spends it in the pubs where the publicans think him the finest gentleman they've ever known. 'Oh, he's a proper gentleman,' they say to my mother.

Those people never see what goes on in our house in Roehampton. They can't understand why my mother worries so much. It's this charm my father's got. He uses it all the time when he's not at home. I've seen it. He stands there at the bar, the tailor-made jacket of his Savile Row suit floppy and open, telling stories. Listen to him, they're all saying and Purcell gets a bit of a kick out of the attention. They pay him all these compliments, which at the same time eggs him on, and he's really pleased with himself. Then he comes home and there isn't anybody cheering him any more, just himself with himself, and that's what he can't take.

There are evenings when David reads to him. David sits at the kitchen table reading and my father sits there in his suit, all untidy, slipping in his chair, until his eyelids close and we know it's all right. Not tonight.

Other nights, and it's now, the hitting starts. That loud voice: Stop, I'm saying. Stop. He's got a cigarette in one hand, and he's lurching at Mummy. Striking her across the chest, and she falls back, back against the kitchen stove. David's going up to him, facing him, looking up from my father's waist into his red, veins-sticking-out face. 'You bully,' he says. And my father turns and swipes David. We both turn and run from the room. We run upstairs. For a while David sits on my bed and we play with the animals. We do a football match between them and I've got Fuzziepeg as goalkeeper on my side. David's got his teddy on his. We make the other animals kick the ball, controlling their legs with our hands. Then my father's voice and the noise of something breaking makes us stop. I tremble, shiver. David sees my shaking and he's starting to make up a story but the yell of my father's shouting drowns it. 'Why should I?' echoes into the room. I lie still.

'I'm going to watch from the top of the stairs,' says David. 'We may have to fetch the police.'

I get out of bed and stand by my door, my head edging round it. Now Mummy's running up the stairs, past us, and into her room. She shuts the door. There's no noise from downstairs.

It's the middle of the night when I hear my father on the landing. I bury myself under the sheets, I bury myself in Fuzziepeg. I stay there until the morning.

Quite a few people have seen my father zigzagging up Roehampton Lane from the bus stop. The zigzag means he's drunk. They stare, pretending not to. And no one ever speaks about it, so you don't know what they're thinking. But they do look at my brother and me as if to say, 'What a lovely pair of boys.' Then there's a pause and they give that look of, 'It's so sad.'

But Michael knows everything now – and so do Mr and Mrs Ivens – and it's strange because they know far more than my own family. Far more. While Granny Blow's prattling on about the Black Prince and Uncle Jonathan's thinking about his genius, they don't care about this on their doorstep. Because even if my mother's said nothing they must realise that things aren't all right.

'Your father should have a cure,' says Mr Ivens, stirring his tea. 'It is curable if he will accept that he needs help,' Mrs Ivens adds, her pink tongue clashing against very white teeth.

'I'll ask a colleague of mine at work,' continues Mr Ivens, between tea sips. 'He has a similar problem with his brother.'

Michael wants me to stay with him. 'I mean, he might strike you too. You're not safe, Simon.' I say it might look odd if I stopped over. And I couldn't when my mother's left alone, that is when my brother's not there. But soon she will be alone as I'm due at prep school in six months. Perhaps I could stay with Michael when my brother's there. And he's there now. So I say I will, and Mrs Ivens is going to get the spare room ready.

'You can go for three days,' my mother agrees, 'but don't forget, darling, we go to Cliveden on Friday. Your godfather's giving a party for you all.'

Cliveden is this enormous house near the River Thames where Godfather Bill lives. It has quite a different look from Granny Blow's house and it's easily two times the size, probably three. It's more like a palace, all golden stone and statues everywhere. My mother talks quite often about 'Bill' – my Godfather Bill – and it goes back to the hamper in the attic time. My godfather's very rich and he sits in the House of Lords. He wanted to marry my mother once and he took her into jewellery shops in Mayfair offering her anything she wanted. But she said no, and married my father.

She wasn't in love with him and just being Viscountess Astor without her heart there didn't mean much. That's why she became Mrs Purcell Blow.

I'm telling Michael this story now, walking towards his home. 'Well, if she had married him then I could have lived with you,' he says, ' and become a lord.' I say to him that I'm not sure living in a lord's house makes you a lord, but we could have lived like lords, I say. 'Except then,' he asks, 'could we still have dreams?' Perhaps their dreams are different, I say, like they want to go a few steps further and become a king. 'Our dreams are better,' he says firmly, and now Michael's running ahead, dodging in and out of the big trees on the pavement. I run after him and hold him against a tree. He laughs and keeps on laughing.

Later that night I think I'm forgetting Roehampton Lane. I stare at the jigsaw pattern on the curtains in my bedroom and they are so tightly and snugly drawn that the mad shouting of my father can't break through. I know it can't and I know I won't wake up trembling. I know it. I turn off the bedside light and close my eyes. I've got Fuzziepeg nudged up against my cheek. I start to sleep and then I'm awake again, lying there looking at the ceiling. I keep seeing my father coming out of the ceiling, and he's walking fast up and down up and down chewing his tongue as he does before he gets angry and starts hitting my mother.

Go away, Daddy, go away, go away, go away. But no, he won't go, and I get dizzy and I'm starting to shake. Then the handle of the bedroom door turns and I hide under the bedclothes. 'Where are you? It's me, Michael,' the voice says. 'Wouldn't it be better if we slept together?' I don't say anything. I want to, but the trembling hasn't stopped. 'All right,' I say at last, but Michael's already lifting the bedclothes and he starts climbing in. Then I feel his legs behind mine. I feel them underneath these pyjamas we both wear.

Now he puts his arms around me. It seems quite natural for this to happen, and without thinking I just take his hands and hold them in mine. His head is soft against my back and he doesn't say anything, and that doesn't matter because I know anyway why he's with me. I put Fuzziepeg close to us too. Then, slowly, Michael turns his head and kisses me twice on the bottom of my neck.

Drifting to sleep without the stomach-churning and with Michael's arms around me is slipping towards places where there's no dark any more – where I can actually see, even feel, light. Like coming across fields of fresh corn with scarlet poppies waving round the edges and in the distance really blue horizons. It's strange, this kind of safety, I'm discovering – not the same as being with Aunt Phyllie in that big house of hers where a little dog barks at her heels. Of course that's another world too. But this new closeness has put the churning terror of seeing a parent mad – going dangerously berserk – out of sight. Except I know the terror's always there because once it's begun, it can't stop. It'll only go away for ever when I die. It's just that sometimes it can go to sleep for a while, which is what it's doing now, with calm passionate Michael beside me, laying the ghosts.

'Good-night kid,' he says.

Mrs Ivens gives me a hug and insists that their home is my home. And I'm saying 'Thank you, thank you,' and thinking of Michael. I'm thinking of Michael suddenly giving me this kiss right bang on the centre of my mouth. It happened just like that, in the middle of the night. There's no point in asking why and making it all cold again. It happened.

I've had a talking-to about chasing a girl. I'm supposed to have chased her three or four times round the tennis court at the school I go to in East Sheen with Michael. Her mother rang up my mother and asked if there was something wrong with her son. The girl thought I was going to kiss her and I've been reported for that. There's nothing wrong anyway. Michael's shown me that. It's a secret, though – a complete secret. The hugs with Michael.

It's Friday morning now and this afternoon we go to Cliveden. That is, my mother, my brother and me. It's a weekend for the children of my godfather's friends. It's all going to happen on a boat on the river, below the house. That's what my mother says. I'm excited and nervous – that feeling when you don't know if you'll know anybody. My mother seems really pleased.

In a few hours our front door bangs loudly and it's my father. He's drunk, terribly, terribly drunk. The shouting starts at once. He goes in and out of rooms and I can see that he doesn't want us to go to Cliveden. He doesn't say it in words but it doesn't take much time for him to make us late. I think, what a thing to do to your own children – because the stay at Cliveden is for us. I dart about the upstairs landing with David, both of us white-faced at what he'll do next.

He's done it – yes, he's done it now. He's hit my mother across the side of her head with that big black telephone receiver.

Mummy's bleeding now, she's leaning against the wall bleeding. Time – dreadful time – passes and the butler is telephoning from Cliveden. His Lordship is wondering what has happened to Mrs Blow and her children. Well, if Godfather Bill could come over and see what's happening there'd be no more questions asked.

'Mrs Blow and the children have been unavoidably detained,' my father tells the butler. So that's it, there'll be no Cliveden, no party on the river. Those words 'unavoidably detained' won't shake themselves out of my head. What horrible words to use, like we haven't filled in the right forms or applied for a passport. It's at that moment I realise that a drinker tells awful lies. But there's no comfort in that.

'Call the police, my darling. David, call the police,' Mummy manages to say to my brother. She's weak and dazed, very weak, the blood thick down her face. David goes to the telephone and dials 999. The police say they will come and investigate. When my father hears my brother talking – his boy of ten on the telephone – he stands there, dead eyed, chewing his tongue. Then he swings quite suddenly on his heel and he's out through the drawing-room french windows, across the garden, past the pear tree and out through the wooden gate by the asbestos garage. He's gone.

We're alone. The house is silent. We wait. I want to run back to the Ivenses. That morning it was light; now it's black dark and dreadful again.

The knocker knocks, three heavy thudding knocks. It can't be those nasty men. They came once and I went to the door but I didn't open it. 'Does Mr Richard Blow live here?' they said, breaking off the knocking. 'A Mr Richard Blow?' That's my father's first name before the Purcell. I was six and I said to my mother, 'There are these nasty men and they keep on knocking.' 'Put the chain on,' she told me. That was my first meeting with the men who take everything out of the house.

My mother explains to the policeman but the policeman stands there rolling backwards and forwards a little on the balls of his feet. We peek out at him from my mother's side. She tells him about the drunkenness and the hitting. The policeman has this round cheerful face and he says very calmly to my mother, 'An Englishman's home is his castle. I cannot interfere.'

The policeman keeps talking like this and my mother thanks him and says that she's sure we'll be all right. Then she shuts the door.

But we can't stay in the house – and we can't go to Cliveden. We're too late and my mother's in no state. But we must go somewhere because my father will come back. She says that she is going to telephone Uncle Christopher to come and rescue us. Uncle Christopher is the brother of the grandmother we see from the tops of the buses. Otherwise, he is Lord Glenconner, the son and heir of my mother's grandparents, Pamela and Eddy.

'You'd better bring the boys and stay with us here,' Uncle Christopher tells my mother. I like that, we all like it, we'll be safe at last. There is the worry that my father will be back before my uncle's car is here. I pack Fuzziepeg into a small suitcase.

We pile into this black shiny car, a Bentley or something. McCubbin, Uncle Christopher's chauffeur and valet, is a small quick-moving black-headed Irishman with a singsong voice that sounds more Scottish because of the years among Scots. He drives us over Hammersmith Bridge and through streets and squares until we come to a large park filled with trees and fenced around by huge cream-coloured houses.

In one these houses lives Uncle Christopher with a wife and children. It's a big tall house with lots of floors and we stay there for four or five days. My mother tells Uncle Christopher everything and he is horrified and he is sad. He is sad for my mother because already she has suffered because his sister Clare would not see her. Uncle Christopher is an indulgent father and he is dismayed by his sister's unnatural coldness. He thinks that my mother should not have to suffer any more after that.

Because Mummy goes on suffering. She does not accept that she cannot see her mother. That is too hideous to contemplate

– as if my mother had been dropped on the doorstep of a foundlings' home by a mother in rags. But Clare is not in rags: she is a society beauty who passes the year moving from one large country house to another.

Clare plays bridge in the large houses – Blenheim and Wilton especially – 'the servants have been at these cards,' she says in a voice of honey soured with sharpness. She stays for three or four weeks making sure the servants are not idle. Clare wears the latest fashions, her photograph appears all the time in magazines, and she never lifts a finger for herself. In London she lunches at the Ritz and Claridge's, though every afternoon wherever she is she lies on a sofa, just lies there, her feet raised a little to let the blood circulate. To refresh her. To keep her beauty.

No time for bothering about Diana. And the excuse that Clare lost her rights to Diana through running off with Lionel Tennyson does not work. Clare made no effort to appeal, to try to see her daughter. None at all.

The hurt that Clare inflicted on my mother at two years of age went deep. Fifteen years go by and Diana, stopping in London to visit the dentist, calls on her mother unannounced. Clare cries: she sees her double; she sees her guilt. Diana returns in two days for lunch with her mother. But a whole circus of friends have been summoned and Clare addresses not one word to her daughter. Oddly, though, later Clare asks her daughter to stay.

Diana, the emergent débutante, was photographed with Clare – by Cecil Beaton, the 'society' photographer famous for his portraits of the great beauties of the silver screen and the drawing-room. The photograph appeared in *Vogue*. And yet beneath the gossamer friendliness of Clare was ice. Still Diana, a seventeen-year-old sylph, persisted in trying to make contact. She wanted, yes, she wanted her mother. So Clare took Diana to a ball, a débutantes' ball. An hour went by and Clare was angry. Why had no one danced with her beautiful daughter? But nobody knew Diana, and Clare made no effort.

Taking Diana home from the ball early, Clare made this comment: 'If you think life is easy, this is to show you that it isn't.'

After that, things guttered. A cup of tea here and there, and then just those sightings from the tops of buses. Diana made light of it at times, imitating her mother's hard voice. At other times she was sad, giving way to the vulnerability that can come to those abandoned. In Roehampton, in the house, there is a photograph of Clare looking down, posing surrounded by flowers that halo her prettiness. Cecil Beaton has done it again. The sweetness and the gentleness and innocence of the photograph are all deception. Always when she looks at it Diana wants to believe the photograph. But Diana is a child deceived, the photograph is a lie.

'You must leave him,' Uncle Christopher tells my mother. 'You must leave Purcell.'

'Must I? But there are no witnesses – only the children.'

'That could be difficult. Then I will ask him to sign something, admitting his cruelty.'

Still Diana wants Purcell as the husband he was meant to be. She sees all the fantasies on which he has been brought up as responsible. She blames the name Purcell and she blames Winifred and she blames Hilles. Now she would like to call him Richard, just plain Richard. To cancel out Granny Blow and all her affectations.

Whichever baptismal name Richard Purcell goes by does not alter the fact that he is no longer the romantic figure who walked down the steps of St Paul's Cathedral with his lovely young bride – her arm slipped through his – at his side. There were no signals then of what is now.

Diana asks herself how. Was it only that childhood? Or was it also the war and the years in the desert? Because if the war did not kill people it changed them; had it changed Richard Purcell? Throughout that time, as she waited, she was in love with this man who had sketched landscapes, drawn her naked, and read her Thomas Hardy. For her, falling in love had happened fast, like a dream, but she told herself it was real. For a while she forgot Clare. And in the years of his absence the dream strengthened.

'I am confused, Uncle Christopher,' she says. 'I need time.'

Uncle Christopher gives a smile to hide his thoughts. Uncle Christopher is a kind man, sitting in the daytime at the head of his chemical empire, and at night with his family. Now he sits in his drawing-room, paintings that go to museums on the walls, his feet on the Aubusson carpet. The blood drawn by Purcell has been removed from Diana's cheek. Uncle Christopher notices the bruises on her arms. He becomes protective. She is his flesh and blood. His mother's first grandchild. He remembers his mother's love for Diana. A love to replace Clare.

'He must sign the admission.'

'I am aware,' he goes on, 'that many find me distant. I have cultivated it, Diana. There is a tendency in our family to live for emotion. My mother introduced this tendency. As you may well remember, she cried at the drop of a hat. I have always had to keep a strong check on my feelings. Be careful in your decisions over Purcell. Be very careful not to allow your heart to dominate.'

'I will try. That is all I can do.'

'I think, Diana, that you are like my mother.'

Uncle Christopher disappears again behind the enigmatic smile.

Now I am a small boy again and it is the night before the Queen's coronation. Uncle Christopher and his wife are giving a party for the family and their children. Laid out in a room are the robes they will wear tomorrow in Westminster Abbey. When the Queen is crowned they will place coronets on their heads. I go into the room and touch the white ermine and the dark red velvet. I wonder at the gold crowns, puffed up with more dark red velvet. This isn't life, I say to myself, it's Madame Tussaud's.

McCubbin, the Irishman with the singing Scots voice, takes us for walks in Regent's Park. He wants to distract us from the unpleasantness in Roehampton.

'Underneath our very feet, my boys, there's a whole network of underground passages.' We listen attentively. Now we are to grasp the sewer systems of London. 'Down there, there're rats the size of my arm running everywhere,' he says, holding his arm sideways in the air. He's telling us this so that we will think rats are worse than Daddy's hittings. To make us forget. So I see in my mind, under the soft green grass of this park, a huge evil-smelling network of tunnels where lice-ridden dank-coated animals with knife-sharp teeth wait. He tells us of all the awful diseases that flow down these rivers of ghastly colour and I raise my head upwards to the bright trees of Regent's Park.

I want to run back to the safe and cosy house where Uncle Christopher lives. Where clocks tick quietly and thick carpets soften footfalls and where nothing changes from one day to the next. But I don't know how long we will be here for. They have these talks in private, my mother and Uncle Christopher; and sometimes his wife, who I call Aunt Elizabeth, comes out of the room too. I see them coming and going in and out of rooms. But there are no loud shouts ever and the house has got these old pieces of furniture which make you feel that the same sort of people have been living there always, quiet and peaceful people, and that nothing has ever gone wrong.

Uncle Christopher's children are in the house. They're quiet too, and distant, because suddenly we've come here and interrupted their lives. They're my cousins, I think to myself, but that's not quite dead centre family, is it? It's something else. There's an awkwardness, as if we're strangers, yet we're not. It must be because we don't live with them day after day. That's why I don't feel as free here as when I'm in Roehampton with Michael. But it's different again when we go to Scotland where my cousins have an enormous house in the middle of moors and hills. Perhaps that's because we go there sometimes for ten days, and everyone's had plenty of warning.

And yet . . . and yet, I still think we're outsiders. Why? Why do I feel this? It must be because they've got this peace everywhere that we don't have. And I don't see any bounced cheques on the breakfast table in the mornings. Uncle Christopher doesn't hit Aunt Elizabeth. We're all one flesh and blood and yet not the same at all. Not at all.

After five days we leave Uncle Christopher's house. I wonder where we're going, I don't know except I hear Uncle Christopher say to my mother, 'I want Purcell to see me.'

And then we're out of doors, on the pavement, and the singing Irishman takes my arm and David's. 'We better get you back to Roehampton,' he says.

So McCubbin – that's the surname of the singing Irishman, nobody calls him John – takes us off again. The days of peace are over. As soon as the Bentley comes to Hammersmith Bridge I start this inside lurching again. My mother sits silent in the back and I sit next to her. She turns her face towards the window. My mother isn't smiling, I notice. She hasn't smiled since we said goodbye to Aunt Elizabeth and Uncle Christopher. We're all worried but nobody says a word.

Now McCubbin's carrying our cases for us, and he gives us all a special smile. I watch the Bentley turning round to go down Roehampton Lane until the black shining car is lost among other cars and the enormous red buses. I stop, turn. I stand looking at our home, as my mother and David go inside the house. I'm going to wait, I say. I'm not ready yet. Then my father comes out all smiles – his double-breasted suit top flopping about like flying flags – and bends down to hug me.

'My darling boy. I've got the most delicious meal for you.' And he takes my hand and I keep looking at the big veins that run across his hand and wonder why they're so large. Does the green bottle mixture get into them? But just now he's so all right nobody would know he'd ever seen the green bottle.

'It's Jekyll and Hyde,' my mother says as my father goes to look at the boiling lobsters. But I don't know what she's talking about and she explains that it's a story about a man who's mad one moment and all right the next. So the two names Jekyll and Hyde are running inside my head and I see one as this lurching monster with eyes the size of gobstoppers and the other as all airs and graces and 'after yous'.

Now we're sitting down at the kitchen table and I'm wondering when we are going to eat. Daddy's taken off his jacket and he's lifting the lobsters out of the water. When he's in these good moods then I think of him as Daddy and I have in my mind a father who takes his children for walks and puts his arm round his wife and sees that there is always a home. A bit like those paintings in railway stations where a family full of smiles is sitting on some beach somewhere and the daddy is helping his son make a sandcastle.

My father builds sandcastles, but they're different.

'I'll make a million fast and furious,' he says to my mother, his throat moving as he chews a piece of this white rubbery fish. Now Mummy has half of a smile on her face and I know she's like this because she's heard it before. David looks at Daddy sternly and not smiling. My mother says nothing, but we go on eating the food he's bought and I think it's going to be much easier when I'm at school because I'll be able to forget what my mother says will never happen. 'There'll never be a million,' she says, but right out loud, now, to my father she says, 'You must take a cure. It's the best thing.'

So he tosses his head up and looks at Mummy. 'Perfectly all right, darling girl . . . I'm perfectly all right.' There's not a word about the bang with the telephone and not going to Godfather Bill and the days we've just spent with Uncle Christopher. No, he hasn't a conscience about anything and I wonder if he's been here not taking a sip at all of the green bottle mixture and pulling out the drawings that are in my bedroom or if this isn't the first day he's been normal – I mean, making sense.

'Herbert Crescent is nearly finished,' my father says. This is a house in the centre of London, quite near to a place where Mummy buys our clothes from. We catch a bus from Roehampton sometimes and go right into the centre of Harrods where there's a banking hall, a food hall, and floors filled with different things. Then sometimes, after Harrods, we walk past these tall buildings – all dark red – to a house on a corner, dark red too. There are builders coming out and going in and dust and noise. 'We'll make a million,' my father says again. And I think of the dust and the noise and the builders' shouts and the million.

That's why he buys these other houses. My father borrows money to buy more houses so that the million will happen quickly. That's why he's always unfolding rolls of drawings and bending over them in Roehampton. He's putting all these houses together again and then selling them as swish family homes. And they are swish. I've seen the ones in Paultons Square. There's a whole row of them there – you can tell them by the big glass windows and the smart copper covers over the front doors. But they haven't made us a million yet. The problem is that my father goes to a public house on the corner. I know the publicans' names – Kitty and George. They're life-size for me. There's one behind the bar pulling pints and the other talking over the bar, cigarette smoke hazing the glitter of her make-up.

'Where are you going?' I say to my mother.

'To find your father,' she says. 'He's with Kitty and George.' And she puts on a coat and ties a headscarf round her, and she leaves the girl who's staying in the house to look after us. But Mummy doesn't seem at all happy because her beautiful face is drawn and her lips aren't large as they normally are, but shrink-ing so that I think she fears the journey she's making. Then she hugs us, and this girl, Michelle, puts us into our beds.

'Leave me alone! Leave me alone!' I hear my father shout. I don't know what time it is but I know it's the night still. Then suddenly the shouting dies away as quickly as it started. That's because my father's collapsed. I know it. He's naked on the bed. Or he's passed out and my mother's undressing him. She does that a lot. I've seen her doing it.

From the next room comes the clatter of the typewriter. My father's secretary never stops. If she eats she only pecks, and she stands tall as a giraffe and trembles. I think it must be my father making her tremble, but she does this quite naturally. She looks after all my father's business and now she comes into the kitchen and says, 'Will you read over these letters and sign them.'

'I'll be with you right now,' says my father. Then she looks at us, trembles, and leaves the room. 'Ann's frightfully highly-strung,' my mother tells us. It's a new word for me, this 'highly-strung' and I'm told that it's because Ann's parents are first cousins. My mother says she comes from a very old family, which means there hasn't been any new blood for ages. I don't quite understand this 'blood' talk. I think about it while I'm eating. But Ann is so good at the typing and I don't believe my father would ever get these letters off without her.

We eat the lobster, but there's no talk to go with it. My father keeps trying to make some joke about lobster pots but it doesn't work. After that it's silence and strain. I want Michael to come over, but he's gone away for two weeks with his parents to a town by the sea and it's all been arranged months ahead. I wasn't allowed to go because we're going to Ragdale to stay with Aunt Phyllie. My mother doesn't like us only going to Granny Blow at Hilles, she wants us to be with her family too. She tells us that we must have stability and that Aunt Phyllie can give us that.

'I must go and see Whelan,' my father announces, leaping from his chair. 'It's terribly important.'

'Try not to be back too late,' my mother says, but I don't sense much hope in her voice. 'Absolutely not, my darling. I'll be home by six.' He tries to give her a big hug but Mummy doesn't want this hug, I can see that. It's all too soon. I watch David's face freeze.

Mr Whelan is my father's estate agent. He puts my father's houses up for sale and brings him the clients. He's a funny, fat little man who wheezes like a pair of bellows and he's got this wife who wears a lot of make-up and a hat perched on the side of her head. Just now I'm anxious to slip out into the garden. My fort's all set up with soldiers, and they're really nice lead soldiers. In a second David's out joining me. We arrange the soldiers ready for an invasion.

'I bet Daddy comes back drunk tonight. And I bet it'll be ten o'clock,' David says, putting a soldier in a turret.

'Do you think so?' I say.

But in a few days we'll be at Ragdale with Aunt Phyllie. Daddy never comes there. Granny Blow and Uncle Jonathan don't come there either. Ragdale's safe. Ragdale's different. Mummy talks about a normal life with Aunt Phyllie. As the front door slams and my father walks down Roehampton Lane to the bus stop, I'm gazing out across my fort wondering what a 'normal' life is. Well, a normal life isn't all this big talk my father goes in for and it's not his green bottle mixture, and it's not those nasty men who bang at the door till it caves in, and it's not those cheques he leaves on the kitchen table stamped in red 'Refer to drawer'. It isn't any of that. Not that.

It's Aunt Phyllie meeting us at Melton Mowbray station, a great smile making a dimple on each of her cheeks. I wish there were hundreds of Aunt Phyllies everywhere.

4

THERE'S A MAN been staying with us in Roehampton. He's gone off now, back to America where he comes from. He's about twenty-two I suppose, and his name is Mark Blow. We say we're all cousins, but we're not one hundred per cent sure what links the American and English Blows. His father, Dick, comes to see us quite often. Dick's tall like my father, and he doesn't work but enjoys himself. Well, he's an artist and he's done this drawing of me that hangs in the room with the french windows. But he doesn't have to sell his art. I think that every American is like Dick, with the Dorchester Hotel to stay in in London, an apartment in New York, and a house outside Florence.

Dick's son, Mark, doesn't seem specially rich. He doesn't say a lot but goes off every day and comes back in the evenings. He's tall too, with foreign-looking skin, but very thin, not that film star, Burt Lancaster build of his father. Once I saw Mark looking very worried when my father was shouting, his white face going whiter than ever. My mother says he's studying for a degree and it's rather put me off that plan. People who study never smile and seem to tremble, a bit like Ann, the highly-strung secretary.

'I think he's a druid,' Michael said. 'It's dead secret, that society.'

'I know. I don't feel quite right about him,' I say. 'He's even more scared than we are when Daddy's on that stuff.'

But Mark's gone now. He was with us for six months, or was it a year? I don't remember. Mark was a shadow who never became flesh and blood. It isn't like that with Uncle Hugh. When my father's out we have games with him. Hide-and-seek and pillow fights. He makes us laugh and we laugh so much with Uncle Hugh our tummies ache. He's my mother's half-brother and they grew up together in a big bleak house in the north, Rise Park.

'What about the Luft?' I hear my mother say.

'As ghastly as ever,' Uncle Hugh replies.

I keep hearing this word 'Luft' and not until I'm at my prep school do I realise it refers to the Nazi air force – the Luftwaffe. But when my mother and Uncle Hugh say it they don't mean the Luftwaffe, they mean my mother's stepmother and Uncle Hugh's mother. I've heard my mother call her 'Cicely', but always in a way that withers up the name completely. Apparently she's not at all nice. That's why they call her the Luft.

We don't see Cicely much but we hear of her. Her cruelty to my mother and her youngest son, Uncle Hugh, makes a bond between them. My mother tells us terrible stories of her stepmother. Adrian Bethell married her a few years after his disaster with Clare. Cicely was the daughter of a Herefordshire baronet and landowner, and as plain as Clare was pretty. She promised to treat Diana as her own. She asked Diana to call her 'Mummy', but after that the promise was broken.

'You thought you didn't have a mummy,' said Cicely to Diana.

'I've not got a mummy,' answered five-year-old Diana.

'You do have a mummy, but she's an evil mummy. And if you ever mention her name in front of your father you'll cause him great distress.'

And they went on walking down the gravel path that is the cedar walk at Rise. Cicely took Diana by the hand. She held her hand tight and then dropped it.

She never showed Diana a moment more of affection after that. Every move Diana made, Cicely corrected. She hung thick curtains in Diana's bedroom at Rise, so no light could chink in at the side. When Diana started to develop her bust, Cicely had it bandaged down. At fifteen Diana's hair fell out through a nervous disorder brought on by Cicely's fierce lack of loving. Diana recovered, her hair returned and ever after Cicely taunted Diana. In any crisis for Diana Cicely would sniff, 'Diana has remarkable powers of recuperation!'

As for Uncle Hugh, Cicely simply wasn't interested.

Under the glass on my mother's dressing table there's a photograph of Uncle Hugh wearing a flying cap and sitting in the cockpit of an aeroplane. That's what he likes doing – flying. I see him flying up and away from the Luft. He's obviously happiest when not on the earth, except that he makes my mother smile and laugh when he's with her. He sparks with life and then one day, quite suddenly, there are no more sparks.

'Uncle Hugh's dead,' my mother tells us. She's not crying now, but I can see she has been. She's packing up to go up to Rise, because that's where they're going to bury him, in the family graveyard, next to my mother's father, who was Uncle Hugh's father too, of course.

I'm eight years old when this happens. I keep going over in my mind Uncle Hugh's last days. He was twenty-two. He was flying in Scotland and his plane struck blanket fog. For three days nobody could find Uncle Hugh. Then finally he was found, his plane crashed, his body inside. He'd hit a mountain. There'd be no more laughter now and no more pillow fights. They slipped him underground at Rise, in the churchyard there where the yew trees sweep low over the family graves. 'My stepmother never attended. She stayed indoors,' my mother tells us. And after that there's a silence in Roehampton, and for the first time I hear that silence – the long, long silence – that is death.

All the time we're going to Ragdale, or Ragdale Hall, or 'the Hall' as the people there call it. We keep visiting. It's like a second home from London. And Aunt Phyllie's car seems to go slowly, too slowly, those five or six miles that separate Melton Mowbray from Ragdale. My happiness always runs ahead, turning to agitation when, in the distance and rising out of the fields, I see the tower that sits on the roof of Ragdale. There's a clock on this tower with some huge bells like Big Ben that strike the hours. Already I smell the new-mown hay and think of the scrambles we're to have in haystacks. Ragdale has battlements, it's like a huge red-brick fort smothered over with ivy, but there's no sign of fighting anywhere, only occasionally the sound of dogs noisily whining in the woods.

We pass through tall gates – the Iron Gates – and down a drive with short, stunted trees on each side and rolling fields beyond, then through a stableyard, and stop at a door on the side of the ivy-covered fort. When I was three or four, there'd sometimes be an elderly man sitting in a summer rocking-chair covered in brown canvas, swinging it backwards and forwards, slowly, by this door. Then, when Aunt Phyllie passed, he'd look up.

'How are we going to keep hounds going, Puppy?' he'd say – grunting, always grunting. Puppy, that's what he called her and she calls him Puppy, too.

'Don't worry. I'll put something in the kitty,' Aunt Phyllie replies, but cheerful, not solemn like Uncle Philip.

'Good,' he says, though you don't hear it much through the grunts. 'Good.' And that's all he says.

Uncle Philip's on his horse riding through the stableyard and my brother and I are tumbling down from a barn. 'Make way for the mare! Make way for the mare!' goes Uncle Philip and he rides past us, a black bowler hat on his head.

'Uncle Philip's the Mayor of Leicester,' I announce proudly.

But of course he isn't, it's the words that sound the same. And I know about Dick Whittington. He's frightening, Uncle Philip, but not in the same way that my father is. It's because he won't speak. And he doesn't pick us up for piggybacks or play at soldiers with us. He's really far away – in fact, all we hear are these grunts. The happiness is being with Aunt Phyllie. Why did Aunt Phyllie marry him? My mother says it's a marriage of convenience. I sort of understand except she doesn't go into detail. Not until I'm twelve is it all explained.

Aunt Phyllie is the sister of my grandfather Bethell. Her childhood was spent at Rise Park where she hunted with the hounds and became a crack rifle shot. She came out as a débutante in Edwardian England and travelled from country house to country house accompanied by a lady's maid. It was in the country houses that Aunt Phyllie was to make a suitable match. She took her album and each page is filled with swirling signatures in thick black ink around a picture of a house.

Aunt Phyllie was not a beauty but there was dignity, comfort and sweetness in her face. Men admired her good sense but the one she truly loved was to die of pneumonia soon after the engagement. Victor Conyngham, Marquess Conyngham of Slane Castle, County Meath, hunted the otter and was loved by Aunt Phyllie. She didn't love again like that and when Uncle Philip courted her she settled for a marriage of companionship. As his wife, she played the perfect county lady – opening fêtes and bazaars, doing 'good works' all around Ragdale, but bearing him no children.

'Uncle Philip was third choice,' Aunt Phyllie said to me one day, many years later. 'You never slept in the same bed with him,' I said to her, surprised by my forwardness. Quite calmly, quite naturally she replied, 'He kicked so much in bed.'

There are Italians at Ragdale. They work on the farm. One is Aunt Phyllie's favourite. Luigi comes over and hugs me. He hugs David too. He's been working here since he came out of his POW camp. Luigi and the other Italians decided they liked being at Ragdale with Aunt Phyllie and so they haven't gone back to Italy. Throughout the war Uncle Philip ignored them because he doesn't know about foreigners. And, anyway, Uncle Philip was making sure the hunting went on. Uncle Philip doesn't bother with people who don't hunt. He only speaks to Mr Ward, his groom, and even then it's kept short. Everybody calls Uncle Philip 'the Major', and I'm getting used to this although I never see any army people with him. Of course, I know he's called 'the Major' because he was in the army during the First World War. But he wasn't in the last war, unless you count the Home Guard. No, Uncle Philip was keeping the Quorn Hunt going.

It's quite a tricky one, saying Quorn. It's said like 'corn' except you have to make a 'q' sound with the 'c.' But I've learnt to manage it and at Ragdale it's bound up with the place as much as the cuckoo spinney and the crab apple tree. Uncle Philip and Aunt Phyllie are always talking about the Quorn and I've seen hundreds of horses racing across the fields, their riders dashingly dressed in top hats, scarlet and black coats, and white scarfs held by a gold pin round their necks. Further on, and usually in woods, are the hounds making this squealing noise. They say that happens when they're on to a fox.

'In the darkest jungles of Africa the name Cantrell-Hubbersty would bring light,' says Mr Ward one day as he polishes and polishes the harness. I think it's a funny name for Aunt Phyllie to have, but it's because she's married to Uncle Philip. And I wander off wondering if I really shouted 'Cantrell-Hubbersty' in a dark jungle in Africa whether all the tribes would gather round me.

Aunt Phyllie doesn't hunt any more, but Uncle Philip has to. He knows every field, wood and place to jump with his horse in the whole of the Quorn country. Uncle Philip didn't notice Hitler and the Nazis too much because he was watching for foxes, talking with the huntsman, and being Master of the Quorn. And the Quorn is the most famous pack of hounds in England. It's famous because you jump your fences very fast, like in a race, and everywhere is grass, grass, grass. You can't have a fast run without grass. If there's one field of plough, Uncle Philip shakes. No devil-may-care rider wants to stumble over plough.

That's why everybody who wants to be somebody hunts with the Quorn. But Uncle Philip's different. He grew up here at Ragdale. It's his family home. He never went to London except to buy and sell his horses. Just the odd day at Tattersall's on Knightsbridge Green, and a few hours hob-nobbing with the dealers, and then, for Uncle Philip, it was straight back to Ragdale. Apart from that it's been hunting, hunting, hunting. There was one young man that came out with the Quorn and Uncle Philip said, 'I haven't seen you for some time.' 'No,' said the young man, 'I've been fighting in the war.' 'Oh,' replied Uncle Philip unbothered. 'You'll find subscriptions have gone up.'

When I mention Uncle Philip to Michael he starts to laugh and tells me that I'm making it all up. I realise that people like Uncle Philip don't fit into Roehampton. He's never been there and I know he's not coming. But I tell Michael there's a magazine that sits on Aunt Phyllie's table called *Horse and Hound* and it's full of Uncle Philips. Although I think nobody can be quite like Uncle Philip; not quite.

I'm eight on this visit and Uncle Philip isn't here any more. He's been killed out hunting: the horse turned its foot in a rabbit hole and over he went. He was over seventy and too old to take the fall. Uncle Philip's neck snapped like that. Aunt Phyllie wasn't there at the time, she was in Italy. My mother says this is how hunting people like to go, killed in the chase. She's not upset, Mummy. She found Uncle Philip very difficult. He didn't even speak much to her. And now he's had the best death. That's what they all say.

My mother tells us about the way Uncle Philip was lowered into the grave and how the Quorn huntsman took off his black velvet hunting cap, pressed it against the buttons of his scarlet coat, and said, 'Goodbye, sir.' About the chorus of hunting sobs from tough-faced ladies, and how Aunt Phyllie wasn't even there. Aunt Phyllie was taking the waters at Montecatini in Italy. It was too far and too interrupting to return. She asked for him to be buried by the side of Ragdale church and later put a sundial on top for a tombstone. 'We'll always be able to tell the time by him,' she told my mother.

'Isn't it quite a good thing Uncle Philip's dead,' I say one day in the dining-room at Ragdale a year or so later. I'm remembering the shouts of 'Make way for the mare!' and Uncle Philip's disturbing silences, broken only by those grunts. I'm remembering my fear.

The room goes quiet. What have I said? Then after a bit Aunt Phyllie laughs, a high-pitched laugh as if a violin was finding its notes.

It's very calm at Ragdale with smells of flowers all through the house and clocks quietly ticking and I spend hours in the cuckoo spinney, which lies to one side of the house, playing at farmers with my brother. Or we're with Hughie, Mr Ward's son, and he's telling us fantastic stories. He tells us that Uncle Philip fell one day into the moat and that a crane had to be fetched to pull him out. We believe him. Then we go playing in a big house on the slope of a hill by the church, a house we call the Old Hall. This house is falling down and it's very sad because once it was very grand and beautiful.

The Old Hall belongs to Aunt Phyllie too, but before the Cantrell-Hubberstys came along all of Ragdale belonged to a blue-blood family called Shirley. The title was Ferrers – the Earl Ferrers. Now there's a story that an earl in the eighteenth century slew his steward while in a temper. It happened in the Old Hall, Hughie says. Because we're in this room where there's a huge hole in the stone floor and that, Hughie says, is where Lord Ferrers chucked the steward. We lean over the edge of the hole and stare into a black mirror of water. 'Are you there?' shouts Hughie. 'We're coming to get you.'

'It's a bit late,' my brother tells him. 'He'd be dead by now.'

'No – no,' says Hughie. 'He's waiting for us.' So we go on shouting down the hole and Hughie distracts us with this bit about the Earl being tried and hanged with a silk cord. Years later

I discover that it's all quite true, but for the moment it doesn't matter because our job is to haul the steward out of the water.

Then we're running through other rooms in the abandoned hall, and in some rooms there's panelling half there and half not and I don't think why nobody's living in the place but that the place is ours and nothing will ever change. And the hours fly past until we're in Ragdale village buying fizzy drinks in the shop and next there's a bell sounding in the distance. The bell means it's time to be back at the new hall — although it's quite old too — where Jean's waiting to put us to bed. So we run back through the park and leave Hughie to go back to his mum and dad while David and I return to Aunt Phyllie, Jean, and supper in bed.

Jean is Aunt Phyllie's maid. Jean isn't young any more, but she isn't old either. I notice her thick stockings and how she walks with a roll as if she's learnt to steady herself because country houses are isolated places, and perhaps not so different from being on the deck of a ship, far out at sea. Every evening, like tonight, she brings the bowl of tomato soup and a boiled egg to our bedrooms. Except that this time as a treat David is being allowed to have dinner with the grown-ups and I'm alone in my bedroom, so Jean comes in and reads me the Doctor Dolittle stories. I sit there listening, my eyes drifting to the hunting pictures on my walls. When I fall asleep I'm thinking of the Push-Me-Pull-You, that animal in Doctor Dolittle with two heads, and the elegant hunting man on a vast galloping horse leaping towards a pretty big river. Underneath the picture there's a remark of the elegant rider's: 'Shall I throw myself off now or take the chance of her jumping it?'

The picture of the elegant hunting man doesn't leave my mind and I think that's all I want to do. One day I'll be old enough to wear those splendid clothes and go out like Uncle Philip or Grandfather Bethell and jump fences and rivers and be really brave. My mother tells me that the best thing that can happen is for a hunting man to take a fall and be carried home on a gate. It's just like a soldier being courageously wounded in battle. Hunting is preparation for the battlefield. But I'm puzzled that she's still a little mocking about it.

'Your father was a Master of Foxhounds,' I say. 'He hunted his hounds himself, you told me. Did you love your father?'

'My father was a good man. But darling, I couldn't marry the sort of person he wanted me to. There were these young men at dances who blew hunting horns in your ear. I couldn't have lived with that. Your father was different. He could draw and he'd read a book.'

Playing in the woods with Hughie and David, I think about this. In fact whenever my father's bad and drinking it runs in my thoughts.

'Hunting won't last,' Luigi tells me as I stand by, watching him straighten a fence. This sends me into a terrible grumpy misery. 'Why not?' I ask. I don't pause to ask myself if Luigi could really know. 'It's too expensive. Only people like your godfather Lord Astor will be able to afford it. You must be very nice to him.'

But we don't see my godfather too much. I want to say that my father's drinking and hitting makes it difficult, but I'm meant to keep quiet. Although David says Aunt Phyllie asks him questions about what goes on at home. Aunt Phyllie's seen these bruises on my mother but just now my mother doesn't want to tell everything. She thinks that perhaps Daddy will get better, but Aunt Phyllie doesn't trust that. She doesn't want to ask my mother about it because it upsets her – and my mother wants to protect him.

'Tell me the truth, David,' Aunt Phyllie says over tea in her drawing-room when my mother's not there. And David looks round at the silver cows delicately standing on a table near the sofa mixed with china figures of people in old-fashioned clothes.

'He hits – he hits Mummy. When he's drunk.'

Aunt Phyllie sighs and puts her hands on her lap. 'We must do something,' she says, the dimples gone from her cheeks. 'I want you to tell me everything.'

But David doesn't go any further. The telephone rings and it's

the huntsman from the Quorn who wants to come over. 'Yes –
do bring them. Give them to Mr Ward.' David doesn't understand who 'they' are. Well, 'they' are two hound puppies that are
going to be 'walked' at Ragdale. After Uncle Philip died Aunt
Phyllie took over as Joint Master of the Quorn, and so the
Quorn kennels are as much at the centre of Ragdale doings as
ever. We're always being taken to meets with Aunt Phyllie who,
although she no longer rides, sees helping the hunt as her duty.
Just as Aunt Phyllie sits on lots of committees that get money for
charities.

In the kitchen Mrs Harvey does the cooking. She's a small
round lady with fuzzy white hair. She doesn't look very well but
that's because she's got her face into steaming pots all day. In her
bedroom she sits in an armchair sipping neat gin. The gin keeps
her going. One day she's walking through the bedrooms with
Jean, stout too, and they go through my mother's bedroom.
Hanging on the cupboard is an evening dress and Mrs Harvey
looks at the dress and mumbles to Jean: 'What's she want to wear
that for – she's 'ad 'er day.'

My mother talks to Jean a lot. She goes to see her and they
drink a cup of tea together. I sometimes hear them talking. 'Oh
Jean, I'm so tired,' my mother will say. 'What you need is a good
rest,' says Jean. And they settle down into these chairs in the old
nursery. They gossip in the same way that we go playing with
Hughie. 'She's been well looked after all her life, has Madam,'
Jean says to my mother, speaking of Aunt Phyllie.

My mother says there aren't going to be any servants soon.
Aunt Phyllie says that, too. Aunt Phyllie's been lucky. I suppose
that's why she talks about her lady's maid, Niggie, quite sadly.
Niggie, who's dead. It's because she knows the Niggies won't
come back.

'Now make your beds, both of you. There won't be anyone
to look after you when you grow up,' Aunt Phyllie tells us in her
violin voice. Then Aunt Phyllie walks out of the dining-room,
her brown lace-up shoes treading towards the kitchen where she

talks to Mrs Harvey. Every morning after breakfast Aunt Phyllie talks to Mrs Harvey about what she is to cook that day.

It is safe at Ragdale. I know that. My father never comes here. There's nothing mad about Ragdale. When Mummy's here with us I see her as she must have been before all the dreadfulness began. The days when Mummy wore those dresses in the put-away hamper, when her father, the grandfather I'll never know, was alive. In the evenings at Ragdale, as I'm lying in my bed and the rooks have stopped cawing, I hear Aunt Phyllie laughing and my mother laughing too.

I love hearing them laugh and I fall asleep with Fuzziepeg, dreaming of white peaches and green figs from Aunt Phyllie's greenhouse. All I say is, 'How long will it last? How long?'

It's harvest at Ragdale and Luigi puts David on a tractor and, standing beside him, lets him drive it. David holds the wheel, reversing the tractor back to the cart. I watch feeling young – too young for anything. So I go to the room where all the bridles are kept. I find Mr Ward there. Uncle Philip's dead but Mr Ward's cleaning as if tomorrow Uncle Philip will come along and ask for the mare. I sit on a table littered with cleaning stuff. I look at the long steel bits hanging like polished skeletons waiting for the mare to clutch at them, to throw white foam everywhere as she jangles them back to life. I watch Mr Ward's quick movements, and his face all pointed and darting like his hands. He wears a brown kennel coat. But Mr Ward tells me it wasn't just one horse Uncle Philip rode because if you hunt four days of every week you need at least eight or ten horses. 'And very partic'lar, the Major – very partic'lar,' Mr Ward goes – he always says everything twice. And as he talks the leather of the bridles gets rubbed and rubbed. But the room is dark, with wooden walls the colour of brown mud brightened a little by varnish, and brightened again by the single bulb that hangs under a white shade on a long wire from the ceiling. Jutting out from the wall on separate iron stands are the rows of saddles which Mr Ward shines too. Mr Ward, as he rubs, tells me that four or five hundred people hunted with the Quorn 'in the old days'. That the Major always hunted on two horses: one in the morning and one in the afternoon. 'Yes, everything had to be just right for the Major. If he saw so much as a mark of the yellow soap on the leather, my God you knew it – my God you did.' So Mr Ward rubs and rubs, his hands going up and down the long leather reins until he lets them drop back into place against the wooden wall. 'Nothing's done as it was – no, not as it was,' he says, going to lift one of the saddles and start on them. In the old days, I want to add, in the old days, and I swing my legs backwards and forwards. Mr Ward's tack room is a chapel. It has the smell of polish that chapels have, and like a chapel it's a place of worship, too – but for things going. Because that's what Mr Ward says. 'We'll never see those days again.' And I feel it, too, in this dark room, as I watch, swing my legs and watch.

My mother says we've got to know what a normal home is like. Ragdale is so solid, so there in its valley where horsemen ride. I know that generations stand behind me at Ragdale, but also that the best of Ragdale belongs to yesterday. I hear the high tones of Aunt Phyllie, comfortable in her cut tweed suit, follow me down the passages: 'There won't be anyone to look after you when you grow up.' There's a ballroom, huge and echoing, but never an orchestra there now. It's filled with these skin-coloured legs which aren't real and white boxes with a red cross painted on them and piles of things you see by hospital beds. My mother tells me that Aunt Phyllie ran the Red Cross in Leicestershire during the war. She had a shop in Melton and the stores were kept at Ragdale. And in the First World War she nursed the wounded soldiers, so there hasn't been much let-up for Aunt Phyllie, what with Uncle Philip's groans and the soldiers' groans. Except that she's never really been without money or she wouldn't be at Ragdale.

In and out of the house go other comfortable-looking women and men, too, all in tweed and often wearing these dec-orated brown shoes – brogues, they're called. I'm inquisitive and eavesdrop on them. They seem so solid and safe. Safe for ever and for ever. How did it happen? Will it happen to us, too, one day? I wonder. I listen.

'Oh, Phyllie, darling, we've had an absolutely topping year with the cattle,' and both stride towards Aunt Phyllie's drawing-room, identical shoes down the passage.

'And we've almost got the harvest in, which is such a relief.'

Their voices grow muffled as Aunt Phyllie gives the drawing-room door a push. I just hear her say, 'I want to talk about the Quorn. I'm afraid there's trouble again.'

Hughie's at the back door. He says there's an enormous rook fallen out of a tree and we're to come and look at it. He says it looks like a parson sleeping and he doesn't think it's ever going to wake again. We run through the stableyard, past the cow shed, and turn down a dry mud track. On one side is the cuckoo wood and, half-way down the track in the grass, the rook.

'We'll have to bury him,' Hughie announces.

'He's definitely dead, isn't he,' I say, touching him with my foot, then running backwards in case he might wake up.

The rook doesn't budge. David and Hughie stand there, staring.

'I think we should bury him with the Major. Poor rook.' Now Hughie pokes him with a stick.

'Aunt Phyllie won't want to be buried with a rook,' says David.

'If we bury him here, there'll be other rooks around him. Do you think he's a man rook or a woman rook?' I ask.

'It doesn't matter any more,' says Hughie sadly. 'Although it's probably a woman and tired with laying eggs all the time. It must be painful.'

Hughie runs off to find a spade in the garden shed. We follow after him. In the distance we see Aunt Phyllie's gardener, Mr Body, and Hughie says, 'Quick, before he sees us.' But Mr Body's walking through the asparagus beds and where the rhubarb is.

Mr Body's old and walks stiffly. He turns his head and we all lie flat, protected by the long grass of the apple orchard. Hughie tiptoes to the shade, gets the spade and we go.

The rook must be buried where the other rooks fly above him. He can't be buried with Uncle Philip because of Aunt Phyllie. And anyway, he's not a Christian. I don't know what religion birds have – perhaps they don't need one, flying so near the sky – that's what I'm thinking now Hughie's digging with the spade. Staring at the dark hole I see worms wiggling out, making these wild lonely wiggles in the air, as if caught at their underground plotting. Once it's dug Hughie says we must roll the rook in and we gently tap him with our feet until he plops into the hole.

Hughie's with us every day. Aunt Phyllie's given us the old servants' hall to play in. It's down a stone passage on the ground floor and on the other side of the passage is the room where Pat, the cowman, separates the milk and where the butter is made. We see him going towards a door that leads to the kitchen, the cream in one enamel jug, the milk in another. The passage has a milk smell mixed with disinfectant. Pat has a sway as he walks from carrying milk buckets, and he's hairy-armed and fair-haired. We hear him swilling out the milk room, the water splashing to the floor. If we're near the cowshed when he's milking, he lets us try ourselves, sitting on his wooden stool and tweaking the cows' udders in that special way which makes the milk spurt. Pat lives with his mother in a red-brick house that's half-way down the drive.

'When you wake in the mornings do you feel something stiff between your legs?' he asks my brother.

It's an odd question, that one. My brother replies that he does, but Pat doesn't take it any further. He moves away with an 'I know what it's all about' glance in his eye.

Without my father's shouting and hitting, suddenly I'm doing what all children are doing. There's so much time and no worries. Hughie thinks we should look at what goes stiff between the legs. At eight, I realise there's something possibly vital there but I haven't a clue what it amounts to. So we climb on to the sofa in the servants' hall – again there's a smell to it; rotting dust, I suppose – and pull a rug over us. Then it's a matter of daring each other to pull down our pants. This done, Hughie touches my not more than three inch willie; in return I touch his. It stops there, with sex not imagined and I'm aware only of the butterfly in my stomach.

Then we forget about that because Tinker, the cat, is in the room. None of us cares for this black cat who spends hours warming himself on Mrs Harvey's stove. There's a strong cat smell everywhere Tinker goes. Hughie runs in and out of other rooms in this empty servants' passage, opens each door to cry 'Tinker! – poo! poo!' and shuts the door fast.

Upstairs at Ragdale are more unused rooms – rooms that were bedrooms once when house parties happened. I'm in this room where shiny top hats are spilled across the floor and there's a pile of white breeches and brown breeches all mixed up and worn red coats and a bundle of hunting whips. That's all that's left of Uncle Philip, I think to myself and I see Uncle Philip not an old man in a canvas chair but charging across a grass field towards a huge fence, scattering other riders with a single shout: 'Out of my way!'

Yes, he shouted like that. Hunting the fox was serious for Uncle Philip.

In that abandoned room filled with Uncle Philip's abandoned things I made my dreams. One day, one day, I said, I'd have that life. I wouldn't shout, though, like Uncle Philip shouted but I'd have horses and stables and a groom like Mr Ward. Perhaps I'd have a house a bit like Ragdale too. If anything is said that takes those dreams away, I fly into tantrums, terrible tantrums. Suddenly I'm on the drive at Ragdale and I might be six or seven or eight years old and I'm pouring gravel from the drive over my head. The little white stones fall over my head and then tears of anger fall too. They don't understand, they don't. Tears pushed aside by my angry hands. It's here that I want, not London. I don't want that house where my father swings from the million promise to the flying knives.

'You must control your temper,' Aunt Phyllie says. Walk round the garden seven times, that's what she says I must do. That's what her mother, Marie-Myrtle, told her. Now I see she's giving me advice, bringing me up, because my father isn't doing that. And when she does this Aunt Phyllie has that worried look on her face that doesn't suit her. It's best when the dimples are there. So I pick myself up and, kicking at the gravel as I walk, turn to the end of the house and head for Mr Body's garden.

I don't want any more of my father's drinking, I'm saying to myself. How could I? I'm his son so this means it's going to happen to me too. Is it? At Roehampton it's close, so close and there's nowhere to go. Then I smile a bit. Apart from Michael, that is. But now I'm anxious Michael's not going to be there for ever. So I'm looking for some kind of always and always – where things aren't ever nasty. That's why I lose my temper for Ragdale.

At night, holding Fuzziepeg, I do wonder where my father is. He doesn't ring up and say 'I hope you're getting lots of riding, darling boy.' He's not making us a million, I don't believe it any more, and this is why. When my bedroom is too full of his drawings, I go and sleep in his dressing-room. One day I had a look in his drawers and out of this small drawer fell lots of cards. On them were the names of clubs. Places I think my father spends most of the night in. That's what I put together from reading their names. Churchill's and the Eve Club aren't places for him to play tennis at, they're for drinking and spending in. And this is why the cheques bounce and why there's going to be no money.

One day he rings up Ragdale and says to my mother, 'How much can you get from her?'

'What do you mean?'

'I must buy these houses. I'll pay her back.'

'Will you? You must.'

'I'm making our fortune.'

'Of course.'

My mother puts down the telephone and doesn't face Aunt Phyllie until the next day. Sitting on the sofa in the drawing-room as Aunt Phyllie pours the tea, my mother explains. I sit there, too, pretending not to hear but hearing everything.

'He's working so hard, you see. It's why he hardly ever leaves London,' my mother starts persuading. Aunt Phyllie listens, then Fluffy – her terrier – starts barking. Aunt Phyllie always has a little dog that barks. Lupo, her Alsatian, doesn't move. He lies there, stretched out on the carpet, hardly opening his eyes.

'I'll lend two thousand. But I must have it back. Money's very difficult these days,' Aunt Phyllie tells my mother. She puts her hand on her lap, a ruby ring and a gold one sitting on her tweeds. Now she asks if my father is drinking and my mother doesn't reply. 'Darling, you must tell me,' says Aunt Phyllie. 'He may need help.'

'He's fine – fine.' And my mother stands up and looks out at the park. The rooks are circling the high trees.

'That isn't true, darling. Irene saw him walking down the King's Road and she said he was drunk. As you know, Irene lives in the Vale.'

'I must stand by him,' my mother says, and she goes on looking.

5

I'M AT PREP school now. I've been here a year. It's in Surrey. There are quite a few prep schools around and we play them at matches. My prep school's called Scaitcliffe and it's near to Windsor Great Park. On Sundays we go for walks there, which means walking two by two with a master at our side. Sometimes we pass the Queen who goes riding in the park and we are made to take our caps off. We wear these red and black caps – the school colours – but the Queen just wears a headscarf and she gives a little smile as we do this.

Suddenly everything's very organised. It's as if home doesn't exist any longer or it's a long way off. Except at night, as I pull the bedclothes over my head, the trembling starts. I keep drifting back to Roehampton and hearing my father swinging up the stairs, clutching the banister, to pull my brother and myself out of bed to show us to some guests who've been there for dinner. 'These are my boys,' he says, swaying above us, his eyes shooting out into nowhere.

'It's far too late for them,' my mother interrupts.

'No it isn't,' my father answers her. 'Aren't the boys splendid.' The guests look at one another and my brother and I keep standing there feeling awkward and silly. Now my father starts chewing his tongue and the guests try to make conversation as if everything's normal. I watch them as they struggle, overdoing it, and feel more awkward. So my mother takes us back upstairs and meanwhile my father's fallen asleep in a chair. The guests sit there in silence waiting for my mother.

'Purcell overworks,' my mother says with earnestness, to convince herself too. 'He wears himself out.'

I'm awake in the dormitory at Scaitcliffe and I stare at the white-painted walls and the huddled shapes of the other boys, their clothes piled neatly on the wooden chairs beside each bed. On Sundays, when we're allowed out, their parents arrive to collect them. The other parents arrive in cars but my brother and I wait in the drive for my mother and father to collect us, crunching their way up the gravel drive on foot. There's a bus stop we go to in the road that leads to Scaitcliffe. It takes us to Egham and at Egham we catch the train to Barnes. And then from Barnes it's only a short walk up Roehampton Lane and we're home.

'We do prefer it if the parents have a car,' Mrs Vickers tells my mother. Mrs Vickers, the matriarch of the school, wants us to be safe. She also wants no indication of us being hard up. Parents who send their boys to prep schools can't be that. My mother tells Mrs Vickers she's an old-fashioned Edwardian snob and at that Mrs Vickers holds the telephone a little distance from her ear. 'Oh, Mrs Blow, I wasn't suggesting . . .' and there the conversation trails off, with my mother saying quite bluntly that we don't have the money for a car. But there isn't enough money for our school fees either because that million my father keeps promising hasn't arrived.

'Shake hands with a millionaire,' Mummy says. And with that she picks up my father's limp willy, which lies there like a dead fish, while he's naked and passed out on the bed. We stand silent at her side. She laughs and I know she's not really being funny but trying to make it all less awful for her and for us. There've been some bad days . . . days I keep thinking about.

This is how it happens on a really bad day. Suddenly the knives start flying and my mother and I are alone in the house. 'How

dare you! – How dare you!' my father keeps shouting, his eyes
bloodshot with fury. We duck into the kitchen and then he's
upstairs on the landing near my room. I duck behind the door
and my mother behind another. Next my father stops and says
he's going to kill himself. My mother stays very controlled but I
see her beautiful lips tremble. It happens so fast that I don't know
what my father will do. He's not my father any more to me now.
I want to shout, scream, 'You're mad! You're destroying us!' But
I don't. The words dry in my mouth, my mouth dried with fear.
My father goes into the bedroom he shares with my mother,
holding one of the long speckled ties he wears with a suit.

'Do it,' I hear my mother say. 'Go on. Do it.'

There's a kind of gurgle from my father and after that he drops
on the bed. I hear him crash on to the mattress. He's dead, he's
dead, I say to myself. I'm worried, and also not worried. There's
that excitement which comes with relief – relief muddled up
with despair. I listen to the silence. It's Sunday and not a sound
from anywhere. My mother goes into the bedroom and I hear
her say, 'He's sleeping, not dead. Your father wouldn't have the
courage.'

She's worn out now and she leans her head against the wall of
the landing as if she's thinking, peace, peace. I'm thinking,
Michael's coming over for lunch today and we've nothing ready.
And I'm tired too. I go to my mother and put my arm round her
waist. She puts a hand on my head. Then she goes down to the
kitchen and opens the fridge.

Minutes pass – half an hour, an hour – until I see Michael
coming into the garden through the wooden slatted gate. He's
always running, always darting as if everything was urgent.
'Hello, hello, hello,' he shouts coming up the stairs. He imitates
a radio comic as he comes into my bedroom, then sitting glumly
on the bed he puts on another voice. He sees my anxiety and
says, 'I know.'

We have lunch, my mother asking Michael about his school. It's
much nearer than Scaitcliffe, only a walk from Roehampton and it's

paid for by the state. 'You shouldn't send Simon to that expensive school,' Michael tells my mother. 'You haven't got the money.'

My mother's thrown by this. She pauses and runs a hand over Michael's shoulder. 'I expect you're right, but I don't want the boys to be isolated.'

If I went to another school – Michael's school – I wouldn't lose him. There's this difference – like the hamper of clothes in the attic – which cuts me off. I got over that one by making Michael part of it. But now I'm going to a private school where I'll only be with boys of my 'background'. And won't I be cut off from them, too, because of home? What's wrong with Michael's background anyway – or anyone's for that matter? I'm thinking of all this when there's a noise from upstairs.

'Simon's safer with me,' Michael announces and, at the same time, my mother lifts her head to the noise.

I hear my father's heavy footsteps going across the parquet floor of the hall. He comes into the kitchen and says loudly, 'We'll go to Ham. I've ordered a car from Daimler hire.'

Ham is this house by the river where one side of Granny Blow's family, the Tollemaches, come from. I've been there once before and my father wants us to go there because he says it's very beautiful, but also it makes him believe he's apologised for throwing the knives. Ordering the chauffeured limousine from Daimler Hire helps too. So I'm sitting in the back of the car with my mother and Michael, and my father's sitting in the front next to the driver. In no time, down a small side road, we enter Richmond Park. He turns his head to explain to us. He says Charles I hunted in the park, and our ancestor, Will Murray, hunted with him. I see these two men in their high boots and a swish of feathers on their tilted hats charging under oak trees and over bracken. Granny Blow is always going on about the Stuart monarchs and she says it's not important what happened after. As we reach Ham my father tells us the ghost of King Charles the Martyr has been seen in the gardens there.

★

'Quite splendid, isn't it?' my father says, turning his head slant-
ways and standing tall, so tall, his hands pushed deep in his jacket
pockets. We're looking up a gravel drive to Ham House. It's all
made of dark red brick with columns of a dark creamy stone. It
has a big wooden door in a stone doorway, a bit like a church.

'Not bad,' Michael says. 'But Blenheim Palace – it's smaller
than that.'

My father, on the defensive now, says these are the true old
houses of England, whereas Blenheim has a foreign look and is
all theatrical. And then he's off down the passages as if he wants
a chat with his ancestors.

My mother, looking pale and drawn, in a long dress with a
black belt, says in a sad strong voice, 'This is where the madness
comes from.'

'Do these houses do it?' And Michael stares at two great
marble figures on either side of the hall fireplace.

'Too much inbreeding,' my mother says. But we don't really
know what she means except I've heard a lot of talk about breeding at Ragdale. That was about horses, and I think then it must
be the same with us.

Michael's staring out of the window now and I know he's
wanting to be set free. So he and I run into the garden while my
mother stands on the gravel drive with the house behind her.
'You want to watch out for these people,' Michael tells me as we
run over the lawn where the ghost of King Charles is meant to
walk. 'Who?' I say. 'These ancestors -- they can inhabit people –
kind of creeping ghosts.' Then we look back and I see my father,
his face against a window, that long face that comes from Granny
Blow's family.

My father's definitely got a touch of what my mother says is
folie de grandeur', because it'll be years and years before we live
in a place like Ham. Except that one day we're going to live at
Hilles. Only it doesn't enter my head because Granny Blow is
alive and she runs it with Uncle Jonathan who never leaves her
side. But he has left her side now as he's always over with us in

Roehampton. He's writing a book about crusaders, but I can't think why he has to be with us.

Uncle Jonathan reads my mother bits of his book. He strides up and down the room, holding the pages in one hand, and stopping every few lines and turning his head to her. 'Tremendous theatre, here, dontcha think,' he says.

Now I'm at boarding school term time comes round quickly and when it comes round, home fades. I know it's there still but it's stopped happening in front of my eyes. It's covered over by my panic of being at school. I have to like cricket, and football and rugger; I have to learn Latin and do PT; I have to learn the boys' names and call the masters 'Sir'; I have to go every morning to chapel and every evening eat Cheddar cheese with a glass of milk – and do all kinds of things that don't happen at home. Like standing at the side of the pitch at section matches and shouting 'Up with Kitchener! 'Up with Kitchener! Down with Jellicoe! Down with Jellicoe!' That's because we're divided into four sections – Kitchener, Beatty, Jellicoe, Haig – and of course we have to support the section we're in. There aren't more than sixty boys in the school, but because they're always rushing past you on playing fields and in the gym it feels like hundreds.

'Hello, Pixie,' a boy says to me. 'Why?' I say. 'You've got a pixie face – that's why.' Or there's a master coming up to me as I'm lolling along on the cinder tracks that go through the school vegetable garden. 'Blow, blow, thou winter wind,' he goes, catching me by the pants, ' thou art not so unkind as man's ingratitude.'

Everyone keeps up this 'I'm all right, don't need anybody' thing. In that way it's rather like home. When the hitting starts and I go on playing with my animals – oh, yes, I've quite a circus – as if my father was doing no more than light a cigarette. At night, in the dormitories, it's different. Some of the boys want to get close to the other boys. It helps them forget how difficult school is. There are boys who climb into your bed and cuddle you and touch your stiff willie and you touch theirs and that's it. It only lasts a few minutes.

The dormitories are called after public schools. The large ones have the names of the schools we're meant to go on to – Eton's the largest, then there's Harrow, and after that there's Wellington, Winchester, Charterhouse and so on, until you come to a very small dormitory called Rossall. I don't think anyone's meant to go there. Everyone at Scaitcliffe is meant to go to Eton. Sometimes old boys come over. They're dressed in black tail coats or short jackets that I'm told are called 'bum-freezers'. That's the Eton dress and you have to be put down at birth or it's not likely there'll be a place. Well, I haven't been put down at birth, nor has my brother, but we keep up this front that we're going there. Well, to Mrs Vickers, at least.

I've got these photographs of my mother and father that I keep on a shelf above my bed. My father looks the OK dad there. He's got on a kind of ordinary tweed jacket and tweedy trousers, and he's sitting in a wood looking romantic, with that I'll-do-everything-for-you face. On his feet are these brown suede shoes. But he looks so normal, he does, with a touch even of the saviour. My mother sits beautiful and calm in a tweed suit, the jacket really held in, in the same woods. They're the woods at Rise. I want my mother and father to look like that when they come for Sports Day, so that I can hold my own with the rest of the school. But as my father comes up the gravel drive he's swaying – not walking straight, those movements of lurching and leaping – while my mother is doing her best to look as if nothing has happened.

I won't notice, I say to myself. If I do that, perhaps nobody else will either. I see my brother's face. He's sad and there's a twist of disgust on his lips. Leaping towards us, my father smothers us in hugs. I wriggle free and look at him for a moment. He doesn't notice my look and throws out one of his isn't-life-good exclamations, 'How wonderful! We are going to have fun, aren't we.' Then we run off to take part in the Sports Day games – the high jump, hurdles, sprinting – and next time I see my father he's leaning over Mr Vickers, who owns the school. He's leaning so far over him that Mr Vickers is reeling backwards, hoping my father won't overbalance and flatten him. He speaks to Mr Vickers.

'How are my boys doing?'

'David's in the first eleven cricket. I'm afraid Simon's a little behind at the moment, but I'm sure he'll catch up.'

'Splendid – absolutely splendid,' I hear my father say. Then I notice Mr Vickers sort of edging away, but very politely with this fixed smile still on his face. I feel upset with my father now. He's made a fool of us but he doesn't notice a thing as he stares into the air, drawing hard on his cigarette.

Things get more embarrassing at the end of the day. My father says he's brought a book for my brother, but he's hidden it in the undergrowth on the road to Scaitcliffe. The idea is that my brother should hunt for his present, which would be fine if my father could remember where he'd put it. So as the other parents' cars drive past, there we are scrambling around on the ground – all of us – trying to find the book.

It's fairly public now, my father's drinking. I've told a friend at Scaitcliffe and next time we go to stay in Scotland with Uncle Christopher I'm summoned into his study. He asks me to sit down. 'Simon, I don't think it's a good idea to mention anything about what's happening at home to anyone.' I want to say, but I've got to let it out somewhere. How can I breathe without letting it out? If I don't tell someone, I'll have pulled all the fur off Fuzziepeg. I pluck at Fuzziepeg at night, a way of pulling him closer. But I can't tell that to Uncle Christopher.

I get lonely in Scotland because they're older than me. There's a lot of talk of expensive parties because Uncle Christopher's son, Colin, is in this big social world. We keep seeing his photograph in the newspapers with Princess Margaret. He's got another brother and a half-brother because Uncle Christopher's on his second marriage. The much younger half-brother, Toby, and my brother go striding across the moors. I dawdle along behind. In the evenings we play cards. One day Colin teaches me how to dance the Charleston. I like that. It's best when we all go skating on the lake together. Skating makes everyone friendly, close.

I don't talk about my father to my cousins. I wonder if they know. They talk about shooting woodcock, catching trout on the loch, in the burns, and these parties. The food's very good here, lots of porridge and thick cream. I forget Daddy for a while, just forget him.

The house is called Glen – although locally I hear people call it The Glen – and it has turrets at its corners a bit like a foreign castle. There aren't many houses around Glen, just sloping moors with Christmas trees running down some of them. There's a village near to a farm which belongs to Uncle Christopher and it's built in black grey stone like I've seen on tombs. At night sometimes the village children come to the house and play 'He'. They speak in these funny voices like the singing Irishman with the Scots voice and I wonder if our voices don't sound as odd to them as theirs do to me.

'Ya dinna know ma saster,' says this boy with a mouth that seems to drop at the corner.

'An ye doon wana knoo'er,' says another boy jostling in with his cap pulled down too low over his forehead.

I notice they're all pretty easy in Glen: there's no embarrassment that it's a very different kind of house to the houses in the village. But I don't know what the people in the village talk about once their doors are shut. It's a sealed-off world. We've got to be the posh people to them. The people who have cars sent to stations to collect them and someone who comes into the room to unpack the suitcase and fold away the clothes.

At home Uncle Jonathan keeps coming over. Sometimes he goes into my mother's bedroom when she's in there and shuts the door. They don't come out for a few hours. After a month of this I understand what's happening – he's having a love affair

with my mother. I can tell from their faces and the way they try
to keep quiet about it. I don't really like him seducing her as if
my father isn't there. Particularly Uncle Jonathan, who swaggers
around 41 Roehampton Lane as if David and I don't exist.

'Has he passed out yet?' I hear Uncle Jonathan say one evening
and I creep into the sitting-room and see Uncle Jonathan eyeing
my father as if he's just a sack on the floor. That's what my father
looks like – a crumpled sack. Then Uncle Jonathan humps him
on to a sofa, makes sure he won't wake up, and turns to my
mother.

'Simon – you shouldn't be here. Go upstairs,' my mother says.
Next Uncle Jonathan is smothering her in kisses and I feel a bit
sick and go quickly out of the room. Sometimes, when my father's
stuck in a pub, Uncle Jonathan takes my mother to a night club.
That's a thing she never does with my father, but my mother and
Uncle Jonathan go to this night club in Leicester Square called the
Four Hundred. She says it's the place where everybody used to
dance – there and the Café de Paris. It takes her back to the
hamper-of-clothes days, and I notice her smiling again. There's a
French song she and Uncle Jonathan like and I hear them singing
it: *'Que reste-t-il de nos amours, Que reste-t-il de ces bonjours.'* It sounds
good and the words go round and round in my head – more than
the 'cat sat on the mat' sentences I'm learning at school.

I want my mother to be happy so I don't make a fuss about
Uncle Jonathan. There are times, though, when he can be quite
funny, and it's 'The Little Bear that Runs by Night' stuff. But not
for long. He's thinking about my mother.

There's no Michael now. I don't know if I'll ever see him again.
The Ivenses have left Roehampton. It happened suddenly a few
months ago when I was going to meet Michael for a film. Going
into the house that makes me calm with its polished pieces of
furniture, I asked Mr Ivens if Michael could come with me to
Scout camp. Michael's a Scout too, and I'd like him to come.

'We may be in the North by then,' Mr Ivens replies, looking down at me, and I look at his tie which is dark blue with old-fashioned motor cars running down it.

'Is that true – are you sure?' I say, looking at his red face.

Now Michael comes running through the house, knocking sideways one of the prints of 'Scenes of London' on the hall wall. Mr Ivens carefully straightens it.

'He says you're going – leaving,' I say to Michael.

'Come on, Simon, we'll miss the film.'

Now Michael and I are running down to the Upper Richmond Road where the buses are. We pass the shops we call the near shops and I see Stowell's where my father buys the green bottle mixture. So many times I've spotted my father making his leaping strides out of Stowell's, holding the brown paper bag with the green bottle and the yellow-label tonic waters like a baby. But he isn't there now. He's far off in Paultons Square – or Donne Place, or Callow Street – where his houses are, or he's not there at all any more but in a drinking club. I push it from my mind. There isn't an answer. There is no answer, I say to myself, catching my breath as I'm running. What bothers me is that Mr Ivens said something about moving.

A huge red bus trundles towards us and Michael says, 'Quick!' We climb to the top and on to the seat at the back. The big silver ticket machine punches our tickets and then I turn to Michael. 'Your father said you were moving North.'

'It's not definite. But it would be a good job move for Dad.'

'So we won't see each other any more.'

'Stop worrying. You're always worrying.' And Michael puts an arm round me and squeezes.

But I know it would be such an emptiness without Michael and the Ivenses. There are friends at prep school but I'm still awkward because of home. And then it's four years Michael's been around and he lives so near. I worry because I have to keep this everything's-perfect-at-home thing going, but I can let

things out to Michael. And if I didn't let all these anxieties out
. . . well, I don't know.

'Is it really expensive, your school?'

'I think there's been a problem with paying the bills.'

'Good. Then you'll have to leave and come to school with me.'

'My mother wrote to our uncle and he's going to pay.
Anyway, you'll be changing schools.'

'You've got all these posh people,' Michael says. 'They come
and look after you.'

'But they don't know me. I'm a relation, that's all. You know me.'

'Out!' Michael suddenly announces. We rush down the
winding stair and on to the street. Then to the cinema, and at
once the scene changes to Roman soldiers marching with
golden helmets down a stony road with bright green trees, a blue
sky and sunshine.

The film's over and we're quiet for a moment. We're walking
up the hill that leads to the Common. Michael says if we were
Romans we would mix our blood, that's what Romans did.

'There's no one for me to talk to if you go,' I say to Michael.

'What about schoolfriends – your new school?'

'It's different. You have to be terribly on top all the time.'

Now we're wandering in and out of the wood and out into
grassy places and we find a place where there's this high grass in
a small space where the trees aren't so thick. I look up at the sunlight coming through the trees and I think, if only Daddy threw
sunlight down on us instead of knives. Michael pulls off his
Aertex shirt. I pull off mine and we lie there staring through the
branches and leaves towards the sky.

'I want a home like yours.'

'One day you'll marry and have a home.'

'Will I?'

'Don't you want that?'

I turn my head and look straight at Michael.

'If you marry, I'll marry, but we'll make the home together,'
I say.

Michael edges towards me and whispers in my ear, 'All right.'
A few weeks later Michael's father got the job in the North.
I went over to spend the night with the Ivenses the week before
they started packing. Michael was in his bedroom putting
together a Hornby-Dublo train set. We played at going on a long
journey. Then I said, 'Let's stop this.'

'Come and visit us in Sheffield,' Michael said. He took out a
penknife and made a small cut in his skin and a blob of blood
rose. He took my arm and did the same. He rubbed the blood
of his arm with mine. 'Better?'

'Yes, much better. Sheffield – to Sheffield,' I said, pointing my
arm upwards. After that we went downstairs where his parents
were watching television. It was all about the war, and Spitfires
kept racing across a dark sky dipping up and below the German
planes which Mr Ivens called Messerschmitts. There were
flashes, explosions, and pilots giving messages in Morse code
from cockpits.

'That was the worst time,' said Mr Ivens. 'The invasion of
Britain. Saved by the Brylcreem boys.'

But nothing could be worse than now, I thought, with
Michael going. Now I was going to be alone in Roehampton
with Uncle Jonathan kissing my mother, and my father all crumpled on the floor, and my brother shrugging his shoulders and
walking away, and cheques bouncing, and the relations far away
on their country estates. 'The family don't understand,' my
mother keeps saying. She hasn't said this before.

That night I lay in bed clutching Fuzziepeg. After a few hours
Michael came and climbed in and put his arms round me and
squeezed. I wanted that squeeze to last for ever. I had this worry
that I wouldn't see him again for a long time.

'Hold my hands,' I said. And he put his hands into mine and
squeezed them. I felt all this warm safety and I drifted off rubbing
Michael's fingers.

'The dear boys,' Mrs Ivens said when she put her head round
the door in the morning and saw us huddled together.

6

THINGS AREN'T GOING well between Uncle Jonathan and my mother. I've been at Hilles and they didn't speak to each other once. I think Granny Blow knows what's going on. She gives my mother her withering face, when the fat skin goes all puckered and sulky. We've been having riding lessons and I'm walking back with my mother when she stops suddenly at the Royal William. That's an inn on the main road just by where you walk up Painswick Beacon. Walking over the beacon I put my hand in the large pocket of my mother's overcoat, as I always do. I touch something like a bottle. 'What's that?' I ask.

'Nothing – nothing,' my mother says.

That evening I'm in bed at the top of Hilles. It's a sort of nursery for us, this bit. I'm on one side of the room and David on the other. I hear footsteps up the narrow stone staircase. My mother walks towards us, not at all steady. She looks at us but somehow she isn't concentrating. Then she puts an arm up to one of the rafters to hold herself still.

'Mummy, you're drunk,' David tells her, his eyes narrowing. No. I don't want to think of Mummy drunk. 'No she's not,' I say, holding the sheets down from my face. 'It's only her high heels. Mummy's not drunk.'

I tell myself that women can't be expected to stand upright wearing those spindly long heels on their shoes, but later I realise

what he said was true. When I saw her standing funny in our
Hilles nursery I didn't know why, and that frightened me.
Mummy's explained it now, because she tells us everything. She
says that Uncle Jonathan wanted to have a child with her and that
child, said Uncle Jonathan, would inherit Hilles. David and I
were silent, more silent than when we watched Scrooge scratching at Marley's grave on the home viewer we've got.

'What did you say to him, Mummy?' we ask.

She looks up and says in her own way, her way that's full of
feeling, 'I said, "You'll never have a child by me to inherit over
the heads of my sons."'

After that she explains we have to inherit Hilles because my
father's the eldest son. She says it's wrong what Uncle Jonathan
is doing and that she can't believe Granny Blow could possibly
approve it. And yet Granny does everything that Uncle Jonathan
wants. My mother says Granny's not that well any more. And her
legs that once were fine and slender are now like swollen tree
trunks, with thick white bandages covering the untidy mess near
her ankles. But she motors Uncle Jonathan here and there,
whenever Uncle Jonathan calls for her.

That time at Hilles, the high-heels time, my mother got
drunk because she couldn't take any more. She went all cold
about Uncle Jonathan after that and she wouldn't let him near
her. And it was worse because Uncle Christopher wants my
mother to leave my father. It's so difficult for Mummy. She needs
us at her side, otherwise she's alone.

One day I am taken out of my classroom to be told by Mr Vickers
with a sorrowing face that Granny Blow has died. For some
moments I don't take it in and I walk back to my class not at all
steadily and as if I'm seeing things double. Granny Blow dead.
What does this mean? What? It means she can never attack me
again. It means there will be a burial. It means I will never hear
her speak again. It means . . . it means. We will live at Hilles now.

My mother says we've got to cry at Granny Blow's funeral.
She says this as if she's not at all sure if she can cry herself. She's
gone to a theatrical shop to buy some lotion that makes you cry.
I have already cried once, but was it from shock or because of
those times when Granny Blow hugged me to her bosom and I
trusted her? I don't know. I burst into tears very suddenly when
I was alone in a classroom at Scaitcliffe. Nobody saw. Now I must
go back to Hilles and cry again. We are allowed two days off
school. The day of the funeral I'm sent into Granny Blow's
bedroom at Hilles and told I must say a prayer beside the coffin.
My head is silent, quite silent. What can I wish for Granny Blow?
I give the coffin a tap with my fingers just to make sure it isn't
hollow. My mother said that Granny Blow's body juices
exploded after her death and I think of all the flesh inside that
box running wild like in a stew. I sort of hope she's somewhere
and then I hope she isn't, and after that I go blank. My leather
soles echo on the wooden floor as I leave the room.

After the service in Gloucester Cathedral, where the choir
sing innocent as angels, knowing nothing of Granny Blow, my
father drives us in her familiar black Ford to the burial place. But
familiar no more because Granny Blow's gone. 'The church bells
will toll for Mother in the neighbouring villages,' my father tells
us, a sob breaking out as he does so. And then another hiccuped
sob.

So we stand at the burial ground which is on a hilltop, about
a quarter of a mile from the house. I've walked all the way from
the house along this narrow lane with Granny Blow's coffin right
in front of me. It sits on a farm cart drawn by a white carthorse
held by a farm man. The coffin is covered with a cross of white
hawthorn blossom and beside me walk my brother, my parents,
Uncle Jonathan, and poor Aunt Luty, weeping badly. The choir-
boys dressed in white and red stand round the grave. They sing
a hymn about there being a green hill far away – their voices dis-
appearing over the hillside – and they tell us how we may not
know and cannot tell what pains He had to bear. Aunt Luty cries

more and more while Uncle Jonathan stands there without a tear, but with a grim ghastly look on his face. My father is sad and about to cry, too, but he just doesn't, and shakes his head instead. Then the elderly man dressed in church clothes with a piece of purple silk round his neck starts to give Granny Blow a goodbye in prayers. Somebody shakes earth on to the coffin. I step forward and have a peep. I have to make myself believe that Granny Blow really is down there, in that narrow earth pit, sealed inside all that wood.

It's a bit of a let-down after that. Everybody goes back to Hilles, and there are all these old ladies and old men who were friends of Granny Blow. They sit there eating cake and drinking cups of tea in the hall. The portraits of the Stuart monarchs look at us, their white fingers pointing. What do they think? Then I wonder how my father's getting on without any drink. Granny Blow drank water only out of big thick goblets. It's a hot June day and I feel uncomfortable in my dark grey Sunday suit. I haven't cried either, except I got a kind of shock, the shock of 'that's it', at the graveside. Haven't I done my crying in that class-room? Death is a shock, and I can see it's a really big shock if you feel you've been quite utterly deserted. Now I know why Aunt Luty's crying all the time. She limps round the room, tears bumping over her face. I'm ten with no pubic hair and I've seen death close. Or close enough. That'll do.

The hall is longer now because the house has altered since the fire. Three years before Winifred's death Hilles burnt down. It started on a summer's evening and the person who spotted it first thought it was a sunset. But it was the thatch on the roof burning. A short in the electric wires had caused it. There was no one in the house except a Hungarian couple. Jonathan, Winifred and Luty were in London. By the time they arrived there wasn't much left. Purcell left Roehampton in the early hours and as the taxi drove down the steep drive that suddenly reveals the house, he wept. What a few hours earlier had been his home, the home where he had stood sketching with his father, was a gutted ruin.

The huge stone walls, the great wooden staircase and charred timbers jutting from the inside of the walls like burnt skeletons, were all that was left; after that it was open, wide open, skies. Christ's lamb cast in stone now stared at the rescued tapestries, pictures, beds, furniture, statues, black steel boxes, bedpans and sheets spread across the lawn.

Winifred felt guilt, terrible guilt that the house built by her gypsy lover, the architect husband, had gone. So she rebuilt Hilles, made it again. And the huge hall, where people wander on this day of her burying, is one room now. It used to be divided up by a screen of old panelling that burnt.

Now, in the changed hall, Jonathan turns to his older brother late in the day. 'Do you want to know the will, Purcell?'

'Yes – tell me,' Purcell replies.

'Everything is half and half between you and me.'

'So we share Hilles?'

'No,' says Jonathan with a swing of his broad shoulders, 'Hilles is mine.'

I'm at 41 Roehampton Lane and Daddy's been drinking again. What Mummy calls 'the unfair cruel will' – the will that's changed everything – is sending him to pieces. It's smashing him and it's smashing us, too. There's nothing now but more of those 'Refer to drawer' cheques, and more drinking. And once one of these men who help him with the drawings had to hold him down when the hittings were starting. He got him down on the kitchen floor and dropped pills into his mouth to shut him up. 'I think I've more or less got Mr Blow under control,' he said to my mother. Now suddenly Daddy's promising not to drink again. Suddenly he is good, very good. Mummy was going to leave him for always, but that was before the will, when she believed our having Hilles to be certain. Now she will not leave him. She wants to rescue half Hilles for us. No, not for my father, but more for David and me. There's nothing for us now, nothing at all. No home, nothing.

My mother talks with disgust of 'the vile greed' of Uncle Jonathan. 'He forced Winifred's hand,' she says to us. 'It's all too clear,' she says, and of course she has the evidence. The child that Uncle Jonathan wanted my mother to have by him that would, on Uncle Jonathan's death, inherit Hilles. 'Heathcliff,' she calls him and it's the first time I hear that new name for him. I learn it's about a man who wanted terrible revenge for being left out. Uncle Jonathan as the second son has got his revenge too. Done what Heathcliff did.

It's not long after Granny Blow's death and Uncle Jonathan wants to explain. That's what my mother's told me. He's asked her to lunch at La Speranza. I know that name, La Speranza, like I know the name Quorn. It's a restaurant in Knightsbridge where I've often fallen asleep on the dark red velvet seats that run the length of a wall. My father spends money at La Speranza. Apparently it's fashionable – that's what Mummy says – everybody uses it. It's in the same street as Harrods. And that's where she's going now. Afterwards, my mother describes the lunch with Uncle Jonathan. He sat opposite her and kept sweeping his head at the sides with his hands, and telling my mother that he was only the custodian of Hilles. 'The boys,' he informed her, 'are to come to Hilles whenever they wish.' My mother looked at him and was silent, quite silent. She has read the will. He is not the custodian, he owns it, he owns everything. So quietly, but with anger, my mother said, 'My children will never go to Hilles again.'

And after lunch, on the pavement outside the restaurant, as Uncle Jonathan chain-smoked cigarettes, my mother delivered a parting shot.

'My sons will get further than you will get after all you've taken.'

Uncle Jonathan went pale, but kept his lips tight. Harassed, he clambered into a taxi. His plump backside dropping into the rear seat was my mother's last view of him.

Months pass and I'm at Scaitcliffe. I'm in a class and Mr

Vickers comes into the room. 'It's your mother for you on the telephone,' he tells me; then, when we're alone Mr Vickers says, 'I have to tell you that your parents are divorcing.' He puts an arm across my shoulders and says, 'You mustn't worry. I'm afraid these things can happen.' I go to the telephone and my mother says, 'I want you to come home at the weekend and to pack up everything that's yours, in particular the animals. I'm leaving Daddy. It's not possible to go on. But don't be upset, darling, we'll be all right. I'll see to that.'

Now I'm at home packing up Fuzziepeg and the elephants and a teddy bear and the toy soldiers and holiday clothes, in secret, without Daddy knowing. The plan is that Mummy will leave him while he is out. She says it's organised for Uncle Christopher to come and collect her and take her to a secret place in London where my father can't find her. At first I'm relieved that I'll never see his violence again, but suddenly I feel so sorry for him. Because I don't believe he can help himself. That's the real trouble, he just can't do anything about it.

Mummy says there's no hope that anything at Hilles will be given to us. Nobody's said anything to Uncle Jonathan. A cousin of my father's, John Tollemache, was going to talk to him and my mother had arranged this dinner where everything was going to be discussed. Once they were very close and Cousin John was shocked when he heard about the will. But at dinner my father arrived so drunk that when he started to eat, the food shot everywhere. It was upsetting for Cousin John as he had just inherited the moated house in Suffolk and with it the title, Lord Tollemache, and at dinner were a number of servants. As my father got worse, Cousin John told the servants to retire. Later, he said to my mother, 'You must leave Purcell. You must save yourself and the children.'

I can see Mummy is sad. Sad because I know she still loves him. Sometimes she quotes lines from a poem to us about how each man kills the thing he loves, and when she gets to this line she puts a special emphasis on it: 'The coward does it with a kiss, the brave man with sword.' I imagine the men, dressed in white tie and tails as my father once was, bending over to kiss their loves, and the wilting girls not realising that there's death in the kiss.

The next thing is she's gone. Uncle Christopher's come over one afternoon and taken my mother to a hotel – Duke's Hotel, it's called, which is off Jermyn Street. She's going to stay there until the divorce is through. Apparently Uncle Christopher got awfully worried that my father would suddenly turn up while he was collecting my mother from Roehampton. Uncle Christopher was right to worry, but my mother insisted that she couldn't leave before she'd found her Eternity ring. So she and Uncle Christopher looked under beds and sofas until they found it. Then the singing Irishman, McCubbin, drove them away.

The divorce happens fast. Daddy doesn't defend himself. Well, he can't – there is no defence. The grounds for divorce are physical cruelty. There are two witnesses of what he did to Mummy – Ann, the highly-strung secretary, and Gladys, who helped clean the house. But the divorce is held in camera. That's a legal term I've learnt, meaning that no press are allowed into the courtroom. Uncle Christopher's requested this, otherwise it will hit the newspapers. I imagine the headline: 'Peer's niece battered by violent husband'. Uncle Christopher has organised the lawyers and paid for it.

'We've got you your divorce,' says the fashionable lawyer from Lincoln's Inn.

'And what am I to live on?' my mother asks. At this the lawyer rearranges the papers on his desk. He picks up an ivory letter-opener and looks up at the ceiling. 'I don't know. That's not our affair.'

Mummy sees all these black steel boxes sitting above a book-case. Painted in white are the names of dukes and of earls, of countesses and marchionesses. The illustrious firm isn't used to questions put so bluntly, if at all. My mother rises from the leather chair, says ' Thank you', and leaves.

Her family arranges a lunch at Simpson's in the Strand to discuss what is to be done. It is unlikely that Purcell will pay his alimony. Diana says that quite definitely he won't. She does not come to the lunch and she isn't meant to. Uncle Christopher is there, and Aunt Phyllie, and Diana's half-brother, the foxhunting squire Uncle Tony, who's come down from Rise Park. Diana's mother, Clare is not there. But then Clare has never been there.

The three relations sit at the table. A good lunch arrives.

Taking some wine, Uncle Christopher says, 'Diana has had a thoroughly difficult time. We must help as best we can.'

'I agree,' says Aunt Phyllie.

'Shouldn't have married him,' says Uncle Tony.

'Well, I'm afraid it's happened,' says Uncle Christopher.

'All right,' says Uncle Tony. 'What shall we do?'

'We must give Diana a yearly sum of six hundred pounds.' Uncle Christopher cuts a piece of roast lamb.

'It's so good of you doing Simon's education,' says Aunt Phyllie to Uncle Christopher. He smiles. 'I'm seeing to David's,' she tells him. Aunt Phyllie doesn't want Uncle Christopher to feel he's alone there.

And over that lunch they arrange between them to make payments by covenant of six hundred pounds. Out of this Diana will be able to buy school clothes for the children. But she must economise, they say.

A little later Diana goes to see her Uncle Christopher. Tea is laid out in the drawing-room and over tea he tells Diana that she must now find a job. He tells her that it won't be possible for her to see the boys and that they, her family, will look after David and Simon in the holidays.

'Would you do that to your children?' Diana questions her uncle. There is no reply; then suddenly Uncle Christopher shakes the tea tray. He shakes the tray because he does not find

the words to say. His situation is different. He has no need even
to consider whether he would have to surrender his children. He
shakes the tray, too, because he does not want to say that he has
money and Diana does not.

Later she says, 'I won't give you up. You and David are all I've
got.' We tell her of course we won't live with relations and we're
going to stay with her. I don't think about what this means, I just
think we've got to make her steady again.

I'm back at school and Mummy says she's taken a job. She
keeps telling us she's not trained for anything. So she's got a job
in a nursery school, looking after children. 'I can do that, but it's
all I can do,' she says. 'I was brought up to marry and to marry
securely. I wasn't taught anything else.' But the job in a nursery
school doesn't last because Mummy's no longer well, although
you can't tell from how she looks. In fact Mummy hasn't aged,
for all the awfulness she's been through. But the trouble's inside,
she's got something called hypertension. From now on she has
to lead a quiet life. But she's very nervy now and I'm thinking,
can she? She goes into these dramatic states, snapping out her
words. 'I'm fine, just fine.' And when David and I say, 'Don't,
Mummy. Mummy, please,' she laughs that sad bitter laugh and
says, 'You mean I should take a pull?' – 'take a pull': that's her
way of saying, I should hold myself together. 'Yes, Mummy,' we
say. Then she stares into nowhere and states, 'But it's not drama,
it's true.'

The trouble is, her life isn't easier. I feel that now, feel the
muddle, the chaos. I wake in the mornings and my head whirls.
Daddy's gone and he's not gone. He'll pay alimony only if he can
continue to see Mummy and us. A few nights after she left him
– that is, after she'd been driven away from Roehampton Lane
by Uncle Christopher – my father was found wandering alone
in Hyde Park. Some friends found him as they drove down the
road he was trying to cross. He was crying. But Mummy isn't
moved by that. She calls him 'the leaner', 'the destroyer'. She
doesn't sing any more that song she sang long ago as she rocked

my pram, that my dada's rich and my mama's good looking. So much is changing, different, not safe again.

We're going to see this film with Judy Garland. My mother insists we see it because it's about a woman living with an alcoholic. She wants us to know what it's like. I want to say, 'Mummy, I know already.' But she won't listen and so off we go to Leicester Square and I look at these colour posters of a woman in fishnet stockings, tails, a black cane and a top hat, and a man to one side with a crumpled, good-looking face. Judy Garland is the rising star discovered by the fading star, fading because he can't stop drinking. I can see Mummy sympathises with the rising star, and she looks a lot like Judy Garland. James Mason is like my father, except he doesn't hit. But Judy Garland sings this song that Mummy really takes to. She keeps singing it. Bits of lines come out, my mother giving some extra punch when it hits its most dramatic: 'The night is bitter, the stars have lost their glitter . . . the winds grow colder . . . and suddenly you're older . . . The dreams you've dreamed have all gone astray . . . That great beginning has seen the final inning . . .' and my mother puts in a punch here, 'The road gets rougher, it's lonelier and tougher . . . with hope you burn up – tomorrow he may turn up . . . There's just no let-up the live-long night and day. Ever since this world began there is nothing sadder than a one man woman looking for the man that got away.'

Now we're going to the Café de Paris with my godmother. My mother knows it of old, from the days when she wore the hamper clothes, back in the prettiest-girl-in-society days. She would have gone there with my godmother, Rosemary, for they were at school together, then they were débutantes, and then both married.

But my father's with us, too, tonight. He insists on sharing the evening with us. He's brought us here in a car he's bought. It's a

cream-coloured Ford Zephyr convertible. He calls it Zellie the
Zephyr. I think he hopes that if he does things like this, my
mother will come back to him. But she won't, I know that. Even
seeing him is difficult for her. She says that she wasn't able to have
complete rights to us in the divorce. My father has to have what
they call 'access'. But she daren't leave us alone with him in case
he gets drunk and then, and then . . . she doesn't want even to
think about that. So for the time being he has to be with us. Also,
it's the only way he'll ever pay any money for us. If he's not with
us whatever money he has goes in those drinking clubs. But as
we go down the stairs of the night club my father makes these
leaping movements which I can't ignore. Legs shooting out suddenly, arms raised and dropped, like Mr Punch in Punch and
Judy. It's not a good omen, I think.

I follow behind Rosemary with her son, and my mother,
who's anxiously watching my father. There's going to be a
cabaret. A foreign man wearing a dinner suit and a black bow tie
lets me see into the star's dressing-room. I look at all the electric
light bulbs dotted round the mirror, and think that's what
happens when you're a star. For a moment I forget my father and
feel tremendously grown-up: I don't imagine lots of prep school
boys do this. Or even if you're at public school, which my
brother is. And Rosemary's son. We sit at a table that looks down
on the dance floor and everything seems to be going smoothly:
the excitement of watching the cabaret and eating in a night club
is keeping me pretty occupied. Except there's a definite strain
between my parents. My father knocks back the champagne as if
it's water. Rosemary's trying to keep everything normal, talking
about old friends and who's doing what or who's seen who –
then suddenly my mother's left our table and is on the dance
floor. Now my mother's doing this solo dance, swishing the
taffeta of her dress to left and right, then raising it, as if she's a
Spanish dancer. And the layers of taffeta all colours of the
rainbow. She's taking up a whole corner of the floor and the
other people dancing have to avoid her. She doesn't notice them.

After quite a few dramatic swishes she looks up at us and says so we can plainly hear – and everyone else too – 'You lika my dancin'? You like?' as if she's Spanish. My face is red, I'm embarrassed. I peer over the edge of the balcony. I look away, I look back. Her make-up's so dramatic. Plenty of lipstick and mascara. Swish, swish, go the layers of taffeta. Oh, Mummy, don't.

'You like – you lika my dancin'?' my mother shouts up at us again. We have to watch her doing her dance now, otherwise it's going to be worse. She'll scream. My godmother sips at her wine, gives these looks to my mother, pretending it's all so amusing, then turns to talk to her son and my brother. The other dancers pretend not to notice her. My father doesn't notice anyway as he's staring about and making disjointed pieces of conversation. 'Frightfully funny', or 'Isn't it all splendid', or 'Aren't we having fun.' Very tactfully, and a little later, the management come to my godmother and ask us if we could leave. It's the same foreign man wearing a black suit and black bow tie. He has a sorrowful, apologetic look on his face. He shrugs his shoulders and opens his hands and seems to be saying he wishes he could do something. I'm embarrassed at my mother's outburst, but I know I shouldn't be. I wonder why no one's explained to the management here how difficult everything is for her just now. Perhaps no one's meant to mention this. Or perhaps they have, but it makes no difference. I want everybody to understand what's happening.

We climb back into the Zephyr. My mother's subdued but giving one of her dramatic looks. She swings this look rapidly round on all of us. Then my father, with another leaping movement, starts the car. He drives rather fast and jerkily but we're all right so far. Now we're going through Knightsbridge and on towards where my godmother stays when in London. Suddenly he jumps a red light and the Zephyr bumps over an island, banging to a halt in the middle of it.

David, sitting in the front, looks at him: 'Now you've done it.'

After that we all get out. There's not much else to do. My father stands hovering on the edge of the island and it's lucky that an AA man is coming up the road towards us on his motorbike. My father flags him down, waving both arms in the air. While this goes on, David and Rosemary's son search for a taxi. My godmother must be got home. At last a For Hire taxi is seen and my godmother and her son disappear into the night. I don't hear anyone say, 'It's been such a lovely evening.' I'm glad about that. It could have been, but it hasn't.

'He's quite irresponsible,' my mother says to me. 'We've got to get him out of our lives.' She's standing on the pavement and we're watching my father as he leans into the engine of the Zephyr with the AA man. It's the wine that made my mother do that dance, like the time at Hilles when she couldn't stand straight on her high heels. She isn't always, no, not always. . . I'm really glad the shock of the accident has made her sober again.

Finally the car starts and my father drives us very slowly back to Roehampton. Nobody talks. There is nothing to say. My father leaves us and then drives off to Hampstead where he's got a room with some friends. I go into the house and it's so quiet. Mummy's still very worked up, in a state, and she says, 'Your father's a wicked man. He's destroyed me.'

I look at her. I look at her and go to my room. I put my arms round Fuzziepeg. I hear my mother go to her room, the door shut, and swiftly the still dark of night. Daddy's gone, and he's not coming back, I whisper to Fuzziepeg. Then I say it out loud to myself, just in case he is here somewhere, in case he can't ever properly go from the house. But nothing. Only that stillness. Only the dark.

'Come on, Blow. The world won't end today,' this boy with curly hair and stringy legs like a giraffe says. I'm back at school and trying to put home somewhere in my mind where it won't interfere. It doesn't as much as I think it will, because boarding school cuts you off. That's what being a boarder is all about. But this doesn't stop it being strange. Twelve isn't old and yet I know I'm seeing things that I shouldn't see. Perhaps no one should see them ever. It's sad there's no Fuzziepeg to hug at school. I'd be teased by the bigger boys, I suppose. Anyway no one talks about their animals. Except it's leaked out about Fuzziepeg and one of the masters has given a dictation on him. In fact, he's become a celebrity and there are boys who come up to me and ask, 'How's Fuzziepeg?' Which means that they'd all rather have their animals at school if we didn't have to keep up this I'm-grown-up-now act.

Sport's the thing here. It's meant to do something to us. 'Pulling together' is what they call it. If we don't beat the other prep schools we're as hopeless as a country that's lost a war. 'Scaitcliffe run like rabbits,' Mr Owen writes furiously on the noticeboard after a football match we lost. Mr Owen coaches us for football in winter and cricket in summer. He's got short, curly silvery-brown hair, and seems rather gruff. At football matches he holds a whistle which he blows in short sharp stinging blasts. When he's not blowing it he twirls it around him on a piece of string. Mr Owen's the real headmaster while Mr Vickers, who's much younger, is a 'kind of headmaster' because the school belongs to him. Mr Owen teaches us Latin and French and if we need a fresh piece of blotting paper we have to get it from him. He likes to write a little something on the blotting paper in pencil. I've just got a new piece and on it he's written, 'Procrastination is the thief of time.' I don't think he's got much time for people who think that life is about lounging around. Well, I know he hasn't. If any of us come over too swanky or posh, he's quick to remind us that 'the middle classes are the making of England'. He writes that sometimes on the blotting paper too.

There's one school we play that's different.

'It's the bungary on Saturday. Shall we make them have a bath first?'

'Do you think so?'

'They stink. And their voices . . . urggh.'

Now several other boys join us as we're walking back from the playing fields where there's been the daily game of footer. We amble along in our everyday games shirts – we wear red and black shirts for matches – and woolly shorts, thinking how nice of us it is to let Staines Grammar play us but I'm thinking, why are we mocking them? I suppose it's because we believe there's only one sort of person who matters and that's our sort. It's all tied in with this pulling together and winning matches. And because Staines Grammar School boys are not as good as we are, not as well-born as we are, we believe we have a right to poke fun at them.

'I don't know if I like all this sport,' goes round in my head. When I'm miserable one day, a boy nudges me. 'Hey, Pixie. Vestey's grandmother sang in an opera house. Heard of Nellie Melba? Well, that's his grandmother.' Amazing what others can pick up on, it really is. I smile.

'You've got to do something about your rugger, Blow,' one of the senior boys says to me. 'Have I?' I say. He gives me that dismissive look. I'm in a dormitory where we play at being priests. The mantelpiece is a mock altar and we make crosses out of our combs, holding them in place with the elastic garters that keep up our socks. There are pretend processions as if we're going up to an important high altar in a cathedral. I know I'd like to be an actor one day so all this is a kind of outlet. Not that I'd mention that to the relations we stay with in the holidays as they would say, 'Look at your father. You've got to be stable.' Acting, I'm told, is one of the very unstable, unsafe professions.

I don't listen, though. I don't. My schoolfriend, Tom, and I are putting on *Macbeth* with the help of a master here. There aren't plays at Scaitcliffe, really, so we're doing this on our own. Tom is much shorter than I am so it's decided that I play Lady Macbeth. She's the bully, after all. Also, I know I've got this delicate kind of face that with stage make-up can easily look like a woman's. Tom's seen the Old Vic production of *Macbeth* in Edinburgh and I've seen it in London. I've written to the Old Vic, too, asking if we can borrow their *Macbeth* clothes, but they've written back saying they're very sorry but they don't lend them. They've wished us all the best for our production. This makes us feel very professional. Now I don't care if the sport swanks attack me for not bothering enough about rugger. I'm an actor.

On goes the play, for one night only, in front of the whole school and the masters. Tom has a tartan rug wrapped round him for a kilt. It looks pretty good. And towering above him in a sort of grey dress that goes to the ground and wearing a wig of flowing hair, I have to chuck him under the chin and say in a big dramatic Lady Macbeth way, which is all right as my voice hasn't broken,

> Your face, my thane, is as a book where men
> May read strange matters. To beguile the time,
> Look like the time; bear welcome in your eye,
> Your hand, your tongue: look like the innocent flower,
> But be the serpent under't.

The whole play was strong stuff. And we got away with it. The boys who didn't like it just ignored us, but quite a few took notice. Definitely a bit odd, the pair of us, but interesting. Soon I'm thinking, OK, I'm not going to be this kind of outsider any more. I'm going to call everyone's bluff. I play football with my left foot, just as I write with my left hand. Within a year I'm playing football for the school first eleven and going to all the 'away' matches, so I know exactly which school serves the best grub afterwards. St George's, Heatherdown, Sunningdale, and so on . . . the smart prep schools of our little group. After a bit I win my colours for being so nippy at left half. I'm quite a little model prep school boy now. Well done, Simon, I say.

It helps, though. There's nowhere at home to get a line on how to keep going. It doesn't help to know that my father was a fine athlete once, not when you see him now. School is useful because it's pretty well all black and white: either you do well or you don't do well. I feel stronger for doing well. That's important because I'm alone here now. My brother's left and gone on to Stowe. Not that we've ever talked together about how to keep going. We just do it, or don't do it. I know he's calm because he wants to be the opposite of his father. If there's something tragic about Daddy, something we could forgive him for, my brother won't sympathise. He's too angry with him. He's angry, not just about the hitting, but about all the small disgraceful things he does, like falling asleep drunk in the cinema and snoring. No way to entertain your children. So David narrows his eyes and gives him these held-in judging looks.

'Ask Mummy which ring she would like,' my father says. From his pocket he brings out two old, beautiful rare rings. We look at them both, David and I. One is a ring with a single blue stone in the centre, and the other has a pink stone with little white ones round it. My father says the pink stone is the more expensive. It's a pink diamond surrounded by little diamonds in an eighteenth-century setting. We both like that one.

'Will you give them to Mummy? I want her to choose.'

But he. hasn't bought the rings yet. He's got them on approval from a Bond Street jeweller he goes to. It's a very good old-fashioned firm and they trust him because he's a gentleman, but what they don't know is that he can't afford them. Not possibly.

'I know I've been a very naughty boy,' my father says to us. 'I want Mummy to choose one of these rings and then we can all be together again.'

We say, 'Yes, of course, Daddy', but we're not sure about that.

'He's got these rings for you,' we tell her. We put them down in front of her. She looks at them. 'He's trying to buy me back,' she says and then she looks sad. She must be thinking of that day when she walked down the long, long aisle of St Paul's Cathedral. Everything was all right then. It can't be made better now, can it? Not with rings. But she'll have to try them out and pretend. Of course, she knows he's got no money to buy them. She knows it's no good saying that to him. He may still be building houses but everything's borrowed, borrowed, and borrowed. If she accepts them, then at least for a while he can still have his dreams. She doesn't have much choice anyway.

In no time the rings are back with the jeweller. But nearly not back, as we're on this train going somewhere and my mother's got the pink diamond one on her finger. We're looking at it and admiring it, then suddenly the clasps of the little diamonds loosen, perhaps it's the shaking of the train, and they spill all over the floor. David and I slide off our seats and scramble to pick up the little diamonds. There's one missing still and we hunt and hunt until finally we see a sparkle by Mummy's shoe. We think the best thing now is to get the rings back.

My mother hands them to my father the next time he's with us. He doesn't say anything about not being able to pay for them. He just says 'Oh, yes' and puts them in his pocket.

He keeps trying to make up for everything. Mummy has to keep seeing him to get some alimony. I know that word well now. Alimony. We go on trips to the country in Zellie the Zephyr and he wants us to look at these country houses which are for sale. He say's he's going to buy one for us. So we go round them with the agent, and my father makes all the right enquiries as if next week he could write out a cheque for two hundred thousand. He must know that it's partly his fault that he lost us Hilles. I think that's why he's doing this. I wouldn't mind if I could trust him but I can't. None of us can, although I want to. Instead I trail after him down these long galleries and Tudor halls as he drags us into a fantasy that can never happen. I'm tired, I think we're all tired. I want to run away from these silly houses.

'I've been very bad,' my father says, and I don't know if the agent hears or not, 'so I'll just sleep in the dog kennel. I've been a bad boy.'

Will it ever get better? I'm saying over and over. Ever?

7

Aunt Phyllie is selling Ragdale. I don't take it in at first, any more than I've taken in losing Michael. Having so much tugged away from under me is making my stomach hurt. She says it's far too difficult to keep it going. Everybody at Ragdale is very upset and Pat who milks the cows wouldn't speak to her for a week.

She's moving to Sussex because the air down there is good for her health. There's a house – kind of another Ragdale, but smaller, and no battlements – with ninety acres of land, that she's found near Robertsbridge. It has a big garden – seven or so acres – and woods. Luigi's going with her and a few others who work at Ragdale. But Luigi's the most important. He's going to run the farm in Sussex. The local papers in Melton put in pieces about Aunt Phyllie – 'Fairy Godmother is leaving district' – and the children's band that she started in Melton is photographed playing to her as she smiles back: 'They beat a retreat on Ragdale lawn,' says the paper.

There's no chance for me to have a last time at Ragdale. It all happens fast, while I'm at school one summer term. I can't say goodbye to Betty at Six Hills. Betty's father was a farmer, and I would bicycle away through the Iron Gates two miles down the road to where Betty lived and share her pony, a pony called Flash. 'I'll never forget the day you fell into the brook at Wymeswold,' Betty wrote to me after Ragdale was gone.

And it means no more chimes from Ragdale's huge iron bell that rings inside the clock tower. Every time that bell chimed it said to me, I'm always here, I'm Ragdale. One day I gave it a push and it rang a single chime in the middle of the morning. Everyone thought it was lunch and came in from the fields. I'll never do that again. And there won't be any more playing in the Old Hall with Hughie. In fact I won't see Hughie again – or Mr Ward, or Mrs Ward. They're not coming to Sussex. No more tea with them in their house that's squeezed between the stables.

My father is coming to Robertsbridge to share us for these holidays. Aunt Phyllie says he isn't to come into her house, Peanswood. He never came to Ragdale except to ask for a loan and she's angry with him for what he's done to my mother. Aunt Phyllie loves my mother. She's been through so much with her that I'm just beginning to learn about. In the evenings I sit with Aunt Phyllie and she talks about long ago. She's never let the grandmother we see from the top of buses into her home either. A hunting friend brought beautiful Clare to Ragdale once and Aunt Phyllie let the hunting friend in, but not Clare. 'She must wait outside,' Aunt Phyllie said. So Clare sat on the wall with moss on it that crosses the baby moat, dangling her sunglasses.

'She caused so much pain to your grandfather, my brother,' Aunt Phyllie tells me.

'Didn't she love him at all?'

' I don't know, darling,' Aunt Phyllie says. 'She wasn't normal.'

Clare had terrible rages and Aunt Phyllie says she would throw herself on the floor and bite the carpet. That's why she made me walk round the garden seven times at Ragdale; she thought she saw that same temper coming out in me. Aunt Phyllie never loses her temper. She's got another dog now, just the same as the one she had at Ragdale and it barks all the time too. I ask her why she always has to have these little dogs that bark.

'They're the last of Victor's breed,' Aunt Phyllie says, and she means Victor Conyngham, the Irishman she loved and wanted to marry. The little dogs are all she has to remember him by –

and the photograph of him on her dressing table beside the looking-glass, with Uncle Philip in a tortoiseshell frame on the other. Victor has a silver frame.

My mother laughs about Victor. 'Why are you laughing, Mummy?' I say.

'He drank,' my mother tells me. 'It was a good thing he died and Aunt Phyllie didn't marry him. That's what my father told me. But Aunt Phyllie never knew.'

How awful, I think. Aunt Phyllie might have had a life like we're having, except that Victor had this huge estate in Ireland. I'm glad now that Aunt Phyllie married Uncle Philip.

My father has to stay in the George Inn by the station in Robertsbridge. He comes up to see us in a cottage we've got on Aunt Phyllie's land. We're not staying in Peanswood because it's shut up now. Aunt Phyllie's in Italy staying in the house she's built for Luigi near Marina di Massa. She still goes every year to take the waters at Montecatini and Luigi drives her out there in the really comfortable Rover she's bought. The shiny black Rolls-Royce that sat under a white dust sheet in the garage at Ragdale has gone. She used that once for travelling abroad and for trips to London, but it's gone now, like Ragdale. Not that Aunt Phyllie's poor – she's got loads of money invested on the stock market. No, she's actually tremendously sensible.

'Never let anyone know what you have,' Aunt Phyllie tells us. I suppose that's for the future because it wouldn't be difficult now.

These shared holidays are wearing my mother out. A year ago my father insisted on taking us all abroad during the summer holidays. We agreed because my mother had inherited a little money from a relation and my father promised, and went on promising, to be as good as gold. 'Tomato juice only all the way,' he said. Now that the divorce has happened we thought he would behave. So we pile into the Zephyr, my father thinking it's so funny because the number-plate reads DHX, which he tells us stands for Diana Hermione, my mother's second Christian name, and then X, ex (wife). Crossing the Channel he drinks masses of tomato juice. We sigh, we're relieved. It's going to be all right.

We get to Boulogne. It's about lunchtime and my father says we must find a restaurant. Once at the table my father looks at the menu, but within seconds he's picked up the wine list.

'You said tomato juice, Daddy,' I say. 'That's what you drank on the boat.'

'The French wines − far too good to ignore,' my father tells us. 'But you promised not to,' my mother reminds him.

'I know, you're quite right. But why not just this once.'

Mummy's looking worried. Really worried. But already my father's made one of his wavy hand signals to the waiter.

'*Une bouteille*,' he says, showing the waiter the wine he wants on the list.

In no time a bottle arrives on the table. Immediately my father fills my mother's glass and his. We watch him drinking the wine fast. 'So good,' he says, swinging his head round. Mummy tries to keep up with him, to make sure he doesn't drink the whole bottle even though she doesn't want a drink herself. She doesn't want Daddy drunk, ever. And . . . I don't even want to say it: not drunk and driving.

We've got to get to the South of France, to Menton, where we've a week in a hotel there. It's going to take three days, my mother says. Well, Daddy isn't drunk after the meal. Thank God. So off we go. My brother sits in front and I sit in the back with my mother. It's not long before I panic, worry silently. Daddy doesn't seem to be in control on the roads. All right, it's a left-hand drive car and we have to drive on the right, but he can't overtake without asking David all the time if he should.

'Shall I go? What do you think?'

'No. There's a lorry coming. Don't.'

But already Zellie the Zephyr is lurching to overtake.

'Pull back. For God's sake, don't!' shouts David.

The car swerves, sways, and he only just tugs it back again. The lorry roars past us. After that we're all right for a bit. Then crunch, we've hit the man in front. We've hit his bumper and we have to stop. There's this throwing of arms around from the Frenchman, while my father tries to apologise but he can't say 'bumper' in French. The Frenchman gets back in his car growling. We speed on. There's more overtaking lurches, and my mother clutches my hand.

While we're in the car Daddy says we mustn't stay in hotels on the way down. We must knock on the doors of the local farmhouses and ask if they've room for us. 'Tremendously important,' my father says, 'to know the local people.' He's got this idea from his father. So driving through France we knock on the doors of farmers and ask if we can stay the night. This is how Grandfather Blow did it when he went through Europe eighty years ago. 'If you don't know the local people, you don't know the place,' he used to say. Amazingly, the locals do put us up, and feed us too, even if they think my father's crazy. That we're all crazy.

Next we're well on the road that takes us to the South. My mother has told me about the smell of mimosa and the noise of crickets which will mean we're in the heat at last. But while I'm thinking of this, steam starts pouring from the Zephyr's bonnet. We don't know what it means. Suddenly we're at a dead halt. The end of the bonnet looks like ten kettles boiling and my father leaps out and opens it.

'Oh, oh dear,' he says, peering through the steam. 'How silly. I forgot to check the radiator. It's empty. The fan belt's gone.'

There's a long wait. Finally a nearby garage finds a fan belt. The radiator's filled and Daddy, back at the wheel, lurches on.

It's night and we're crossing the Alpes–Maritimes and the car's headlamps go dim. We have to take these frightening sharp corners on the Grande Corniche, a road which winds and winds up high hills and along the road with drops into nowhere. My father keeps his lips tight and his long arms around the steering wheel. 'How are we doing?' he says as we crawl along with no more light from the headlamps than a candle. The car lurches near to the precipice, one wheel crunching the edge, and swings back again.

At last! At last! Menton. We climb a hill to the Hotel Astride where there are separate bedrooms for my mother and father. But my father keeps going into my mother's bedroom as if they were married.

'I can't keep Daddy out of my room,' Mummy says to us. 'He thinks we're still married.'

'We're divorced, Richard,' my mother tells him, calling him Richard not Purcell now. Mummy finds the Granny Blow Purcell stuff affected. She doesn't want anything to do with my father's family. 'The Blows are cursed. Hilles is cursed,' she says. And I think I'd better steer clear of them too. Except I am 'a Blow'. Or perhaps this family name I carry doesn't mean much anyway?

The palm trees, the sound of crickets, the excitement of being 'abroad', is being shattered. Daddy's seriously drinking again. I like all these new places, but where's the fun in my first trip out of England? We might as well be back in Roehampton. At every meal my father orders wine and more wine with money he doesn't have. I watch him stagger down the palm tree streets, his eyes staring and swivelling. I long to be back at school. I long to be where my father isn't.

'We must see Florence,' he says. On we go and I get dizzy with the car jerking to a halt as my father draws back – that overtaking bit – or makes the car do sudden leaps, putting his foot too jerkily on the accelerator.

We reach Florence. My father in his sober moments tries to tell David and me about the buildings, but we don't take much in. Turning our heads away from the cathedral, we watch a funeral instead. My father gets angry, his upper lip held firm and tight over the lower, like a visor clamped down. All we want to do is get away, go home, finish this holiday. But he says we must go to Bologna and look at the towers. No chance of that. He loses his head in Bologna. He goes out on his own. I spy him eating and the table is cluttered with empty bottles. Is it my mother pushing him away that's brought on all this drinking? It's not been so bad for a long time, not since Roehampton. Now David's got an ear infection which means he must go into hospital. The doctor says he must have an operation. But we've no money to pay for it. The surgeon says if we can send him some kind of medicine he can't get in Italy, he won't charge.

So David's in hospital now having his ear done. I find my father has walked in and out of the hotel seven times in eight minutes. And gone up and down in the lift the same number of times.

The manager of the hotel, standing behind the desk, says to me in funny English, 'Eez your fader all right? Or eez 'e mad? Ee comes in and out. Goes up and down. Do you know what ees 'appening?'

I tell him that I'm sure my father is all right. I tell him that there's nothing to worry about. I'm shaken, dazed. I don't even know I'm lying. I go up to my bedroom, fall on my bed and tremble. It's hot and these sticky goose pimples break out.

Aunt Phyllie before she leaves for Italy with Luigi explains firmly, 'He's not to come into the house.' But my father doesn't complain. He knows what he's done, he can't stop it, and that's the saddest bit of all.

We're in a cottage on the edge of Aunt Phyllie's land, with the woods behind us and a small road that runs down to Robertsbridge in front of us. I want to carry on my riding here, I say to myself. It's these hunting figures I've got attached to. They seem so calm, jolly, and untroubled. I rode whenever I could at

Ragdale. I ride when I go and stay with Uncle Tony at Rise. I had my first day's hunting from Hilles. I jumped stone walls, and jumping them made me feel really well. When I ride I think of Grandfather Bethell because my mother's told me so many stories. Grandfather Bethell kept about twenty horses and hunted his hounds himself. She says he sold Great-grandfather Bethell's collection of porn books to keep his riding going. I've got this dream of Rise and my grandfather riding through the villages round Rise – Ellerby, Skivlaugh, Withernwick – surrounded by his hounds and jumping these big ditches as the hounds run. It's a dream where everything is calm and unchanging.

Why won't Aunt Phyllie buy me a horse? I keep thinking. But she won't. We've got to cut our coat according to our cloth. We've got to learn to live with nothing when all the relations seem to have everything. So what I should be doing is hanging around street corners with a quiff and black pointed shoes. That's what lads do who've got nothing and expect nothing. But I've got this passion to jump fences bravely and to follow the hounds as hard as they run. My father says to me, 'Hunting's so good for your riding. Do it as much as you can, darling boy.' But my father's blown the money to do it with. Worse, much worse, he's given me this book, *Memoirs of a Fox-Hunting Man* by Siegfried Sassoon and it's all about this person who's really on the inside of it all. Reading it makes my heart break with longing. I wish I had a groom as this chap, George, in the book has and could spend hours learning about it all; I mean talking to the huntsman and living in the kennels.

There's a riding stable at Robertsbridge where Aunt Phyllie says I can ride. It's run by a woman who's quite gruff but friendly underneath, and another woman. Every morning I go there and one day I say to my father, 'Why don't you ride again, Daddy?'

'What a terrific plan,' my father says. 'I'll come with you tomorrow.'

'You rode in all those races, didn't you? I mean when you were at Cambridge.'

'At Cottenham. Quite right.'

'What about your horses?'

'I had one terrific horse – Noble Boy. He won races.'

'All right,' I say. 'Pretend you're back there tomorrow.'

It'll do my father good to ride again. He doesn't have any jodhpurs or breeches, but he puts on a pair of old corduroys. He seems a little unsure at first on the horse. He'll be fine, I'm saying to myself. And as we're jogging along the road, I give him sideways looks. His arms and legs are going all over the place and he just about controls the horse, but I don't know how as even his hands are making the reins dance like waves. Is this what drink has done to him? I turn and look the other way. However much disgust I feel, it is sad. The two emotions fight within me. We go on jogging until we hit a grass patch. 'Let's give them a canter,' I say. We break very gently into a canter and my father goes all lopsided then manages to pull himself straight again. Goes off again, centres himself finally. I'm embarrassed. I want to shout out to anyone who recognises me: 'He won point-to-points once, I've seen the photographs. My father won races at Cambridge, you should have seen him then!'

'So good for one, this,' he announces suddenly, shooting his head round, and making his whole body lopsided again. Steady, I want to say, for God's sake keep your balance! But I can't. How can I? I just want this ride to be over.

Nobody's seen my father for a long time. That is, no one who knew him well when he was young. There's a lady a few miles away who took quite a fancy to my father when he was a debs' delight. My brother's been over to play tennis with her children. 'I'd so love to see your father again,' she told my brother. 'Do bring him over.' David tells my mother. My mother looks out into the woods because we're going for a walk. Then she swings her head back to us, 'What on earth will she think?'

But they take my father over. I'm not there. I'm up at the stables and I hear about it later. The lady who had so liked my father – now a lady-in-waiting to the Queen – reeled in shock.

Before her was not the dashing man who had enchanted so many, but a leaping, uncoordinated wreck. 'Don't think we're married, we're not,' said my mother, quickly explaining. And I realise how for my mother everything has to be explained about the gap between the life she once had and the life she has now.

'What can have happened to him?' asks the lady in her drawing-room.

'He's ill,' my mother replies. 'Ill.'

'Oh,' replies the lady-in-waiting. 'How awful for you.'

'We're divorced, though,' my mother goes on.

Nobody quite understands. Not quite.

The strain is hard on my mother, and hard on my brother and me too. We can't put across the awkwardness of it to the relations. Aunt Phyllie understands the most because she sees us most. But her life is so different. There are no sudden things happening for Aunt Phyllie. The friends who look down from their photographs come and visit – Irene, Aunt Marion, Lavinia – Luigi sells the pigs at the market, every year Aunt Phyllie goes to Italy, and she's never been in a bad way with money ever. But sometimes Mummy talks about Aunt Phyllie's feelings: she says Aunt Phyllie had an operation years ago so she can't have babies. After Victor, Aunt Phyllie didn't want anybody else's child.

I've had a letter from Michael. He's done really well at school and he's met this girl he goes to the cinema with. He's thirteen now. He says Sheffield is quite different from Roehampton and that everyone up there speaks in a different way. He writes that I'm to go and stay and that Mr and Mrs Ivens worry about me. I've never been to one of these big cities. I wonder if Michael would put his arms round me again or is he too grown up for that now? I write back saying I'd like to come up but we've got to go to Italy next summer and I don't know when I'll find the time. I sign it 'love and lots of memories, Simon'.

Is that a bit soppy? I wonder afterwards. I don't know. Perhaps I'll never go to Sheffield anyway.

★

My mother's sold 41 Roehampton Lane. She's bought a small house off the King's Road in Chelsea. It was a kind of workman's house once – that is one hundred years ago – but it cost the same as we sold our house for, which is twice the size. Roehampton Lane was bought with the money Grandfather Bethell left my mother. So the house was never my father's. That's lucky, I'm thinking, very lucky. But for that we wouldn't have a home. Or we'd be staying all the time with relations. Mummy doesn't want to depend on the relations. She's got the idea that she's failed because of the marriage to my father. It took my mother three weeks to write to Uncle Christopher asking him if he could pay for my education. Three weeks of worrying and worrying.

Number 12 Burnsall Street, that's our address now. It's got two rooms at the top, two on the ground floor, and apart from the kitchen one in the basement. They're all small rooms and there isn't space for anyone to stay. Sometimes we find the kitchen too small even for breakfast. And it's depressing having breakfast in a dining-room where the only light comes through a half-window. My mother takes us up the road to an Italian coffee bar to have breakfast most mornings.

Aunt Phyllie says, 'If you want a friend to stay, bring them here.' She does understand, Aunt Phyllie.

I'll be leaving my prep school soon, too. David's already at Stowe. We couldn't go to Eton in the end. It doesn't bother me but it's hard on my brother and Mrs Vickers is upset. 'I can't understand you two Blow boys going to Stowe. Only the other day they said to me at Eton, "There's no boy we like better than a boy from Scaitcliffe."' The trouble is it's like entering for the Derby, going to Eton – and after my brother had passed twice, taken his Common Entrance twice that is, and passed into the Upper Remove twice, there still wasn't a place for him.

My mother's upset about it. Her father went there and Uncle Christopher's children too. She should have put us down at birth, like other boys. That would have guaranteed a place. But Daddy went to Stowe. So that's why we're going there too.

'I want your names changed,' my mother says to us one day. 'I want you take one of my family names – either Tennant or Bethell.'

'Is Blow the wrong name?' I say.

My mother thinks that because everyone knows my father bounces cheques it's going to harm us. I feel it's a bit strange suddenly being called Simon Bethell or Simon Tennant when I've been Blow. Of course, he's been terrible with the cheques. He bounced one at the Connaught Hotel and that was awful. The Connaught is Aunt Phyllie's hotel in London. Luigi opens the door of the black Rolls-Royce and out steps Aunt Phyllie all beams and smiles as the tall doorman in his brown coat lifts his top hat with a black cockade on the side, and says, 'Very nice to see you again, Madam.'

I pulled my weight in the end at Scaitcliffe. I joined in. Schools like that. I got into the first fifteen rugger as well as the first eleven football. Mr Owen gives a talk to us at the end of term and mentions me. 'One boy who's surprised us all in the last year is Simon Blow. He's shown that it's possible to catch up if you want to. From not being interested in being part of us, he's shown determination and spirit.' He goes on to talk about how the Empire was made by people putting their backs into it. 'Nothing comes without work,' he says. He wants us to remember this when we're in our next school and in all the years ahead.

Mr Owen takes his spectacles off, wipes them, and goes on to talk of matches lost and won. Bits of what he's saying reach me. I see playing fields and people running and classrooms filled with boys whose heads are bent over desks scratched with initials and stained with ink. Then it's fading and there's my father, all six foot four of him, coming to strike my mother. She falls against the wall of the post office in the King's Road. All she's done is ask for the alimony – money for us to live. He knocks her again and she's on the ground. I reach down to pick her up and she puts her arm round me. I don't hear Mr Owen any more. I don't see any more playing fields. Everything inside me freezes and I wonder. I wonder what's going to happen in the years ahead. There are no playing fields there.

8

MY MOTHER HAS gone to Aunt Phyllie's doctor. He's in Harley Street where all the best doctors are supposed to be. Dr Pierre Jonescu is from Romania and Aunt Phyllie swears by him. He tells my mother that she isn't really physically ill at all. The word he uses is 'psychosomatic'. That means the whole lot's imagined. Then he thinks it might be anaemia and he gives her insulin injections. My mother's in a nursing home having some tests done. Aunt Phyllie says Dr Jonescu once saved her life.

'He's been so brave himself, darling,' she says to my mother, 'getting out from the Iron Curtain.' Escaping like that and giving Aunt Phyllie the right injection one day at Ragdale has made Aunt Phyllie trust him for life. Dr Jonescu's secretary tells my mother one day that, apart from Aunt Phyllie, he has virtually no patients at all. This makes Mummy think again about his diagnosis.

When Mummy was in the nursing home David and I stayed with Aunt Phyllie. They've done these tests but still don't know what it is. I'm not worried as Mummy's never been ill before and I don't suppose it could be anything serious. She's too young for anything serious to happen.

My mother still hopes that she might see her mother. Uncle Christopher is trying, trying to see if anything can be done. And while we wait my mother can't even pick up the telephone to ring her mother. It's odd and so horrid that I feel it too. But now she needs to ask Clare to agree to break what Mummy calls 'my parents' marriage settlement'. I don't understand that much about these things except that if Granny Clare agrees it will give us some money. So my mother says she's going to get to her mother through her half-brothers, Harold and Mark, who are Clare's two sons by Lionel Tennyson. My mother says they see Clare quite a lot. She calls them and lunch is arranged at the Connaught Hotel.

I'm going to the Connaught with my mother and she still looks so young. She's nearly forty now but strangers think she must be our sister. She's taking David and me with her because my father's not here any more, and we're all she's got. I don't know my half-uncles that well, although they've been to Roehampton Lane. Uncle Mark's in the Royal Navy – Commander Tennyson, RN. He was going to take David and me on his submarine and let us spend a night on it. In the end it never happened, but I've got this submarine all imagined in my head. Uncle Mark is always very well dressed, and wears either a suit, terribly well pressed, or his blue naval uniform. He looks like Granny Clare. Uncle Harold is rather fat and he wears spectacles that have thick lenses. I don't quite know what Uncle Harold does, but I know he likes playing golf. My mother says that Granny Clare was horrified when she saw what Harold was turning out like. She says Clare used to write to Harold when he was at Eton saying, how could a beauty like me have produced something like you? But now Clare leans on him because he's so very nice. Uncle Harold's now Lord Tennyson and Clare likes that too. 'If I'd married a duke, my mother would have made it up with me at once,' Mummy says. My uncles know there's this awkwardness over Clare. They're definitely both fond of my mother, but they're worried too. I think it's because they can't all say lovely things about their mother.

Today Uncle Harold and Uncle Mark are both in very correct suits and we sit in the Connaught Hotel dining-room, with snow-white napkins unfolded on our laps.

'Speak to her. You must speak to her,' my mother tells them.

'We will broach the subject,' says Uncle Harold. 'I can't say how Ma will take it.' Uncle Mark says nothing except to make movements with his tiny lips.

'I can't go on, don't you understand?'

Now Uncle Mark puts his hand on my mother's arm. 'You know how we care about you, Diana.'

'Care? Nobody cares about us. Make her break the settlement.'

Uncle Harold's spectacles get a little steamy. 'We will do everything in our power. Please, Diana, keep calm. I'm sure that Uncle Christopher will speak to her too, if necessary.'

A waiter wearing a long white apron hovers around the table taking away plates and putting down clean knives. Another waiter with a grape embroided on the red lapel of his tail coat pours wine. Mummy pushes her empty glass forward.

Uncle Harold looks at my mother anxiously. Uncle Mark, speaking through his mouth that seems stuck on rather than real, asks David about Stowe.

'Have you got a steady?' Uncle Mark says to David. He means a girlfriend. I watch David going red, because it's quite a question, that one. And Uncle Mark, with his neat tidy suit, isn't the sort to suddenly go personal with.

My mother interrupts before David can think up a reply. 'Why's my mother so awful?' She sits erect, and stares with big actressy eyes at her brothers. First Uncle Harold, then Uncle Mark. I'm thinking, oh no, Mummy, don't.

Uncle Harold freezes, only his neck moves. Uncle Mark tries to continue talking to David as if he hasn't heard. My mother drinks the wine in one go. 'Shall we find the waiter. I need another.'

I notice that she isn't quite steady any more. When Mummy drinks – and I've seen it a few times now – she doesn't just fall about, she goes all dramatic. She gives these frightening looks as if she's very angry and the person she's looking at is the reason.

Uncle Harold tries to pretend it's nothing and he says to me, 'You should enjoy Stowe. It's nice to be at a public school that's really in the country. I wish Eton hadn't been in a town.'

Yes, I say, I am looking forward to Stowe. Well, I've got to say that, although I'm scared stiff of the whole routine that goes on in schools. I think that if you follow the routine the chances are you're going to be killed – the person that's in you, I mean. I'm not allowed to talk like this in front of the grown-ups as it's such a big deal going to public school. I'd rather be with Michael in Sheffield. So I sit there, neat and looking cool, until my mother suddenly says to Uncle Mark, 'Is there anything to my mother? Anything at all?'

This throws Uncle Mark. He keeps making patterns with those lips, and I wish he'd leave those lips alone. He looks at the cuffs on his shirt and plays with one of the gold cuff-links as if the answer is somewhere tucked up in there. Uncle Harold is putting some runner beans in his mouth, so there's no noise but eating from him.

'Ma,' Uncle Mark says, and there's a pause. 'Ma,' he says again and I think it's some kind of animal sound, 'keeps a lot inside her, Diana.'

My mother isn't listening any more, or what she does hear she doesn't reply to. There's a handkerchief coming out and a face mirror, from her handbag. She wipes away some mascara from under her eyes and puts the mirror up to her face. Next she takes lipstick from her bag and drags the lipstick over her bottom lip then rubs both lips together. She holds the mirror a little bit higher and has another look. Then she snaps it shut, looks at Uncle Harold and Uncle Mark in turn and says, 'Right! OK! Fine!'

This puzzles both of them. I know they are both trying to help and now my mother's embarrassed them. She's had too much to drink, I know she has. It's the worry over money that's made this happen. We're in the Connaught Hotel but that doesn't make the money situation any different. It isn't the Ritz which is all showy, and it isn't the Dorchester where the Americans stay, but it is the Connaught – the hotel where the quiet county families go. It's really quiet everywhere in this hotel and in the sitting-room there's calm in the sofas and the flowery curtains and the polished mahogany writing desks and the paintings of flowers on the walls. Now I'm wondering how we're going to get my mother out of here. She's from one of the quiet county families too – this is Aunt Phyllie's hotel, her father's hotel – and what is to be done? What, what?

Uncle Harold disappears to pay the bill and David and I keep an eye on my mother as we both see she's losing control. The words aren't coming out and she's making odd movements with her body, like a trapeze artist about to fall off the rope.

'Which sport do you enjoy most?' Uncle Mark says to David. There's nothing safer than those questions. I know that. The normal questions which smother the fact that my mother's about to fall. David holds her arm. 'Are you all right?'

'I'm fine. Absolutely fine.'

Now Uncle Harold comes back. He looks at his sister (although they have different fathers, my uncles always talk of my mother as their sister). Now she tries to stand on her feet and she takes a breather, holding the sides of the table and swaying, as she gets there. Uncle Harold takes her by the arm. She leans on his shoulder and they walk down the panelled corridor where the food is laid out on silver trays. The waiters in the long white aprons smile and give semi-bows as if everything is, as my mother says, fine. Uncle Mark, David and myself follow, Uncle Mark pulling at his white cuffs and holding his lips like they're on show.

The revolving door is a bit of a problem. My mother doesn't make it in one go – she misses the exit and goes round again. The doorman with the black top hat and coffee-coloured long coat looks away, not wanting to make it worse, into Carlos Place, the opposite direction. But there's no Granny Blow coming down the steps of Number 3. We're just with my mother now and worrying with her over what can be done to make things better. She's been to see a film called *A Streetcar Named Desire*. As she leaves her brothers outside the Connaught, I think how pretty she is – but dreadfully sad. Her eyes so dark. 'What is straight? A line splashed across a street.' That's what Vivien Leigh says in the film. My mother says it when she doesn't know where to turn. She says it now, on the steps of the Connaught.

Uncle Harold gives my brother and me a leather wallet each, with our initials on. He looks embarrassed doing this, and I don't know why. Perhaps because there's nothing to put in the wallets, but I really don't mind that. At least not now. It's my first grown-up wallet. I like Uncle Harold and I think how cruel of Granny Clare to ever have been angry with him. My mother says she was never angry with Uncle Mark, but only because he was good looking. That mattered a lot to Clare – I've got to stop saying 'Granny Clare' as I don't feel as if she's a granny. I ought to, of course, and she ought to make me feel it too. I find this distance frightening – more frightening than when I was eight or ten – and now it makes me shiver. It's gone on for too long.

The Tennyson brothers give my mother a peck on the cheek and promise to talk to Ma. My mother is too wobbly to thank them, and I think perhaps she doesn't have to – she didn't make the problem of my grandmother. But I can see that neither of her half-brothers wants to face up to it. It doesn't fit how they've decided to live. There's Uncle Harold playing golf at Sandwich and a member of White's Club where everybody talks about horses or shooting or who they've been staying with, or if they've got one of these ancestral houses, who's been staying with them. Then there's Uncle Mark and that officer's uniform of the Royal Navy and shooting at Glen whenever he can and worshipping Ma whatever she's done. They both worship Ma and this is why my mother's swallowed far too much wine. They don't want to understand what's happened and this makes my mother nervous and makes her feel she's got to fight.

David and I take my mother's hand. I'm thinking now how

she stood here once wearing that long white wedding dress with the gold cross round her neck in the moment before she climbed into the Rolls-Royce with her father, Adrian. And the car would have gone along the Strand and down Fleet Street and up the hill which takes you to St Paul's. I've seen all the pictures in the wedding book. There's a big green album full of newspaper cuttings about it. The saddest remark is a line in large print which says, 'St Paul's stages a real romance for city workers.' It's all too much for me when I think of it now. 'Why did you marry at St Paul's?' I ask her one day. 'That was Winifred's wish. She organised everything, as usual.' Then my mother goes on to tell me how Winifred took over the whole wedding. It had to be at St Paul's because that was where she had been married to Detmar, and this happened because of Detmar's descent from John Blow who wrote the music for the opening of the new cathedral after the Great Fire. On account of this connection a special licence was granted for them to marry there. 'Are we really related to this composer?' I ask. My mother laughs. 'Winifred was very keen on establishing the Blow lineage. She was a Tollemache and she wanted the Blows to be at least some-where.'

As we go back in the taxi from the Connaught she tells us that her life is not a drama but the truth. This confuses me. Why can't drama be true? The trouble is the class she comes from doesn't have dramas, or if they do they push them aside at once. That's why Mummy keeps saying, 'The family don't understand.' But we do have Aunt Phyllie and Uncle Christopher. They understand. They're not like the ones who just think my mother's 'frightfully neurotic'. I have heard that word 'neurotic' used. It's like a brush to sweep anything nasty away. And then I'm thinking, the taxi stopping at traffic lights and going on again, she never was like this. At Roehampton she was always calm, controlled, sensible – only as the years passed I saw this sadness

growing. Like now at the Connaught. It hurts all the time inside
watching it. Hearing it. 'Your broken-hearted Mummy,' she put
at the end of a letter that came to me at Scaitcliffe. This letter
was written the week before she left my father.

She's not in love with my father any more, but she's still terribly upset. I know she needs someone to love her. Of course
David and I do, but she needs this physical love. There's a man
called Mike who's been to see her in Burnsall Street. Mike was
an ace fighter in the war. His plane roared through the skies
dropping bombs on Germans. But Mike's got a wife, so my
mother says there isn't any future. My mother needs someone to
look after her and he can't do that. He's taken me out to dinner
– and my brother too. We went to a restaurant in Chelsea and he
gave us a talk about how life wasn't black and white. What I
suppose he's saying is that nothing is clear. He talks about life
being covered in mist. He must see it like that from his time in
the air.

Later, in Burnsall Street, he finds a record of the march from
the film *The Dam Busters* and he puts it on. Then he goes and
sits on the sofa with my mother and puts an arm round her. He
is good-looking, I think. He's got dark hair and a face like the
actor, Richard Burton. He doesn't mention his wife, but my
mother's told us that she nags him a lot. Then, after that night,
we don't see Mike again. But always running in my mind is that
conversation in the restaurant about nothing being clear.

I miss Mike. I've no father in the way of someone to talk to.
Mike was a help like that. It's difficult without an older person
around. There's Mummy, but that's different. We've got to stand
by her now, look after her. Yes, Aunt Phyllie's a second mother,
but she's not a father. I'd like my mother to have a boyfriend who
could be like another father for me.

I'm still at prep school when Mike is around. The years of
being twelve, thirteen and fourteen stretch out like they're never
ending. And I'm with my mother so much when I'm not at
school that I learn all these things about her life before she

married my father. She's got a soft spot for this man called Valerian. She says they had a real love affair. And that when it ended she was very unhappy. I wonder if she misses him now that my father's gone, and if she sings the songs of her débutante time to bring it all back, in a way. That's it. Suddenly she'll be singing 'Blue Moon', that song I know so well now that I can sing it as she can. And when she sings she dreams. She dreams there's someone, somewhere, and that's why I hear her singing these words over and over. They're words that every time you hear them, you believe them.

Blue Moon you saw me standing alone,
Without a dream in my heart, without a love of my own.
Blue Moon you knew just what I was there for,
You heard me saying a prayer for, someone I really could
    care for,
And then there suddenly appeared before me,
The only one my arms will ever hold
I heard somebody whisper, 'Please adore me'
And when I looked, the moon had turned to gold.
Blue Moon! Now I'm no longer alone
Without a dream in my heart, without a love of my own.

9

I'M ON A train with my mother going to a wedding. It's a special train laid on to take guests and it's going to Norfolk. All the guests on the train are dressed as if they're at some cocktail party on wheels. The men are in tail coats as if it's Royal Ascot. When we stop in Norfolk, buses take us to the church. It's a country church, not big like a cathedral – though there ought to be a cathedral for all the guests that fill it. My mother and I are given places with other members of the family, because it's the wedding of Uncle Christopher's eldest son, Colin. It's a real social affair, and there's the Queen Mother and Princess Margaret sitting in the front pew. My mother says her cousin Colin is 'very social' and for a time it seemed as if he might marry Princess Margaret. In the end he married this pretty, noble girl I met at Glen.

My mother and I are sitting in our pew waiting for the bride to arrive. So my mother points out to me, in a whisper in my ear, other relations. She says, 'There's Hermione Baddeley. She's a famous actress and she married my mother's brother, David.' I don't see this Uncle David who used to own a night-club in London, as our eyes turn to watch the bride going up the aisle. My mother whispers again, 'Daughters never inherit. So they've all got to marry well.'

This is what my mother hasn't done. I know she thinks about it, and when she sees Colin's bride it reminds her. After the church we're taken to the family house, and as the bus turns in between the stone entrance lodges and swings down a long drive, Holkham Hall – the stately home of the Leicester family – looks like a cardboard cut-out in a hollow of an enormous park filled with trees and deer. I'm wearing my prep school grey Sunday suit and I wander around the reception. The rooms are rather like those I've seen in photographs of Buckingham Palace. I see Princess Margaret standing with the Queen Mother and both are a little smaller than I am. There's a heavy smell of women's scents which mixes with trails of cigarette smoke, and the noise of conversation makes my ears hurt. Do all these people really keep talking like this all through their lives? What a lot of breath to use up.

The next moment I'm standing in the hall of the house, by the front door with my mother. Behind us is a great stone staircase with a red carpet running down it. Suddenly there's a woman on her own coming down the staircase towards us. 'There's my mother,' my mother says. I look again at the woman and the great marble columns and the huge domed ceiling above me. It's like in a film when there's silence before something happens. My mother keeps looking at her mother, who all the time is getting nearer to the foot of the staircase. She's not tall, my grandmother, not so tall as my mother, and she has a lot of white powder on her face. The face seems to be tucked away in the silk shirt and suit she wears. I'm looking too and my mother puts an arm round me to push me forward. 'I want you to walk past my mother so that she knows who you are,' she says.

I step forward, and everywhere there's more silence. I think, what if the whole house fell down now like when Samson pushed the temple apart. That would be it and I'd never have to worry whether my grandmother was going to say hello or not. But I keep walking, my arms straight by my side and my hands hot against the grey flannel of my trousers. My grandmother comes closer, and I notice her neat leather shoes and her stockings. I've got to raise my eyes soon, I've got to look

at her but so that she won't think I'm staring. I'm going to pass
within two inches of her, that's how close we're going to be.
What is going to happen? Will she stop? Will she say something? I pass her, and take in what I can because she doesn't
stop, she doesn't turn her eyes to mine, only the faintest glance
and she walks on towards the front door.

Surely she'll say something to my mother? But I can't look
round quite yet. Not yet. Then as I reach the bottom of the
staircase I turn and there's my grandmother, her outline sharp
against the sunlight of the day. And there's my mother standing at the side of the door, ignored. Clare walks past her
daughter as if they couldn't talk because they had never been
introduced. I keep looking at my grandmother as she goes into
the distance and wonder how she can walk so lightly, carrying
with her all the trouble and all the sadness she has caused my
mother.

'Did she know me?' I ask my mother.

'Of course she knew you.'

'But she didn't speak.'

'That's my mother. That's what she's like. She lives for her
beauty – nothing else.'

My mother says that Uncle Christopher is still trying to bring
her – his sister – into our lives. And I think to myself, well, if it
happened would she change, suddenly be all loving? My mother
told us that when Clare's twins by her last husband, an American
my mother calls Jimmy Beck, came to say goodbye to her she
sent a message to say she couldn't see them as she was in the bath.
The only remark that's been passed on from my grandmother
Clare is that she understands that my mother is a very good
mother. The way my mother told it was as if Granny Clare had
never put a motherly foot wrong in her life.

On the train back to London there's a man talking to my mother.
I hear him asking her to a dinner-party he's giving in London.

This cheers my mother up quite a bit as she often says, 'There's no place for a divorced woman.'

At the dinner-party she meets Alun. She comes home and tells us about him. He's a diplomat and he's somewhere around forty. He starts to take my mother out and my mother tells us he's dropped all his young girlfriends for her. Alun is a well-known womaniser. That's the word my mother uses for men who can get women quickly into bed. But he stops all this for her. He comes to Burnsall Street one evening and he's very charming to David and me. We think he's the first reliable person in my mother's life since before she married my father.

Will he really make her happy again? This is the worry. Because I don't know if she will ever be like she was before my father hurt her. She used to have this happy smile when she chatted with her girl friends. She hardly sees these friends now and she tells us they're all far too conventional. If she meets one of them, she can be very dramatic. 'They know nothing of life,' she says to us. This means that they don't know about the nights growing colder and how the stars have lost their glitter. Sometimes in the daytime she slips up the road to the pub and sits at the bar alone. She orders a glass of wine and sits there, with her headscarf tied under her chin, hiding her dark hair cut short. But whatever the worries, she looks so beautiful still, like a woman of twenty-five, not forty.

From Sussex, Aunt Phyllie says, 'There's always Bill Astor.'

Aunt Phyllie wants her to marry the kind of person my mother should have married. My mother has been to Cliveden – my godfather Bill Astor's house on the River Thames – but Bill still doesn't appeal to her. We agree with Aunt Phyllie and we want her to marry someone who will look after her.

'What's wrong with Bill Astor?' I say to her.

'I could never love Bill,' she replies. 'I find him unattractive physically.'

She tells me this and I'm thirteen and I've got to understand it. In fact when she went to Cliveden for a weekend, my godfather made a pass at her. When she got back she told me the story. I said to myself as I heard it, 'Mummy, you've made a mistake.'

Bill was married at the time, but apparently that doesn't stop him. He's always wanted my mother, and she's always said no. My mother was sitting up in bed reading when a piece of panelling in her room shifted. From this secret door Bill appeared wearing a dressing-gown, although the first thing my mother noticed were the slippers with his initials WA in gold thread. My mother put her book down, startled. 'Bill,' she said.

Bill went towards her and sat on the end of her bed. 'You're not happy, are you? You're in difficulties with money,' he said.

'It's hard just now,' my mother said, 'but it will pass.'

'I want to help you, Diana. I want to give you money.'

'No, you mustn't do that. I'll be all right.'

Bill looked at her directly. 'I like to help my friends before it's too late.'

Still my mother refused. But then he moved towards her and made a pass.

'What did you do, Mummy?' I ask.

'I let him go ahead.'

'What? You mean he made love to you.'

'Yes.'

But I'm not shocked. My eyes are far too open for that. Once you've seen your mother being beaten to pieces there aren't many surprises left.

'Perhaps you should have taken his offer.'

'I would have been trapped.'

'I'm sure he was being kind,' I say, but my mother has this thing about not getting help from friends. The family, the relations, are another matter, but not friends. Only the covenants aren't nearly enough to live on. She says she's going to let our bedrooms in term-time while we're at school. The house is so small, though, I ask if there'll be any room for our lives.

'You'll have to pack your things away, and then put them back again in the holidays.'

'Of course,' I say. I don't complain because it will be worse for her than it is for us. She'll have two lodgers in the house using our sitting-room and kitchen, which aren't big enough to swing a cat in.

'If the family had done more I wouldn't have to do this,' she says. When she says this it makes me sad. 'The family covenants', as she calls them, don't help as they should help. And I begin to realise, too, that there's a gulf and that the family are on one side and we're on the other.

Alun's been round quite a lot. Sometimes he spends the night and we see him briefly before he goes to his office. He takes my mother out to restaurants and one day he invited David and me to have lunch with him in his club in St James's. I had to put on my grey suit for that. He's very well mannered and I've never seen him in a temper or out of control. We think he could be just right for my mother.

'Would you mind if I married Alun?' she says one morning as we're having breakfast in the coffee bar opposite our house.

I'm not upset, I'm pleased. And David is too. There'll be somebody to give her all this love she needs. 'He's dropped all his eighteen-year-olds for me,' she says proudly. And she tells us that as they walk down the streets at night he says to her, 'The stars on the pavement are shining for you.' It's so good he's steady and not dull with it. It's as if everything's suddenly quiet and calm after all the noise of my father. So my mother says she's going to show the family that she can pick a sensible person. She doesn't want them to think of her as 'a failure with men'. She's sensitive about that. So she takes Alun to dinner with Uncle Christopher who's moved to a house off the river in Chelsea.

The next day she talks about the dinner. 'It all went so well,' she says, 'but Alun got a little over-excited and became rather free with Uncle Christopher.' After dinner he slapped Uncle Christopher on the back and said, 'She's worth fifty thousand on the open market.' Uncle Christopher responded with a thin smile. He's not too keen on members of the family being sold, my mother says. At least, not like slaves at the market. No, not keen at all since the Tennants are aristocracy. Not that Uncle Christopher would ever say it, so he left it to the thin smile. My mother laughs, and says, 'I don't think that went down too well.'

We get used to Alun and we like him. There is an evening in Burnsall Street. My mother has cooked the dinner and we're in the small dining-room in the basement. Dinner is over and Alun is sitting there talking to my brother about the world situation – David's really gone on politics. I'm thinking about the book I'm reading. If I bury myself in it I'll be able to escape. It's called *Vanity Fair* and I'm half-way through and I'm wondering how it will all end for Becky Sharp. George is dead and Amelia doesn't know. The reader knows and I'm worried for Amelia. David's talking about Egypt and President Nasser.

That's what's happening in this room that's half beneath the pavement. I'm getting tall and I'm feeling the smallness of our house in Chelsea. I can touch the dining-room ceiling with my hand. I know Chelsea is where smart people live but I think their houses must be bigger than ours. Suddenly I'm angry that we don't have money and I bury myself back in the book.

My mother's sitting at the table, looking darker and darker. She stares and stares at the table, nothing but the table, then she lifts her head and stares at Alun. She doesn't say anything, just stares. I know something's going to happen, for she makes these quick exaggerated movements, like an actress on the stage.

'Do you love me more than your Calvados?' she says to Alun. She faces him directly, cutting the conversation. It's all too sudden. Alun looks at her, and she goes on looking at him. She wants an answer. Alun's caught off his guard.

'Well?' my mother demands.

'This isn't the moment, Diana . . . but' – he swallows and we notice – 'of course.'

So that's the reply: not much good, but it has been made and she has to accept the broken answer.

My mother's affair with Alun lasts for a year, perhaps a month or two less. It's Mummy who breaks it off. 'Why?' we ask her. 'Alun's very tough. He's very hard. He would destroy me,' she says. Or is it that Alun doesn't give her the attention she demands? She's been starved for so long.

Now Mummy sits in the pub that you cross the King's Road to reach once you are at the top of Burnsall Street. The Commercial, that's the pub's name, and sometimes I've been in there with her, not for long though, in case the people who run it find out I'm under age. Because I'm already six foot, I get away with things. The Commercial is filled with very clever intellectuals, like writers and painters, who've usually got no money. They go up and talk with my mother, and I think they're intrigued. And my mother finds them much more sympathetic than the hunting hearties she grew up with. She damns the whole world she came from because they're not interested in life with a capital L. 'What is Life?' my mother asks. I like talking to them too, because they're the sort of conversations I can't have with relations. There's a freedom with these Commercial people. They talk and talk, cigarette stubs crowding dirty ashtrays, and the hot smell of whisky mingling with the funny sour smell of beer. 'Life,' I hear my mother announcing to one of them, 'is a boxing match. It's just a matter of how many times you can stand up again.'

We're at Glen for the holidays. It's all normal again. I go fishing on the loch that we walk to along a rough track with moors all around. There's a boathouse at the side of the loch where sometimes we have picnics with my cousins. In the house there's a ping-pong table and I play against Colin, who's very quick at it. My mother takes us into the huge woods on the hillside and shows us a fairy ring. Emma, another cousin, is now a débutante like Mummy was once. She plays a record by Frankie Laine over and over on the gramophone. It goes, 'All day I've faced a barren

·waste without the taste of water.' Uncle Christopher strolls in and out of rooms, smiling.

But my mother's not well this time. I could see that unhappy look as nice McCubbin, talking all the way, drove us from Galashiels station to the house. Now Mummy says she's found a medicine which she swears will keep her nerves steady. It comes in a bottle and its colour is brown, and the recommended dose is a few teaspoonfuls a day. She asks for twelve bottles from a chemist in Edinburgh. It's delivered to Glen and I watch McCubbin carrying the box of bottles up the steps of the house.

That same day my mother comes into the Glen drawing-room wobbly. It's early on a hot summer evening and I'm desperately hoping no one will notice. After dinner she sits on a chair and I have to keep a hand on her to keep her upright. I'm waiting for the house to be in darkness. This will happen soon as the dynamo that powers the electricity will go off. Then everybody reaches for candles and nobody will realise that my mother's lost her control. But I know that they know because they've been talking to her as if they knew she wasn't herself but were determined to treat her as normal.

'Diana's gone to her room and come down quite another person,' Uncle Christopher's wife, Aunt Elizabeth says, looking up from her knitting. My mother should be there with her knitting too. The sweaters she's making for us. But Aunt Elizabeth's noticed that the piece of knitting she's taken from her bag is the same one as last year. 'Is that the sweater you were knitting last time?' she asks. Mummy tries to think of something to say. 'Oh, no. It's for a friend of the boys.'

'You are quick,' says Aunt Elizabeth, impressed.

'My knitting, my knitting!' my mother shouts just before leaving. Knitting is the done thing in these houses where we stay. At Glen it happens in the evening, in the quiet drawing-room with the thick carpet and the smells of flowers. But my mother can't do any knitting at all this time. She's spaced out on this nerve medicine called Elixir Gabail. So David and I help her up the small white-painted staircase that leads to her bedroom. I'm glad it doesn't have to be the other staircase where you're too noticed. The house is dark now except for the flicker of candles and faces only partly seen. We get my mother to her bedroom with its views to the garden and heathered moors. They're dark now, too, behind drawn curtains. And my mother sits on her bed swaying and telling us she's Mary, Queen of Scots. Whenever Mummy compares herself it's always with someone tragic. She draws a wild and unhappy comfort from the tragedies of others.

I'm trapped inside her tragedy, too. I've lived it with her through the years, and I think I should have been living other things like kicking a football around or reading the stories of Hans Christian Andersen with lots of fantasy. Being a child, being free. But I'm caught in her tragedy. It's so strong that it empties my mind. David is learning to detach himself – to save himself – although I can see he's often desperately worried, like the day my mother fell off her chair in the dining-room at Glen. Nobody was there, only one Tennant cousin who helped us to pack as we had to leave later that day. The nice cousin, a distant one, had played with my mother when she was two. That was when my mother's grandmother, Pamela, was alive, and her grandfather Eddy. My mother was at Glen then, protected by Pamela. I keep 'if-ing' – *if* Pamela had lived longer, *if* my grandfather Bethell had lived a bit longer too, everything would have been different.

I can't do anything but look back. I can't. If I look back I can reconstruct a whole time when nothing awful has yet happened.

'I'll wait for the real Galahad now,' Mummy writes in a letter to me. But how can she find Galahad if she sits in the pub at the top of the road? She tells me that she just stares at the glass of wine on the polished bar top. Sometimes she'll stare at it for five, six, seven, ten minutes, her face cupped in her hands. But if they're there, the bohemians, as she calls the always talking group, they draw her towards them. They know about messed-up lives, and that's why she needs them. They're educating my mother too. Because she didn't really have an education except to marry the right person. The bohemians talk of the Spanish Civil War, of Honoré de Balzac, of their friend George Orwell, and the power of Dostoevsky. There's a tall, brown-haired man in the pub and my mother says he keeps looking at her. He's in the group and he can't stop his eyes drifting towards her.

One evening at closing time the brown-haired man said to my mother he'd better take her home. 'I live very near. I'll manage,' my mother replied. But he insisted. 'So he saw me home.'

This man's called Peter and my mother writes to me at school saying he's been ringing her up. By the time we come home we find Peter is in Burnsall Street most evenings. I'm having to get used to my mother's boyfriends. I don't mind them as long as it's good for her. It's odd, but we've got to look after her when it should be the other way round. It's difficult. I'm not old enough.

I don't think Mummy believes Peter's really the Galahad she's looking for but he tells her that he loves her passionately. Also, she says Uncle Tony's been round, the squire of Rise, with a television set. She thinks he's given it 'to keep me in'. They're worried she might keep the wrong company now she's on her own. Of course, this isn't said but Mummy says she can feel it. 'There's always Bill Astor,' Aunt Phyllie says again from her house in Sussex with the bluebell woods.

I've made a 'best' friend already at Stowe. He came the same term as I did. His parents live near Esher in Surrey. I've been to stay with them. Ian's father works with Lloyd's and their house is quite big with a good-size lawn where Ian's parents do barbecues. There are lots of houses down the road. It's very green and leafy, sort of countryside without country. I'm told this is where stockbrokers live. I couldn't tell you why I've made a friend of Ian. We look pretty funny together as he's half my height. We don't really share much, although I pretend to him that we do. I made him my friend in case nobody else became my friend. He's very keen on racing cars and he's always talking about Brooklands. I shocked his mother one day and I don't think she's ever looked at me in the same way since.

'I've got this debt. A bill I haven't paid.'

'Oh,' says Ian's mother. 'You must pay it. Always pay your bills at once.'

'It's difficult just now. I don't have any money.'

'Then you shouldn't run up a debt. Surely your parents have taught you that.'

I look ashamed and I feel hot. Should I explain? My father? The divorce? No, I decide. It would go on for ever. So I go on feeling hot, awkward, until Ian proudly takes me for a short spin, down the drive and back, in their bubble car.

I've got these different worlds running together. They don't connect at all. There's Glen, Aunt Phyllie and Rise, which is one world, and this other world of Peter's. Apparently Peter's a social-ist and he's always spouting Lenin and Marx. 'Your relations are utter shits,' he tells my mother. He stands there in our small sitting-room pushing his hands out as he's talking to make what he's saying seem very important. 'It'll all be over for you lot soon,' he goes on. He says she should stop having anything to do with her family and join the Labour Party. Mummy listens to him as if she believes every word he's saying. I'm thinking he wants to make us all feel guilty . . . he wants us to apologise . . . he wants to be the only person who matters. But my mother's being taken in a little because she was never educated like Peter's educated himself. She was brought up to glide through the days with a smile, and this intellectual jousting, well, it wasn't quite . . . it wasn't done. You can tell he's angry that he can't dominate my mother on the social ladder, so he dominates her like this.

Of course it's bullying and it's below the belt, but I say nothing. I say nothing because my mother needs him.

My father's disappeared for a while, we don't know where, and we've given up about the alimony. My mother's managed to let our bedrooms for the next school term, but the worries that don't end are making her drink a lot now. Except Mummy doesn't drink like my father drinks. She doesn't start at nine in the morning and go on through the day. It'll happen suddenly in the afternoon, or evening, and the drink will be drunk as suddenly. One day it's six o'clock and we've planned to see a film at one of those big cinemas in Leicester Square – Mummy, David and me. There's a bottle of wine in the kitchen and my mother's drinking from it. She fills, refills, and fills her glass again quickly.

We're in Leicester Square and Mummy can't stand straight on her feet. She was going all blurred in the taxi and the outdoor air's hit her and she's gone. David and I decide not to go into the cinema with her. It's going to be terribly embarrassing if she starts talking loudly or falls over the person next to her. So we leave her in Leicester Square after she's given us some money to go in. She says she's going to be all right: 'I'm fine,' she says, but I can see she's not because she's swaying badly. 'I'll see you at home later,' she says. But I don't really take in the film because I'm worrying whether she's all right.

When we get back to Burnsall Street her bedroom door is ajar. I put my head round and there she is curled up in bed. Her dark hair is all tangled across her face. 'She's fast asleep,' I say to David. Next morning we ask her how she spent the evening. 'Oh, I ran into a man I met at Cliveden and we had dinner and he saw me home.' I suppose the man must have known she was in a bad way – or perhaps he didn't. I wish we hadn't left her alone in Leicester Square. I really do. I think it's going to public school that does it. It makes you so ashamed if your parents don't behave correctly. Even if something really terrible has happened. It makes you feel really ashamed. And I know.

Peter isn't married but he's had more girlfriends than you'd expect. I mean, he's not that handsome. He's got these narrow eyes that make him appear shifty. Then he doesn't shave that well and there are often patches of hair on his face. I find his nose uncomfortable, as if he's about to peck at something with it. But he does make a great fuss of my mother at times. Still, that doesn't explain it. I can't understand how someone as beautiful as she is can sleep with him.

'Why do you sleep with him?' I ask her one day.

'He's a good lover,' my mother replies, as if that settles it.

This life isn't any more safe than the life at Roehampton. My father may be out of the way but all my mother's past is stirred up now. I hate Cicely for being so hard on Mummy – that's what we call her: 'Cicely', never 'Granny', as she writes on the note at Christmas with the handkerchiefs she sends David and me. My mother says that since she was six Cicely has tried to make her feel terribly small. She never liked my mother being pretty and she struck dead centre at her vulnerability. 'You're far too emotional for an Englishman,' Cicely informed my mother, looking down her beaked and crooked nose on which the horn-rimmed spectacles sit. We try not to see Cicely but sometimes she telephones. She starts by playing the loving Mummy bit, so my mother then has to go and have lunch with her. Then the loving Mummy bit ends and she throws my mother these cutting remarks. It takes my mother back to Rise before her marriage and coming down into the drawing-room where guests are gathered before dinner.

My mother tells us how she once entered the room, her dark hair falling over almost bare shoulders. From her place by the fire, Cicely turned her head and, seeing Diana, levelled her eyes. 'Diana, you look quite ridiculous in that dress. Go upstairs at once and put on something more suitable.' Diana looked away from her stepmother. Her father, his bow tie straining as he turned, pleaded with Cicely: 'Cicely please don't say that to Diana. Please.' But Adrian Bethell's gentleness did not work with his humourless wife. 'The girl must learn,' said Cicely. And Diana, whom the guests now stared at with pity in their eyes, went back to her room. A friend of my mother's was there, and the friend told my mother afterwards how, once my mother had gone, Cicely turned to Adrian: 'I want to help Diana. Anything that resembles her mother's disgraceful behaviour must be extinguished.' Adrian, sad now, but silent, returned the conversation to next day's race card at York.

My mother tells David and me these stories and it's all so vivid that I can see it.

But I keep asking myself why my mother's gone for a man like Peter. The way he takes her over and tries to tell her what she should do annoys me. He doesn't know anything at all about our lives really, just what he thinks he knows. My father broke my mother's heart and he doesn't care tuppence about that. Mummy doesn't believe in herself any more and that's why she listens to Peter's jibes about where she comes from. That's why Cicely haunts Mummy, too.

'The rich waste their money, but they never give,' Peter tells my mother, thrusting his arms out.

'We're hardly rich,' my mother states.

'Oh, but you're related to them all. Your Uncle, Lord Glenconner – he's worth millions. The boys' cousin, Lord Tollemache – all that beer money. What's it called, "Tolly Ale". And your Aunt Phyllie with all her servants. That's not poverty. You don't know what poverty is, Diana.'

'Not your poverty, perhaps. But when Aunt Elizabeth tucked thirty pounds into my suitcase at Glen, that was meant to help.'

'And your sons go to public school,' and Peter wrinkles up his nose.

It's true that Peter went to a state school and he would have gone on to a university if his parents could have paid for it. They couldn't, and he's blaming us for that. I'm learning about class hatred fast from Peter. It's not nice at all, and when he's ranting this nausea starts inside me. It's because I want to tell him to shut up, but at fourteen I'm not sure of anything yet. Then he's all concerned about my mother but it's ruined by the ranting. It's then I ask my mother again why she can't look up her friends from her débutante days. 'Surely they'd like it,' I press on. But what I get is one of her dramatic looks and, 'There's nothing to say to any of them now.'

If my mother could shake off Peter, her life would improve. He takes her to his drinking clubs because he keeps telling us that that's where the 'real' people are. These clubs, which I haven't been to yet, she says are full of drunks and people at the end of their tether. I don't understand what he means by 'real'. I think it's his way of putting us down about where we come from. Then he claims to be getting my mother off drink. Anyway, he's had a victory with my brother. They talk about Socialism, with a capital S, and Dostoevsky for hours on end.

'You can't understand life until you've read Dostoevsky,' he spouts. I wonder about all the many many millions who've never read him. I see them plodding in the dark until someone throws them a copy of *Crime and Punishment*. Then all these books by him tumble out of the skies and housewives look up from their ironing, builders stop midway on scaffolding, accountants close their ledgers, squires lock themselves in their unused libraries, tramps and down-and-outs dance, and the Queen of England removes her crown.

I don't feel safe with the bohemians. They like living without a thought for tomorrow. They despise anyone who's practical. But I've noticed they're not slow to take money from anyone who's got some. Sometimes one of them rings our doorbell, not for money, but to look at my mother. They admire her freshness, like a country girl's, still there despite everything. One of them, a writer, stood at the door one day and told her he wanted to come in. 'I've got an erection,' is what he said.

'And what did you say to him, Mummy?'

'I told him to take it to Piccadilly.'

They are different, but they're not the people I want to be with after life with my father. I want to go down to Aunt Phyllie and ride through the woods. I'm sorry and unhappy about her selling Ragdale because Leicestershire is the best for riding. If I knew I could tear across open grass with fences in front of me, as they do in Leicestershire with the Quorn, it would make London and the bohemians more bearable. I feel awkward in front of them. That's because Peter's mocked us so much for having posh relations. And he makes me feel clumsy whenever I open my mouth.

I've had a letter from Michael. 'If you don't come to Sheffield soon, I'll come to London and find you. Your friend from six years of age, Michael.'

It's five years now that I've not seen Michael. It'll have to wait until next holidays. But I want to go to Sheffield. I do. Another eight weeks of slog at Stowe, then freedom. These term times seem to run for ever but at least I'm away from Peter and the nasty twist he puts on everything. My mother says he's started ringing up the family, making telephone calls and pretending he's got inside information on money deals. He rang up Uncle Christopher and said he knew about some collapse of the market in South Africa. Uncle Christopher behaved with restraint when Peter said of course he'd expect a rake-off for the information. Peter found it wonderfully amusing. 'I'm not a rich man,' Uncle Christopher replied. 'Lord Glenconner not a rich man!' Peter exploded in Burnsall Street later. If Peter did some work, he might be less bitter. He's told us he's a journalist but he never shows us anything he writes. I wonder what he does do. Perhaps he's a Communist spy.

10

'AWAKE, MY SOUL, and with the sun thy daily stage of duty run. Shake off dull sloth and joyful rise to pay thy morning sacrifice.' This is the hymn we chant from the school chapel once a week. But I'm not lazy – I'm afraid. I'm afraid of older boys, panicked at being in a strange place and frightened of what will be expected. Afraid, too, simply of more school and it going on and on, but I show none of this. I appear cool and detached. My father's written to tell me to get in all the hunting I can. There's a rule in something called the Red Book that allows a boy to go fox-hunting once a term. This means that once a term I can escape the routine for one whole day. Twice a year, really; there's no hunting in the summer.

I like riding more than it's ever possible to say. It's taken over my life. Ever since I read Siegfried Sassoon I want to have the hunting life that he had. I identify with the book's hero, George Sherston. He doesn't have a proper family and he grows up with his comfortably off spinster aunt. I turned Aunt Evelyn into Aunt Phyllie, and George Sherston, lonely and shy, into myself. I want to open out and find companionship with earthy hunting people as Sherston does. I dream of having a season with one pack and spending evenings learning and talking hunting to the huntsman, like Sherston. It is a world with clear borders, with horses at the centre, and when I'm on a horse all that nervousness and churning that started in Roehampton stops. This calm is made stronger by my imagination. I'm always imagining, as a way out of the present. There's a place where the boys can go for riding in the grounds and I set off there as soon as I can.

How am I going to deal with Stowe? 'Enjoy Stowe's palatial setting,' my father has written. He's not paying for me to be here, but he can write that with no conscience. Of course he was a boy here, too, and my mother says that his years at Stowe were the best, far the best of all, when he showed such promise. I don't like to think of that, it only makes what's happened more horrible. Instead in class I daydream about my Bethell grandfather hunting his hounds over that great drain country in the East Riding of Yorkshire, where he so belonged.

'Blow, come here,' says the prefect sitting at the centre table in the houseroom. 'You've been talking. I saw your lips moving.'

'Yes,' I say. 'Right,' he says, 'I want you to write out one hundred times, "I must not talk in prep."' I nod obediently and sit down.

Later I knock on the prefect's study door. He's sitting in his desk chair. He looks me up and down. 'Well, what is it?'

I tell him I think it would be more useful if I learnt 'The Ballad of Reading Gaol'. I explain it has a lot of verses. His eyes blink and, rather than show his ignorance, he says, 'All right. Do that.'

Two days later I start reciting to him. He sits there in his rugger shorts and stares at me. I get to verse seven which goes:

> Yet each man kills the thing he loves,
>> By each let this be heard,
> Some do it with a bitter look,
>> Some with a flattering word.
> The coward does it with a kiss,
>> The brave man with a sword!

Winterbourne's eyes go blank. I notice that all the time he has been staring at his crotch. In the changing room I've seen him with his arms round this young boy with wavy gold hair. I saw that during my second day at Stowe. Everybody says it's just replacement for girls. Anyway the poem unsettles him. 'Stop there,' he says. 'Enough. You can go . . . And don't talk in prep again.'

There's a girls' school not far away, but it's out of bounds. Some boys risk it, but not long ago two boys were caught and punished by not being allowed to leave their houses. I've risked it, too, and got into trouble. This girl I met over the school fence has been writing to me, but there's nothing I can do about it. That's why boys do it with other boys. There are boys who try to get into my bed at night. If I like them, I let them play with my willie. Our willies go stiff. We don't kiss properly but kind of smudge our faces together. I like the warmth of their bodies. Something wakes in me that hides the loneliness.

'The Ballad of Reading Gaol' is not quite classroom reading. And of course I didn't get to hear of it in class. Nobody talks about Oscar Wilde, not the masters. It's because of the lines that Mummy keeps quoting: 'Each man kills the thing he loves', and after that come the coward with his kiss and the brave man with his sword. Like the quote from Tennessee Williams about a line splashed across a street. They're her props in stress. But for me they're vivid, and they're disturbing, and once they're in my head I can't get them out of it.

It's because of home, too, that school is strange. It's as if I've already done this growing-up stuff and I've somehow gone beyond school education. Other boys at Stowe refer to 'the parents' and talk of them as if they're people who lay down rules and that's it. But there's been no space for rules where I've come from and I've only known where they are by watching my father break them. It's too late to turn me out, hand-stitched in tweed jacket and flannel trousers, to be that stiff-upper-lip English type. It's Stowe the house, not the school, that I go for. I keep making places into home and dreaming of how the ancestors lived. It's not difficult at Stowe with all these temples in the grounds. But best by far is the one day's hunting we're allowed. I get my *nihil obstat* – the day-off chit – immediately.

Suddenly there are no classrooms and I'm with the hounds running through the woods, viewing a temple or an obelisk from a distant landscape. The hunting people dressed in scarlet and black canter down ridings while far away I catch the big classical front of the house which again sets me dreaming. Elderly women in black habits and black bowler hats, their white hair bunned by a black veil, bounce past me. There's the Master, a severe-faced man who could shout at a regiment and who reminds me of Uncle Philip as he rides with utter determination at his fences.

I soon learn that the hunting's better away from Stowe. There are too many woods in the grounds for the fox to run far in the open. And there's more jumping where there are just fields. Once a season the Grafton Hunt meets at Stowe, and that's treated as an extra day. On that day Stowe's grandeur comes back. With the horses and hounds, the scarlet- and black-coated riders, Stowe's once more the most romantic setting in all the land. I've seen things go, Ragdale most of all, and the soul of a place goes away with it. It hurts me thinking of it. That's why I don't treat Stowe as a school. And it's another reason why I go hunting, and riding through the grounds, all the time turning Stowe back to what it was.

'Hunting at one's public school sounds rather upstage to me,' Mr Owen writes from Scaitcliffe and goes on to tell me of football matches won and lost. Does he think I'm not preparing myself properly for what's to come? Am I not taking seriously enough his grounding in the middle classes, playing fields, and all that? The thought of having to play up and play the game appals me. I fight against this jingoism. I dig my toes in, more than I ever did at Scaitcliffe. I show openly that I don't bother about rugger. Then one afternoon I do play, running hard with the ball and tackling, which impresses the prefect in charge.

'You see, Blow, you can do it if you want to,' says the prefect, who has a lisp. I don't reply, but carry on walking with the others the long walk from the playing fields to my house.

I bicycle away from the school as much as I can. There's a family about two miles away that I visit often. I met them one holidays and I go over to see them for lunch at weekends, and in the weekdays, too, if I can steal off. The old lady is the widow of Admiral Sir Roger Keyes and in the hall is a life-size torpedo with ZEEBRUGGE marked on it, on a brass plaque. Lady Keyes, a large woman with a bristle of moustache, sits down on a *chaise-longue* in the drawing-room and takes me through the battle, moment by moment. This is far more exciting history than I'm learning at school; there's emotion thrown in. There are horses in the stables, too. Her daughter, Elizabeth, rides them. One day the old lady comes down the stairs with a grey-black hunt coat.

'You'd better have this,' she says. 'It was Roger's May hunt coat.' And she explains how once they hunted as late as May. I bicycle back to school that day, the hunt coat tied to the handle-bars.

They're worried at Stowe that I'm not making myself part of the school enough. But I don't see the school as a family, whereas I do with the Keyeses'. I'm being prepared for confirmation and the school chaplain, tugging at a small lock of red hair above a pasty forehead, says to me, 'At one's public school one should, Simon, grow inwards rather than outwards.'

My mother comes to visit but she's not conventionally dressed. The boys notice. 'Pretty amazing those bright red stock-ings. Is she an actress?' Of course, that's what she should be. I've seen cuttings of her when she used to model and I wish she'd gone from modelling to the stage. She modelled because Cicely made sure she got as little money as possible. But girls of her sort

– I'm told – didn't go on the stage then. I worry about her when I'm at school and whether she's safe in Burnsall Street.

My mother wants me to do well at school. 'You must get high marks in exams,' she keeps telling me. Only I'm so easily distracted from school work. I've got this fear of something slipping, falling out of place, going wrong. Fear that there's going to be a crisis at home.

'I'm afraid your mother's had a miscarriage. I found her bleeding on the floor at Burnsall Street. She's had to go to hospital.' That was how the news was broken to us by Anne Phillimore.

Anne and Claud Phillimore are two of my parents' oldest friends. We've been many times to stay in their house, Rymans, which is by a village near Chichester. Claud is an architect, like my father, and he's tried so hard to make my father have 'a cure'. He says my father has so much ability but there is no confidence there. Claud and Anne are kind, and I don't know many kind people. If Anne hadn't called by chance that afternoon my mother would have bled to death. 'I was haemorrhaging badly,' she said to us later. 'It was Peter's child.'

We don't go home at the end of that term. Luigi comes and collects us in Aunt Phyllie's car and takes us to Sussex. My mother's in a nursing home now and we go with Aunt Phyllie to see her. Aunt Phyllie wants her to give up Peter, in fact she's really concerned that she might marry him. 'Any news of that man?' she's always asking David and me, a nervous look on her face. 'It's such a worry, Mummy and the men.'

'You've got to learn to mix,' Aunt Phyllie says, and she sends us to the Saturday night dance in the nearby town. Off we go with Luigi to Hawkhurst and Luigi buys our tickets so that we can go into the dance hall. It's a big room with a bar at one end. At the other end is a band and the room is lit by spotlights thrown on to a revolving mirrored ball, making rainbow colours round the room. There are groups of girls with piled-up hair-dos keeping to themselves. The men, wearing rather sharp suits and bootlace ties or coloured dickies, crowd round the bar. I'm a bit nervous, but Luigi's with us so I can't be left on my own. As the night gets under way I dance with quite a few girls and don't have any difficulties. They don't think I'm posh and in the wrong place.

Aunt Phyllie's modern, I'm thinking, she knows that we won't ever be living the same life as she's lived. Except that living with her I get lulled into a security that makes me want to believe that none of it will go.

'I'm going to Sheffield,' I say to Aunt Phyllie, 'to stay with my friend Michael.'

'Do be careful,' says Aunt Phyllie.

'He's been my friend since I was six.'

'Don't stay too long then. And come back safe.'

I've never been to one of these industrial cities. The train journeys have always been to a relation's house. The Ivenses are there to meet me at Sheffield station and Mrs Ivens gives me a big hug. Michael's got quite tall and the freckles on his face are still there, and they spread apart as he gives me a smile. He puts his hand in mine, then puts an arm round my shoulders and squeezes me.

'I've told my mates I've got my posh friend coming.'

Now I'm embarrassed. I don't want to be thought of like that. 'I haven't changed,' I say.

'Where did you get that voice from?'

'It's the same. It's just grown up a bit.'

Mr Ivens drives the car very carefully and I look out of the window at the buildings and think, these cities are too big really. Cinemas flash past, and people hurrying along streets, then groups of boys my age or Michael's, not hurrying but leaning against walls in drainpipe trousers and quiffed hair, talking, then smiling, now silent, then hanging around again.

'Is it rough, Sheffield? Are there fights on streets and that kind of thing?'

'It isn't Roehampton, Simon,' Michael says. Then he remembers, and touches my hand. 'Sorry. I didn't mean that.'

Michael's parents don't ask me questions until we're in the house. We've driven out of the centre of the town to a quiet street of detached houses all looking the same. They've got front gardens, with a garage and a path that leads you to the front door. The ground-floor windows are arched like a sunrise and the roof is brown-red tiles which curl and the outside of the house is speckled white. In the sitting-room I notice the same furniture that was in Roehampton. Mrs Ivens goes to make tea. Mr Ivens takes down his pipe, starts prodding it with tobacco, sits down and lights it. Michael says, 'Come on. I'll show you where you're sleeping.'

'Here,' he says. 'I knew you'd need a good-size bed. You're tall now. Normally, it's my room.'

There are posters of Elvis Presley on the walls. A guitar leans in a corner. Michael's school books are cluttered on two shelves to one side of the bed. By the window is a desk with more school things. There's a poster, too, of Nietzsche – every rebel's hero – and a smaller poster of my great-grandmother, Pamela, and her two sisters by John Singer Sargent.

'Thanks, Michael,' I say, looking at the Sargent.

'I saw it on a school trip to London. I really like it.'

'Do you remember what she used to say?'

'"Take two cows, Taffy. Take two cows, Taffy."' And Michael draws out the words in a cooing sound. 'She said that's the pigeons when they talk.'

I laugh. 'Where will you sleep?'

'I've got the spare room. It's been five years, Simon. I want you to be comfortable.'

Then we go downstairs where Mrs Ivens has the tea all laid out. It's not just tea but sandwiches and cakes. Mrs Ivens pushes a plate of fish-paste sandwiches towards me.

'And how's your dear mother?'

'She's OK,' I say and don't know whether I should tell all now.

'She's a beautiful woman. I used to say to Henry she had the most charming smile – so inviting and warm.'

'She's left my father,' I start. 'They're divorced. My brother and I live with my mother. We've got this small house.'

Mr Ivens looks up. A sweep of black hair falls across his forehead. His pipe sits on the table by him, gone out. 'A great sadness, your father, my lad. I'm sure your mother did everything she could.'

'Yes. Too much. My dad'll outlive her. My mother says he's strong as an ox.'

Mrs Ivens beams at me; her white teeth have edges of lipstick on them. 'She could have married anybody. Why, as I've said to Henry, with a face like that she could have been a princess.'

'Everybody noticed her in Roehampton. She was a star,' says Mr Ivens, talking gravely and slowly. Suddenly I'm awkward and seconds later a belt is drawn round my stomach: that belt I hate so much. I hear my breathing shake. I'm back there with my father shouting, shouting till the veins stick out on his neck and my mother's there too, slumped against the wall bruised, bleeding.

Michael, one leg crossed over the other, moves restlessly. 'Drink your tea, Simon. We're going into town. You haven't seen Sheffield.'

'Give him a minute, Michael,' Mr Ivens interrupts. But Michael says we'll be back for dinner and he grabs my arm. Soon we're walking down the street and it's not long before we're in the centre of town. Michael leads me to a coffee bar. The inside is decorated with music notes. He tells me a friend is arriving. I look around and see lots of quiffed haircuts. There are girls with these huge big hair-dos sitting like beehives on their heads and all looking like the singer, Anne Shelton.

'Who's the friend?'

'Amanda. She's at my school.'

So we sit there waiting, stirring our cups and Michael looks at me with that half-smile I recognise from the days we unpacked the hamper.

'Does your mum have a boyfriend, then?' Michael asks, perhaps thinking like I am of days long ago.

'Yes. I've got used to all that. She needs to be happy again.'

'And you. Do you have a girlfriend?'

'There are these girls I meet . . . at dances. We don't have any girls at my school.'

'So do you fancy any of them?'

'A few. There's one but she says she's too old for me. She's nineteen.'

One of the drainpipe haircuts goes over to the jukebox, presses some white plastic buttons and puts money in a slot. The croon of Elvis starts: 'Love me tender, love me true . . .' drowning the mumbled conversations. Two of the beehive hair girls stand by the jukebox, tapping their shiny high-heel toes on the floor, and chew gum in silent ritualistic movements. Now another girl comes into the bar. She looks round, spots Michael, and comes over.

'Amanda. Meet Simon.'

I give Amanda a nod and she sits down. All at once I'm wondering how long she will be with us for. I didn't take in until she appeared how much I want to be on my own with Michael. They're talking now and I'm not properly listening. She's got peroxided bouffant hair, wide-apart eyes with false lashes and a bouncy Marilyn waistline. They talk these kind of nothings and then Amanda says to me, the false eyelashes lowering, 'Staying long?'

'I don't know. A few days. I don't see Michael often.'

'Funny place, Sheffield. It's not for everyone.'

'Simon'll be all right. I'm looking after him.' And Michael puts an arm round my shoulders.

'Better find him a girl then,' Amanda says abruptly.

Then Michael says will I wait for a second and he gets up and takes Amanda to a corner of the room where it's darker. I sit at the table looking down into my empty cup. The waitress comes to tidy the table and I ask her for another. The jukebox goes on playing – Paul Anka, Cliff Richard, Tommy Steele. There are none of the songs I've heard my mother singing, and I think of the speed of generations passing and I'm hearing that nightingale the poet writes of when he says the voice he hears this passing night was heard in ancient days by emperor and clown. I like that. The clowns and the emperors go round and round in my head with bits of jukebox songs breaking in, then the poem again. And I say to myself there's still time for me – no hungry generations have taken me yet.

Next Michael's standing over me. 'Are you ready, Simon?'

Amanda's with him, chewing gum, 'Are we all going?' I ask.

'Why, anything wrong with that?' says Amanda.

'Where are we going?' I ask.

'To Amanda's place. Her parents are away.'

I want to say I'll see Michael later but I can't say that. So we bounce along the road in the bus until we come to a stop about a mile away. We walk up the road and there's the house – Amanda's home. In the sitting-room are all these high glasses with swollen bases on display. I sit down on the green sofa and stare at the mirror with a pink glass surround, over the fireplace. Michael and Amanda sit together in one of the big armchairs. I see Michael peeking down her bra. He puts a hand there.

'Wait,' says Amanda.

'Why? Simon doesn't mind. He can join in.'

But Amanda pouts and Michael pulls her leg up, and leaving the room says to me, rubbing the top of my head with his hand, 'We won't be long.'

I decide I won't stay, but I still sit there for a bit. Then I hear these sighing noises start from upstairs. They go on and on. I feel sick. I get up and tiptoe to the front door, which isn't necessary, as obviously no one's hearing, open the door and close it behind me. I run down the street to the bus stop and I wait and wait. I've got Michael's address and I ask which bus when I'm in the centre of town.

'Where's Michael?' says Mr Ivens, looking puzzled. 'He's on his way,' I tell him. 'He had to see someone and he thought I'd better get back in case you were worried.' Mrs Ivens takes me to the kitchen and wants to make some food for me. I say I'm not hungry but she insists. She puts down a plate of hot gammon with tomato and mashed potatoes. Then she makes me a cup of Horlicks. I pick at the food.

'I'd like to go to bed.'

'Of course, you must be tired,' and Mrs Ivens puts her hand on my arm.

They say they'll make sure Michael doesn't wake me and I go upstairs to his room. I pull the cotton curtains over the white nylon hanging and undress. I brush my teeth in the washbasin, put on a pair of pyjama bottoms and climb into bed. Fuzziepeg's at Aunt Phyllie's. I haven't got him because I don't want to be thought soft, which is silly, as I feel so lonely without him. Then I start thinking about Michael. In Roehampton it was just Michael and me – the two of us together. Now all these years have gone by and others have come between us. I look at the picture of my great-grandmother. Michael remembered the stories I told him. She's fairly exotic in her satin evening gown, her fingers delicately set above a bowl of white peonies, and her two sisters, one sideways towards her on the sofa, the other perched on the back, with faces declaring their breeding and painted in part profile, only great-grandmother, Pamela, staring out, saying, 'Look at me. I'm an aristocrat.' It's funny Michael liking that picture, which means he understood the hamper-in-the-attic stories. I stare around at some of his school books. There's a Latin grammar, the complete plays of Shakespeare, a book to do with science, the collected stories of H.G. Wells, and novels by D.H. Lawrence. But I'm too weak to pull any down, too exhausted, I mean, after the journey and the sudden change from Aunt Phyllie's to here.

I sleep. I'm wandering in a dream where my father's not drunk any more and he's taking my mother, my brother and me to Hilles. He starts talking with Uncle Jonathan about the inheritance and Uncle Jonathan goes very pale and struts around the place like a stung peacock. He admits he bent his mother's arm over the will,

'I was only trying to do my best for this house,' he keeps saying. 'Don't you see, Purcell.' Suddenly my father's forceful and he says he will contest the inheritance and divide the property half and half, or even get complete power over Jonathan. There the dream ends – snap – and my head is falling down and down and I'm waking to the reality that we have nothing. I remember how cruel Uncle Jonathan was to me then. That morning I sat in the back of the car, Uncle Jonathan in front dressed for hunting. I say, can we stop, I want to wee. Uncle Jonathan turns round and picks up his hunting whip that's beside me. 'If you don't shut up, I'll whip you with this.' And he gives the whip a shake in my face. Another time he pushes me forwards into a bed of stinging nettles. I drag myself out screaming, running until I find dock leaves which I grab and rub over my scalding legs. I don't realise then he's burning up with wild envy of us. I keep on thinking, Why? Why? Why did nobody stop him? . . . Because . . . because, and there I stop thinking, my jaw jittering, trembling.

'Hi, Simon, it's me' – and those arms are round me. Michael's in the bed as if we were back in Roehampton. His thin body presses against my back and he entwines a leg with mine. It happens naturally as if he's a part of me like my own hand. I say nothing but put my hands round his arms and hold them. If bodies don't touch, I'm thinking, that's where this coldness is. In the country houses of relations there's no touching. It's all formal. Then Michael turns my face towards his and says, 'You look like her.' 'Who?' I say with sleepy eyes. 'The painting, you fool,' and he puts a kiss on my lips. I touch Michael's forehead and say, 'We'd better get up soon.'

Mr Ivens has left for work when we come down. Mrs Ivens puts a fried breakfast in front of me and she keeps saying 'We must build you up', but I'm quite built up enough, even if I am fairly skinny. I've got this long straight body and small waist, and I'm already close to six feet tall at fourteen. She's a good soul, Madge Ivens. It's only a way of getting affection to you, people wanting to take you over, I think to myself. But after Michael and me have been together I don't need any other closeness. To please her, not to offend, I struggle though this heavy, thick, cold-weather food.

Mrs Ivens starts questioning Michael about coming in late and she beams with secret pleasure when she guesses. 'He's a one, my son, a right lad,' I can hear her saying to herself. Then she asks us what we're going to do today. 'Loaf around,' says Michael. 'It's holidays.'

So we wander round Sheffield, sit in the same coffee bar, and hang about with Michael's schoolfriends. They're suspicious of me, I know, because I belong to a part of Michael's life that happened before he came here. They call me 'the posh one', and I know that I can never be a part of their life. I can never be a part of my own either, because I'll never be one of those who goes off shooting in Scotland, or hunts in Ireland, or goes to county shows with a tweed cap on my head and a crook in one hand. It's best when I'm on my own with Michael, then all these class bothers aren't there any more.

'What about Amanda?' I ask Michael as we're walking in the open hills round the town.

'You've got to have a girlfriend. That's all.'

'Like having a bank account when you're older.'

'That sort of thing.' He pulls at the strands of thick grass. 'Everybody has a girlfriend.'

'What about love?'

'I've got you, Simon.'

'I don't live here.'

Then he smiles and takes my hand. 'I'm going to leave England for good one day,' he says. He says he's going to marry a foreign girl and live somewhere like Italy, or Greece, or Scandinavia. 'It's grim up here. Grim.' And we look down on Sheffield with its smoking chimneys and big buildings. We go on walking over the hills and Michael suddenly turns to me and says, 'You can live with us too.' But I think that would look funny. 'I know my parents are divorced,' I say, 'but they're still my parents and they're still alive.'

'Perhaps your mother will remarry. Then you'll have a home

again.' 'That would be nice,' I say, but what I really want to say is that of course I'll come to where he is with his wife. I don't say that because the present is all I know. The present is staying these few days with Henry and Madge Ivens and Michael in their speckled white house on the outskirts of Sheffield. It's grim to Michael, but it isn't grim to me. We sit down by a stream and watch the bubbling fast-running water.

I'm on Sheffield station waiting for the train to come in that's taking me back to London. The Ivenses are there too. I sit with Michael on the edge of a platform where old stock stands and we swing our legs backwards and forwards. I think I'll be a kind of star for him in a secret heart of his, but somehow I know we won't see each other again. He keeps glancing at me with his brown eyes and he tells me he'll take a scholarship to university if he gets good School Certificate passes. His dark hair falls low over his forehead. Then he stops swinging his legs and looks down at the cinders between the rails.

'Do you think we'll ever be children again?'

'Not as we are now. But I think we'll want to be children,' says Michael seriously.

'How will we do that?'

'Second to the left and straight on till morning,' Michael says looking up with a smile.

'Never Land. I don't believe it,' I say.

'You've got to, Simon. You've really got to.' He kicks his shoe against the brick wall.

'All right, I'll believe it,' I say. Over the loudspeaker an announcement comes that the train shortly to arrive at platform five is for London, King's Cross.

'We've been there. The hamper in the attic. Our cuddling in bed. That's Never Land.'

'Yes,' I say and hold Michael's hand. 'The train's coming.'

He kisses me on the side of the neck. We get up and walk over to where Michael's parents are. Mrs Ivens looks at me. 'You boys. I think you two could chatter till the cows come home.'

The train is steaming towards the station. It halts abruptly, making loud hisses. Michael picks up my case and walks ahead. I catch him up. The Ivenses follow us. Michael and I find an empty compartment. He puts my case on the rack. Vividly coloured advertisements for seaside resorts hit my eyes. Now Michael, my height within inches, is looking into them. 'My love to your mum,' he says. 'I won't forget', and he holds my arm. Michael's parents are standing outside the window and I go to lower it.

'You do well at school now, Simon,' says Mr Ivens in fatherly tones. 'I will,' I say. 'And we're always here for you – you know that,' Mrs Ivens says, giving my cheek a squeeze with her fingers. The train slowly starts to move and Michael gives me a last pat and rushes from the compartment. After that I'm looking out of the window at the three waving people who grow smaller and smaller. I keep waving and I see Michael running to a place where he can still wave back. The train jolts round a corner and he's gone.

The compartment smells musty and the thick zigzag pattern on the seats makes me dizzy. I lean my head out of the window for air and see fields, farms and pylons running faster and faster into the distance. Back in my seat I turn the pages of an H.G. Wells story. Michael got me a copy of his stories, but I can't take them in. I read pages of *The Time Machine* over and over. Sentences go and come, broken up by the noise of the train. In three hours I'll be back in Burnsall Street. Michael will be going to a dance with Amanda, so what will I do? I'm going to Rise to stay with my uncle and aunt. I'll be there on my own because David's off to Spain with a schoolfriend. My mother will be in London with Peter; she's out of the nursing home. Already I can only imagine Michael's arms round me. I'm alone, now, alone. I can feel it like a pain in my body. Then comes panic as the train speeds through a tunnel. There are no lights: only darkness, terror, memory. The tunnel ends and daylight washes in. My stomach turns again and I slump against the seat and stare at the clouds rushing and the sky and I'm crying. Goodbye, Michael. Goodbye.

11

THERE'S A LOT of banging of doors when Uncle Tony comes
down to breakfast. On hunting mornings especially. Bang! bang!
I hear as I sit at the breakfast table and stare at the running silver
fox set in the centre. 'Beasts of the chase that are not worth a
Tally-Ho!/ All are surpassed by the corse covert fox', says the
inscription. On the other side it says the fox was presented to my
grandfather when he gave up the Holderness Hunt. When
cancer hit he could no longer hunt his hounds. Like my mother's
quotes, this is another that sticks in my head and won't go away.
I puzzle and puzzle about the corse covert fox. I've never asked
my uncle what it means. I couldn't on a hunting morning
anyway. He'd explode.

Uncle Tony's a squire, a real out-in-the-fields squire. At
breakfast he opens letters and reads farming journals. A radio by
him keeps conversation to a minimum. My aunt sits at the opposite end of the table and reads *The Times*. My mother says he's
irritable from losing half a leg in the Normandy landings when
the tank he was in was shelled. 'His leg gives him a lot of pain,'
she says. On hunting mornings he wears an artificial leg with a
boot already over it. He's Master of the Hunt, like my grandfather, and he also farms the six thousand acres that he's inherited.

'Why don't you read a book?' my mother says to her brother.

But Uncle Tony doesn't hold with reading. He says it's too much education that's messed up the country. He's not too happy over me reading and one day he asks me where I got the habit from. He says it as if I was doing something very wrong. I'm silent with confusion so he fills in. 'You get it from those Tennants, I expect. They're all mad.' Uncle Tony was brought up by his mother, the beak-nosed Cicely, to assume that my grandmother Clare had introduced some very odd genes into the straightforward Bethells.

When I first stayed at Rise everything happened for me in the nursery. There was David, myself, and Uncle Tony's two daughters, my cousins. A nanny named Alice looked after us. We went downstairs at teatime, otherwise we ate in the nursery. Now I've two other cousins, two boys, and they're quite a bit younger than David and me. Sitting downstairs for meals now I hear my uncle and aunt planning their lives. It all seems to go like clockwork – entertainments, friends, school, and the rest of it. When we were younger my aunt organised children's parties with a conjuror. All the other children from the nearby landed families came. Now it's Pony Club events, hunting and racing. I hear it all, but from the outside. I feel very isolated and I look out from the dining-room window to the park hoping that Grandfather Bethell will be there, will come towards me and say to his lost grandson, 'And what would you like to do, Simon?'

I've been at Rise for these Pony Club dances. Once Uncle Tony told me off because I danced with a girl who wasn't in our party. 'You dance with your own party first,' he said, not smiling. Other people heard and I felt clumsy.

What Uncle Tony knows about is his farms. He's pulling the estate together as it nearly went under in the Depression of the 1930s. My grandfather had to sell his father's collection of pornography to keep the hunt going. Great-grandfather, Willie Bethell, was keen as mustard on sex. His wife, Marie-Myrtle, died when he was only forty and so he took off to London whenever he could. In London he had rooms in Albemarle

Street, Piccadilly, and there ladies of the easiest virtue came to please him. He would say he was going to have his corns seen to.

The stories my mother tells me are enlarged on by an old retainer at Rise who was a groom to my grandfather. 'Yes, old Willie,' says Bert with a Yorkshire chuckle. 'Corns? It wasn't corns. He went to see the ladies.' A great beam slowly grows on Bert's face which is as broad as a giant turnip, and he gives a twinkle.

I feel awkward going round the farms with Uncle Tony as I never know the right questions to ask. Also, he might think me inquisitive and that I'm after it all. 'You don't get a look-in here,' he said to me one day after I'd asked a simple question. He was quite fierce as he said it, as if I'd struck something in him. I hadn't meant anything. I shut up after that. Uncle Tony doesn't like any questions, really. So I keep quiet as the Land Rover bumps from farm to farm down the narrow roads where the old man's beard spills from the hedges at one side. He talks to the men and once when I was with him got out of the Land Rover and swung himself on to a tractor to show one of the men how to turn a furrow. I sat there watching, with Uncle Tony's terriers, which were squealing loudly for him to return. He never goes any-where without the terriers. 'C'mon, c'mon,' he shouts to them as they leap into the back of the Land Rover.

The old house, Big Rise as we call it, was given up by Uncle Tony when he came back from the war. My uncle rented it out to a convent school, and when I look towards its huge entrance propped up by four vast columns I see grey shapes with starched white caps dart like scurrying mice on to the gravel then vanish again. I've been over it in holiday time when there's no one there. There's no furniture there now, just a few family portraits hanging on the staircase wall. My shoes skid on echoing polished floorboards. I imagine my mother here as a child, and then a girl, and finally a young woman. I think of the stories told to me by Bert about her hunting. Grandfather Bethell wished she wouldn't put on make-up. No women wore make-up for hunting, just white powder. But my mother did. And if her horse fell, the horse ran off in one direction while my mother took out her glass to see that her face was all right. 'It was always her face, with Miss Diana,' says Bert. 'Her face came first.'

The house stares out over an enormous park with two small lakes in the distance and behind them some woods. In my mother's time the entrance was through the lodge gates at the edge of the wood. The drive wound across the park, where deer idled, through a gate that opens to the wide expanse of brown gravel in front of the portico. The drive can be seen still, two faint grass tracks, but the deer have gone.

Big Rise is just a memory now, that's all. My uncle's family live in what was the vicarage at the far end of the park, near to the stone lodges. Big Rise needed so many servants. Aunt Phyllie says that in her day there were twenty-seven laundrymaids, and by the end of the war it needed money spending on it. My mother's told me how Grandfather Adrian – it's my first name too – was a spender, but he ignored essentials. In the 1930s, when tenant farmers were unable to pay their rent and there was no income for the landlord, Adrian Bethell wanted all the mahogany lavatory seats in the house changed to cedar. 'Why, Adrian?' a friend asked. 'So much warmer to sit on,' was the reply.

I mooch about the old stables, which are older than Big Rise. They belong to an earlier eighteenth-century house, which a Bethell squire pulled down to build the present one. He built it as plain and as bleak on the outside as possible. On winter days, when no sun shone and the trees were bare, and five miles off was the cold North Sea, my mother saw no difference between Rise and Wuthering Heights. So she invented a new expression when she was going for a walk: 'I'm going for a Brontë.' And she always used to say to us, 'Shall we go for a Brontë?'

Old Jim used to live in the tack room of Rise stableyard. Jim was bent, with a moon face, and he slept wrapped in horse blankets among the tack. He preferred it like that. When I was seven or eight he liked to show me the ceremonial dress my grandfather wore when he was a soldier in the Second Life Guards. The most exciting parts were the silver breastplate and the plumed helmet. Jim would take the uniform out from a black wooden box, dropping the buckskin breeches, then reaching down further for the plumed helmet. His face shone with happiness as he handled it.

I live in the past at Rise. I have to. I can't join in with much of the present. I'm a visitor here. To belong I have to go back to the time when my mother belonged. I still see Big Rise standing there, looking out over the park, a house and not a school, just like when she was a girl here. The woods are used for pheasant shoots and the lakes for bringing down duck. Uncle Tony shoots duck and pheasant. Grandfather Bethell shot them too. I use the woods for my daydreams. My feet trample the fallen branches and leaves as I walk the avenues, a pheasant whirrs noisily from thick undergrowth, making me jump. I walk on thinking of the bohemians, of their tipsy stories and their empty pockets, and what Grandfather Bethell would have made of them. Perhaps he knows. My mother said he came to her soon after he died and told her that she was going to have a very sad life but that he would be near her. She laughed at the time and brushed it aside. She doesn't laugh about it now.

I don't talk about the bohemians to my uncle, or about my mother and Peter, or about visiting Michael. No, that's not what's talked about at Rise. It's point-to-points, or where the hunt's new whip is coming from, and what's happening in the county, that make the short bursts of conversation at meals. The bursts are always short. Uncle Tony really doesn't care for conversation.

Uncle Tony isn't interested in the past. And my aunt is busy organising Pony Club events for my cousins. So I sit in the small sitting-room at the vicarage reading a book and looking up occasionally at the handsome Georgian door frames or often at the Jacobean portrait of one Hugh Bethell, a child, holding a racquet in one hand and wearing a cream gown, painted in folds, that runs down to his feet.

'Would it be possible to move back into Big Rise, one day?' I ask.

'You would think that,' growls Uncle Tony. 'No, it wouldn't.' After that I'm pretty well silent for the rest of the meal.

In the evenings it's different. As course follows course at dinner, Uncle Tony changes. Drink makes him less irritable and when the eating is over, and his glass is filled with port or brandy or Cointreau, he becomes quite kindly. He tells stories. He remembers the only question Uncle Philip at Ragdale ever asked him. Uncle Philip, sitting in his study, with no noise except the inhaling of a cigar, would turn his head slowly from gazing at the smoke rings on the ceiling and say to young Bethell, 'How's the sport in the North?' He would barely wait for the answer before his head stared upwards again.

I'm back in London. Two more days and then back to Stowe. I'm half an adult, and half a boy. They call us teenagers but I don't like that. It sounds like an illness – 'I've got teenagers. Stay away, it's infectious.' My friend, Leo, who's at Harrow, has taken me to a coffee bar in Soho. We're sitting there, stirring the coffee, when my mother and Peter spot us. I don't want Peter to come in. He's bound to make some uncomfortable remark. But in seconds they're standing over us.

'Introduce your friend, Simon,' says Peter.

'Mummy's met him,' I say. 'Well, I suppose you haven't. OK. Leo, this is Peter.' Leo puts out a slender hand. I notice his long fingers, the blue veins close to the surface. Peter does too. He looks at him.

'Simon's mentioned you. You're at Harrow,' he says. 'And your family have some palace in the country near Vienna. Disgusting.'

Leo's thrown by this. So am I, but I shouldn't be. Peter doesn't believe in putting people at their ease. My mother changes the subject. 'Peter's taking me to the Colony Room, darling. He says it's full of real people.' Leo and I are silent. Peter breaks in again. 'When you're older I'll take you there,' he says, looking at me. 'You need to meet people who've got something to say. You won't meet any Masters of Hounds there.'

'I'll be home soon,' my mother says to me. 'Don't be late.'

Leo has almost no accent all. His family are well-known and have places in Paris and New York. I'm a bit envious of that. Leo talks about Fifth Avenue and the Champs-Elysées and I know whatever I say won't shape up to it. I mention Italy and the American Blow with his villa near Florence, and it turns out Leo has relations there, too. I think my life's been small, so small. Walking down a side street towards Piccadilly Leo says, 'Put your hand in my pocket.' 'Why?' 'Go on. Put your hand there.' I do this. There is no pocket but I feel Leo's leg and a tangle of pubic hair. I take my hand out again. 'Coward,' Leo says. He gives a smile through slightly slit eyes. I feel myself blushing.

At Stowe there's a boy who follows me down into the dark bicycle shed, dark because it's underground. The bicycle sheds were air raid shelters in the war. This boy thrusts his erect cock against my leg. He hovers around me, leaning and pressing himself against my back while I'm trying to get at my bike, and I find the only way to get rid of him is to play with his cock, with my face turned away, until he's satisfied. I would have gone further with Leo, willingly, but I'll never know if he knew that. After a few meetings Leo vanished and we lost touch. I remember his slit green eyes, his slim elfin figure, and his tales of being seduced by his family's servants in Austria. He becomes a ghost, a ghost that haunts me.

My father turns up at Stowe in an enormous green Jaguar – Mark 8 – and he brings this very attractive woman with him. We don't really want to go out with him and when we hear he's in the grounds looking for us, my brother says we've got to disappear, hide. Then my father calls on our housemaster, who becomes confused and says he will find us. He comes into the houseroom and goes through into the boys' changing-room where he spots us both crouched down, close to the floor, hiding well below window level.

'I don't know what you're doing,' says Mr Macdonald, bending down too. 'Your father's waiting for you. He's outside now.'

I look up at Mr Macdonald's circular lenses above his walrus moustache.

'We can't see him,' says David. 'He's a monster.'

'Come, come,' replies our housemaster. 'He's your father.'

'Tell him we're not to be found, Sir,' I say.

We're still crouching there with Mr Macdonald still peering down.

'I can't do that,' says Mr Macdonald, looking uncomfortable. 'I've told him you're here.'

'Blast!' says David. We stand up now and we follow Mr Macdonald who wobbles as he walks, moving rather like a walrus.

Outside the house is the Jaguar and my father is standing by the car waiting. There's a smile on his face, which makes me sad. My father gives each of us enormous hugs as if he's been permanently the most wonderful father we could ever want. 'My darling boys,' he says several times over, 'my darling boys.'

Then he introduces us to the attractive woman. Her name is Catherine and she's his wife. I hadn't seen her since the day my mother spotted her with my father as we were going down Piccadilly. They were getting out of a taxi to go to his bank. She wore a full dress and a large hat.

'Look!' my mother exclaimed. 'There she is.' And we stared. We'd heard that my father had remarried, and my mother was stunned. David and me too. How could anyone want to marry him? Apparently they met in a drinking club. We've heard she's from Scotland, which possibly accounts for her red hair. And she looked very glamorous this woman, stepping out of the taxi with him. With the same posture as models in magazines, one foot pointing forward and the head erect. Which is how she's standing now. She gives me a gloved hand. I shake it and look at her.

'I want to give you both dinner,' says my father. 'We're going to have a simply splendid evening.' One of his over-the-top expressions again. We get in and off we glide in the Jaguar down the main avenue, past the two classical pavilions, over the moss-pitted stone bridge, and on to Buckingham. The Jaguar jumps with my father's foot going suddenly on and off the accelerator, and then his swift jerking of the clutch.

Over dinner at the White Hart Hotel, where nearly every boy from Stowe goes to eat with their parents, I keep looking at my new stepmother. Not so that she would notice, but observing. She has these refined gestures and her voice is refined too. There's a lilt of an accent layered over by London. She talks about her brothers in Scotland, up in the Highlands. She says there's a farm, although I can't imagine her as she's dressed now anywhere near a farm. Towards the end of dinner my father starts to make out two cheques – one for David and one for me. Five pounds each. 'Some pocket money for you, darling boys,' he says. He tells us how everything is going to be wonderful now and that we must come and stay in the house he's bought in Chelsea. He's bought four houses in a street called Park Walk, and he's doing three of them up and selling them and keeping the one on the corner for himself.

'No don't, Daddy, please,' David tells him. 'We're all right.'

'I insist,' my father says, offering us the cheques.

'Do accept the money,' says my stepmother, fixing her eyes on us both in turn. 'He does so want you to have it.'

We each put our cheques in a pocket.

The next day I cash my cheque with the school bursar and my brother cashes his at the school shop. A few days later the bursar tells us that both cheques have been returned 'Refer to drawer'. I'm disappointed. David's furious. That evening I walk into the room where the five hundred boys gather before meals, sure that every boy knows that I'm the son of a man whose cheques are bounced.

When Mummy hears, she tells David that he must write to my father and say we will never, ever see him again. David writes to him at once. His letter begins, 'Now when you get this don't go to the first pub and drown yourself in alcohol. Your behaviour as always has been utterly irresponsible...' My father doesn't reply and we don't hear any more from him. 'Thank God,' my mother says, 'we've got him out of our lives at last.'

The Jaguar never returns to Stowe.

It's the summer of my fifteenth year and I've got a part in a school play. It's *A Midsummer Night's Dream*. I've been chosen for the female lead, Titania. It'll be performed on the steps of the Queen's Temple in the school grounds. It's a temple that looks over a valley towards the Palladian Bridge. Anyway, the setting's really stunning. I beat another boy for the part and I feel chuffed about that. There are quite a few lines to learn but I like my first line best: 'What! jealous Oberon. Fairies, skip hence: I have forsworn his bed and company.' Then I have a great long speech where I tell Oberon that I haven't been unfaithful and it's full of wonderful images which I can't get out of my head: 'Therefore the winds, piping to us in vain,/ As in revenge, have sucked up from the sea/ Contagious fogs; which, falling in the land,/ Have every pelting river made so proud/That they have overborne their continents.'

A lady in Buckingham makes my dress for me and most of that summer I'm rehearsing with boys much older than myself. Oberon, for instance, is a sixth-former and that's pretty high. He's seventeen to my fourteen. Soon it's just like in real life because Oberon falls for me and I fall for him. But there's no sex, it's all spiritual and on my side very emotional. It's emotional on his side too, but he's much more in control than I am. Nothing is seriously discussed until the last night of the play – it's on for two nights – and once it's over Oberon, who's really called George, and I go for a walk. We pause at the Temple of Ancient Virtue, a small temple with a domed roof and stone columns. Walking round and round the temple on the ledge where the columns start, we decide whether to kiss or not, whether to be physical.

I've got my head leaning against the rounded wall and George is looking at me, standing a few inches away. He says it will spoil everything if we kiss and I don't know what I want except I've got these butterfly feelings inside me which have to be a sort of desire. So we go on walking round the temple and George starts talking about the French symbolist poets and T.S. Eliot. George is about to take a scholarship to Oxford and I've begun writing poetry in prep. I neglect my prep work but at least I can release anxieties that I suppose go back to those days at Roehampton.

He's not the obvious good-looking sort of boy. George is tall and thin limbed, fair haired, and very clean looking. Often he wears spectacles, with a black rim at the top and nothing at the bottom. I don't think either of us knows quite what it is, this attraction, but for me it is something powerful and it doesn't really seem to matter that we can't define it. There are others, though, who define it for us.

One evening I walk across from my house to his, which means walking the full length of the school, across the south front and down a small hill. I go to his study and for an hour and a half we continue talking about T.S. Eliot. We dig meaningfully about in 'The Waste Land' and 'The Love Song of J. Alfred Prufrock.'

Outside George's study prefects wait, timing my arrival and departure. They report back to my housemaster. They assume that we have definitely 'done something': sex has happened, they are sure of that. Mr Macdonald gives me a lecture. His moustache rising and falling, he tells me that I shouldn't be seen 'going around in older boys' pockets'. Odd way of putting it, I think. I don't argue, but hang my head with lines from Prufrock running through it. I must keep the bottoms of my trousers rolled and keep my hands only in the pockets of Leo.

'I can't wait to get my hand round your arse, Blow,' the head of house bites at me. What he's saying is he can't wait to beat me, and it's certainly not sex-fuelled. Not from him. He has curly hair and a red face which looks older than eighteen. He's a sporting all-rounder, always coming into the house with a golf bag over his shoulder and telling us how many silver trophy cups we've got to win. The trouble is, I've broken a few rules and I've got away with it. Now I decide to go one further. I'm going to buy myself a horse. In the Red Book it says that boys are allowed to keep a pet. Nobody does any longer, although my father kept a dog in what are called the Boycott Pavilions – two lodges that sit on a rise half-way up the main drive. I've got a few hundred pounds in the Post Office savings because Godfather Bill has been sending me a hundred pounds every Christmas. I know he does this because I'm the poorest of his godchildren, but I haven't touched much of it so far.

Tonight I'm sleeping with some of this cash under my pillow. I keep lifting it up to look. I've a plan to bicycle to a local horse dealer tomorrow afternoon and see what he's got. The important thing is not to ask anyone's permission but to go and do it.

Morning classes are finished and now I'm anxious for lunch to be finished too. After lunch we trail out of the long dining-room that smells of piled-on years of mushy food and I run all the way to the bicycle shed. Then I'm cycling away from Stowe down small roads where the air wafts grass and cow dung, taking me back to days at Ragdale. After four miles, I turn down a long gravel drive at the end of which is a clutter of stables and farm buildings.

The horse dealer, Mr Welton, is in a field with some of his animals. I dump my bike and run up to him. 'I want to buy a horse,' I say.

He looks down on me over a vast expanse of stomach. He

wears a reddish brown smock with a yellow handkerchief round his neck.

'Good horse over there,' he says, pointing to a brown horse with an elegant walk. 'Five-year-old – suit you well.'

I'm about to own a horse, is going round in my head. My first horse. Suddenly I feel less alone, as if I'm on the verge of belonging to a world of Dickensian people in smocks and breeches and brown boots who lean over railings of fields talking horses. Just horses.

'Can he jump?' I say, not knowing what else I should ask. 'I need the horse for hunting.'

'She'll do you well. She's a fine mare.'

I walk with him across the field to catch her. I keep looking at Mr Welton's gaiters and thinking how time really does stand still in the horse world. He's like one of those people in the hunting pictures at Ragdale. I feel warm and safe.

He gives me a leg up and I ride the mare up and down the drive, walking and trotting. After that I canter her in a field. Then, to get the whole thing done with, I say, 'All right. I'll buy her.'

Mr Welton takes the cash and I turn the horse round and, saying I'll be back for my bike, trot away down his drive. I look back once and notice Mr Welton putting the notes somewhere under his smock. Then he goes back to his field.

I've already arranged to keep the mare, Moonlight, with a farmer nearby. I put her in the stable and the farmer gives me a lift back to the dealer to get my bike. Next day I go and see the headmaster. 'I've bought a horse,' I say. 'I've stabled her down below the Corinthian Arch with a farmer there.' The head takes off his spectacles, but I know he's a horseman too, so I'm not too anxious. Except, except ... you never know. 'You'd better show her to me,' he says. So I go off later that day to get the mare.

Now I'm circling with her in front of the headmaster's house, which looks across the golf course and down to one of the lakes. He studies me as I ride, then I hear him say, 'Well, now you've bought her, you'd better keep her. And perhaps you can exercise mine for me, too.'

From now on it's no more house games. I'm allowed off in the afternoon to exercise my horse. This makes the prefects in my house boil with rage, particularly the head one who's already keen to thrash me. I'm a junior boy with privileges. They can't stand that.

Every morning now I bicycle down to Moonlight and clean out her box, like a stable hand. In the afternoons, after exercising, I clean my saddle and bridle and make her feed. My life's filling out and I've got this sense of importance that owning a horse gives you. It makes everything worthwhile. At last I'm putting to use all those things I've watched happen or been taught, from swinging my legs in the tack room at Ragdale to the East Sussex Pony Club. But, and I sigh with pleasure, there are no fierce horsy women around me here like there are in the Pony Club – just me, the farmer's family and Moonlight, my fine-looking mare.

I've had to tell Aunt Phyllie and my mother. 'Darling, you can't possibly afford it,' says Aunt Phyllie. 'Why not?' I say. 'Why not? Your brother kept twenty horses in the stables at Rise, and I've only got one.' Uncle Tony writes from Rise to say that I've got no money and I'd better sell her. But my longing for a horse has nothing to do with reason. So in the end everyone gives up, and accepts that from now on it's Simon plus horse. What suffers is school work. I become hopelessly inattentive, which is not difficult as most of the masters teaching me are a lousy, exhausted bunch. Except for my English master who introduces and explains W.H. Auden to me and the tutor who teaches my brother, who says I must carry on so that one day I can be a historian. After I've passed my School Certificate and I'm a senior boy, he wants me to be in his group, the Historians. He's published good history books, too, and is one of Stowe's most

civilised masters. But I'm stubborn: the horse and my riding
come first.

I'm difficult. I misbehave. 'Manners sometimes make fools,' I
tell the Latin master, who every time he takes us writes on the
blackboard, 'Manners makyth Man.' I'm beginning to understand that if someone has manners and nothing else – the stuffed
shirt kind of person – there may not be much to them. That
evening my housemaster bends me over and gives me three
whacks on my backside for cheek.

In the holidays we go to Italy to stay with Aunt Phyllie in the
house she's built for Luigi. I leave Moonlight to be looked after
by the lady who runs the riding school in Robertsbridge. Aunt
Phyllie tells me there's no one at Peanswood to look after horses,
it's not like Ragdale, but she says she'll pay for the stabling. Aunt
Phyllie always has herself driven out to Italy in the Rover by
Luigi. David's travelling with them. I'm going out there by train
with Mummy. Aunt Phyllie's pleased to get my mother away
from 'that difficult man', as she calls Peter.

My mother and I are at the Gare du Nord and we need to spend
the night somewhere. My mother doesn't know Paris, but she
speaks fluent French, almost without an accent. She says she
spent the first night of her honeymoon here in the Hôtel Lotti.
It's one of those grand hotels in the centre of Paris, quite near to
the Ritz, where her father-in-law stayed when he travelled. I
don't know much about all this except that we can only afford
to stay in the cheapest place. If my father had made that million
we might be going to the Lotti now. But that's a thought that
gets us nowhere. Not here, close to midnight, on the Gare du
Nord. Then a small Frenchman approaches.

He asks my mother if he can help us. My mother explains that
we're looking for somewhere to stay, and I can tell she's feeling
stressed. He quickly shows us to a hotel and insists on carrying
my mother's case upstairs. He puts it down in her bedroom and

next I hear him ask my mother if he can sleep with her. She says no. Nicely, but firmly. Then he follows me to my room, hovers around my door, and asks the same question. I say no, too. I want to laugh – it hasn't made me that embarrassed, though I put on an innocent, shy face when I refuse. *Am* I putting it on? No. I don't have to. Because I've got this butter-wouldn't-melt-in-my-mouth face. Faces can be like that at fifteen. So much can happen inside which doesn't show outside.

Next day there's a long train journey and finally, in the early hours of the following day, we arrive at Massa where Luigi meets us. It's funny seeing Luigi in Italy, I'm so used to being with him at Battle market watching him buy and sell Aunt Phyllie's pigs. He comes from a village near Carrara, where the marble is, and he's going to take us into the mountains to watch the marble being cut. His family are very simple and poor. But one day Aunt Phyllie says to me, 'Luigi's so intelligent, I'm sure there's noble blood in him.'

The house Aunt Phyllie's built for him is about four miles out of Marina di Massa. A rough road takes us there and other houses and small farms are dotted along it. In the distance are the marble mountains. The house is just like those whitewashed modern villas with an upstairs that you see by the roadside in Italy. Aunt Phyllie spends hours sitting on the balcony by the outside staircase gossiping with Signora Andreani. The trouble is Aunt Phyllie doesn't speak more than three words of Italian and Signora Andreani's English is half fluent. They make a curious pair.

It's summer, the weather's hot, and my mother's cracking. There are days she's in a hysterical state and drinking far too much wine. She gets it from a bar across the road. 'Oh, Diana, I wish you wouldn't,' Aunt Phyllie says. 'Right!' my mother says dramatically. 'If my father had lived none of this would have happened,' Mummy goes on. And then she does these bits from songs about the nights growing colder and suddenly you're older. She walks nervously around in the house, with odd twisted frightened looks on her face. Then the next day she's better and we bicycle to the beach and laugh with Luigi's sister and her friends, but it's the other days that send my spirits dipping. It makes David feel pretty awful too.

Some days when I go into the bar and delicatessen where my mother gets her wine, the large Italian lady who owns it comes up to me. '*La mama multo nervosa*,' she says and she raises her hands and repeats it: '*Multo nervosa*.'

The evenings are often bad. Today my mother's not sober and she's shouting at Luigi: 'You Italians who never faced a British gun!' Aunt Phyllie, so worried now at what my mother's saying, comes down the shiny marble floor of the hall. 'Darling, please. Please.' But nothing stops my mother when she's had a drink. 'Cowards!' she shouts. 'All of you, cowards!' I see Luigi, nice patient Luigi, his head almost bald from washing his hair with petrol during the war, when there was nothing else, trying to keep up a smile.

My brother's met a girl who's a friend of Luigi's sister, Elisha. They go for walks together, but I don't think there's much else going on. Except I know David's very romantic about her. My mother's not angry, but she's definitely interested to see how far it will go. '*E la Georgia*,' she says, imitating the way Italians gesture as they speak. Hardly imitating, though: it comes quite naturally to her, as if she's spent her life making dramatic gestures in foreign rooms. No, I think as I watch her, she doesn't seem at all like the daughter of an English fox-hunting squire. When she's at her most hysterical I wish she was.

We haven't heard from my father since my brother wrote to him. And we've completely given up on the alimony. The last hope was putting a detective on to him. This was the idea of my mother's new solicitor, a very friendly man who doesn't charge much because he knows we have no money. But it didn't work. My father was quicker than the detective and all we got back were dismal reports. 'I followed Mr Blow down into Green Park underground, but the tube train doors shut just as I was reaching him. I will continue my efforts.'

'The havoc he's made of my health,' my mother writes. The havoc he's made of our lives, too, I want to say to her. But I don't. I don't because my mother would be upset. She wants us to know that she's protected us, that she's saved us. The opposite of what Clare did to her. She loves us as her mother never loved her. Except that we have to look after her now, watch her when she's losing control, and accept that she's not at all the same person who stood strong through the long, long years at Roehampton.

That Italian summer we go on to Florence. Dick Blow's villa is up a road that winds out of the city. It's called Villa Piazza Calda and I think it's one of the prettiest villas that could possibly be. On one side it looks over a valley and the Tuscan hillside and if you go up to Dick's studio there's a view down on to Florence. Dick paints here. In Florence he's reviving the mosaic industry and he takes us with him sometimes, into workshops where men in aprons are bent over carving out the semi-precious stones. I say to myself this must be what it was like in the Renaissance.

Dick lives alone in the villa with his manservant, Dante. He's old now, Dante, or old to my fifteen years. In the last war Dante guarded the possessions in case the villa was occupied by the Germans. He buried all the silver deep in the earth. He looks at Dick adoringly, saying, '*Si, Signor. Si.*' Dick's had two wives – the first one, Eleanor, was murdered in her apartment, but that was after she and Dick divorced. Her lover shot her after she'd told him she was going to leave Florence and live in New York. After he'd shot Eleanor, the lover shot himself. My mother tells us this, she likes the story because it's so awful and sad. It's about life. It was their son, Mark, who came to stay with us once, ages ago. Dick never talks about Eleanor. He never talks about Maria, his second wife, either, although there's a piece of sculpture by her in the villa.

Dick's restless, very restless. The villa's so comfortable but Dick's so restless. He spends perhaps an hour in his studio, then he's downstairs wanting company. We set off for Florence. He takes us to museums but walks through them before we have finished with the second room. On we go and always before lunch to the Anglo-American bar, Lelands, where everyone in Florence meets.

My mother isn't drinking any more. She's stopped. I'm trying to cope with her mood swings. Sometimes it's her family who make her tense. Not that Aunt Phyllie's done anything wrong but Mummy thinks she's failed them. She can't forgive herself for marrying my father, so she gets angry and strikes out at herself in front of Aunt Phyllie.

Next we're in Venice. Dick's taken us and we're in a gondola, on the Lido, and going fast round museums. He's generous, Dick, he doesn't think twice about paying for everything. I know he's very fond of my mother and sorry for what she's been through. He's not at all close to anyone else in my family. He's just singled out us for his attention. I remember Dick drawing me in Roehampton when I was six. I've still got the drawing. It's a good one. As a young man Dick studied at art school, but he never finished the course. 'Michelangelo didn't need qualifications, and neither do I,' said Dick to his tutor. And with that he shrugged his shoulders and walked away.

I watch Dick walking fast through St Mark's Square and I think how cut-off he looks. His face seems to be shut against the world. It's a good-looking face, and in build he makes me think of Ernest Hemingway. I've been reading him. Dick does the same kind of tough things – he's an ace pilot, with his own plane, a first-rate swimmer, good at tennis ... but still the face is closed in. When somebody hugs Dick he says, 'Ouch.' It terrifies him.

In the villa there's an old gramophone and Dick keeps playing the music of Falla, and Segovia on the guitar. It reminds him of his free and easy youth in Europe. My mother's told me that the American Blows lived in Yorktown, Virginia, in the house where General Cornwallis surrendered, ending the War of Independence. There are cannon-balls lodged in some of the brickwork. Dick and his brothers inherited a fortune from their mother, who was an heiress.

'Where did her money come from?' I ask my mother.

'Westclox,' my mother says. 'They're the clocks that tick in almost every kitchen.'

The only clocks that tick in the villa are very old antique clocks. Everywhere there's panelling and my bedroom has green shutters with a sheet of mosquito wire over them. In the afternoons it's siesta time and I lie on my bed dreaming. It's so safe and far away here that nothing miserable enters my head. I don't hear Granny Blow any more coming down the narrow stone staircase at Hilles. I don't hear Uncle Jonathan or my father. I wake and there's warm sunlight coming through the slats of the shutters, making soft lines on the worn carpet. I think I'd like to live in a villa like this one day. It carries the past with it, but a Florentine past which I don't know and must imagine. Drifting off again, I'm in Florence and we're going round some museum and then we're having lunch in a restaurant that looks over the River Arno.

'I get my suits made in London,' says Dick.

'Goodness,' I say, 'that's expensive.'

Dick laughs. 'Not a bit. I fly to Europe twice a year.'

Later my mother tells me that Dick spends the winters in New York and the summers at the villa. I dread going home; if it wasn't for Moonlight I'd ask Dick if I could stay for ever.

12

I'M BACK AT Stowe and what's left of the holiday is in the photo-graphs. There's one of Dick sitting in the hotel lobby in Venice, pork-pie hat on his head. There's one of my mother in the villa playing planchette with Anna, a tennis star friend of Dick's. My mother's hand is placed dramatically on the upturned glass. She believes firmly in signs from beyond. One of my brother and me standing outside our hotel in Venice, two tall boys in khaki shorts, our legs like poles. Another of me sitting next to Dick in a gondola, with a gondolier's straw hat on my schoolboy head. Endless different views of the villa and its garden. The pond-like pool and grotto where every morning before lunch Dick dived in.

Now my mother's back in Burnsall Street with Peter. He still hopes she will marry him, but she promises us that she won't. Aunt Phyllie's back in Sussex and nothing more has been said about Mummy's hysteria in Italy. Aunt Phyllie writes me letters, kind loving letters, telling me the price her pigs are fetching at market. And I sit in the houseroom, a junior boy, wondering about the years of school still to be endured.

I can see the prefects are irritated that I've been allowed to go my own way. In the afternoons while everyone else plays rugger, I ride my horse. As I'm riding I keep thinking, worry-ing, about what to do next. I seem to have become a rebel, sort of accidentally. I don't see myself as a rebel, but I do think I'm an out-in-the-open kid. After Roehampton Lane, I've got a fear of being shut in. They say that if you get to university, after that you get a good job in the City. This means a merchant bank or something. That's shut in. And anyway, I'd add everything up wrong, or I'd be sitting there without the right look of earnestness on my face. I'd be found out. I need a passion.

'Daydreaming, Blow,' one of the boys says to me.

'Why not?' I say. This boy nudges up to me. 'If you were a bit smaller, Blow, you would have been a crush boy.'

That's what the boys think about all the time here. Sex, sex, and sex. 'It's going round you've got a crush on Hartley.'

'Is it? Well that's none of anyone's business.'

'Have you raped him yet?'

'Bugger off.'

George has left now. There's no one for me to talk to any more. I've got Ian, who's loyal, but he's too doting. George could teach me things, help me; Ian can't. One of the masters has given me my first pair of boots. They belonged to Dr Huggins, who was the music master here and for a time he was also Master of the Grafton. He played the organ in chapel and kept his horse tethered to a post outside until the service was over. I like that. I'm going to spend my term riding and hunting Moonlight from now on.

I've just cut four classes, getting other boys to cover for me, to take Moonlight to a meet of the Grafton. I hacked for four miles and when I got there the meet was cancelled. Damn! I've made up my mind that I don't like formal education and I want to find an excuse to leave as soon as I can.

One day I've got it. Suddenly it slips into my mind like that. I'm doodling away in class, not concentrating, and I think I'd like to leave Stowe and learn about horse-racing. Why don't I do that and then I can become a racehorse trainer? I want a break from everything that's happened in my life so far. When my mother next comes down I tell her of my plan.

'But you must take some exams, darling,' she says.

'You don't need any exams to be a racehorse trainer,' I reply.

We're going for a walk across the fields near to the Green Man where we've just had lunch. The Green Man's a creeper-covered old-fashioned inn near to Stowe where the parents take the boys on weekends.

'I thought you wanted to become a priest,' says David.

'That was last year, before I knew what I really wanted.'

'I do insist on the exams,' my mother stresses, looking towards David.

'You're going to find it impossible to get a proper job if you haven't any school certificates.'

'I don't want a proper job. I'm going to be a trainer.' I've got my head down now, staring at the grass I'm kicking over as I walk.

'What do you think we should do?' says my mother, turning to my elder brother.

'I don't know,' my brother says, beginning to be exhausted and wanting to talk about something else.

Of course, I'm thinking, they don't understand. All I want is to be on my own where nobody knows anything about me. And I know that I'm really happy with horses, and will be much happier than I am now.

'I'd like to ride over fences, too,' I go on. 'It'll be good for my riding.'

'But, darling, there's no money. It's for rich people, that.'

'Don't worry. I'll make it work.' I give my mother that determined I-won't-budge face.

'Well,' says my mother, 'I'll ring Bill Astor. He's got horses in training. He'll know.'

Nobody knows how to deal with me. Aunt Phyllie's brow furrows and she tuts. Then she looks at me and says, 'If you do go ahead, don't bet till later in life.' Perhaps, secretly, she's pleased. She's raced horses herself, but she's worried because I've no balanced father to give his opinion. I've no male guidance. But

Mummy's spoken to Bill Astor and she says I'm to write to him. So I write to Godfather Bill and he says I'm to come down and discuss it. I get a *nihil obstat* from my housemaster, who is puzzled but agrees, and soon I'm on my way to Cliveden. Bill's chauffeur meets me at the station and next thing I'm getting out under the awning of Cliveden's front door. A proud-faced butler escorts me to 'His Lordship'.

As we walk through the hall I hear a voice shouting: 'You should never have had this house. Look what you've done with it!' The butler ignores the voice and leads me into a small drawing-room. I see my godfather with an old lady. She isn't tall but she has a rather haughty face, although the skin is wrinkled with quite a few big brown spots, like oversized freckles. The old lady is Godfather Bill's mother. 'Do you know my mother?' he says. I don't.

I hope the old lady won't start shouting at lunch. But she's small, not large as an omnibus like Granny Blow. Still, if she shrieks I'll curdle inside, Granny Blow looming again. At lunch she sits small and erect and Bill talks. He doesn't say anything discouraging. In fact he has a trainer at Newmarket whom I could learn with.

'I'll contact Fergie Sutherland. Perhaps you could go to him,' Bill says. 'He took over from Joe Lawson who trained our horses.'

Bill's mother, making a pecking movement with her face, interrupts. 'I think you're very young to be leaving school.' She has this kind of American accent, under an English lady's voice. I let the remark glide by. I smile and go on eating. 'Well?' she says.

'I love horses. I like being out of doors.'

The old lady keeps studying me. I can feel her eyes on me.

Bill changes the conversation and asks about my mother. He wears corduroy trousers and a tweed jacket with a flower in his buttonhole, like a pink carnation. It's true, I think, he's not handsome. He has pop-out eyes that twinkle and a hook to his nose. 'She's well,' I tell him.

'Your mother needs cherishing,' Bill says.

After lunch I'm packed into Lady Astor's Rolls-Royce, because she's going back to London too. I sit in the back next to her and she starts talking at once, the moment the Rolls's wheels turn in the drive. I hear about her being the first lady to become a member of Parliament, how Winston Churchill wouldn't talk to her for years. 'Too silly of Winston,' she says. Then suddenly she swings to my godfather's private life and how he can't keep his hands off any pretty girl. 'I said to that girl's mother, "Don't you let her near Bill."' She drops me off near Sloane Square. As I step out, she says, 'Why did you see Bill about racing?' I say, because he's my godfather. 'Well, you should have seen Jakie. Bill knows nothing.'

Seen Bill's brother. But I didn't, because Bill's my godfather and my mother's friend. Goodbye, I say. Then the strange old woman with a black hat perched on her head like an upturned bird disappears off in her big black car.

It's my last term at Stowe, in fact it's my last two weeks. Everyone seems to have accepted that I'm leaving two years earlier than I should. I'll be sixteen on the 23rd of July and term ends two days later. I've had a letter from Fergie Sutherland telling me he's expecting me and where I'll be lodging and when I'm to start with him. Am I making a mistake? I don't think much about that. I know it's a worry to my mother and perhaps I shouldn't do this after all she's been through. But deep down I know it's all right. I know it is.

'So the horse won,' my housemaster writes in the book of school hymns that everybody who likes you signs when a boy leaves. So many boys sign it, too, that I feel sad now at going. I won't see some of them again and perhaps when I'm older these schooldays will seem so short. I wasn't aware of being popular. I feel I hardly got to know the school. But I'll be leaving Moonlight behind with the farmer for a bit, having made no arrangement for her at Newmarket. It's the summer now and she's at grass.

That's it, Stowe. No more public school. Nor more that kind of education. I look down at my school tie for the last time. The school train puffs and steams with hundreds of us boys towards Euston.

The first couple of days I'm in London. My mother's still terribly worried. She makes me promise to come back and take the exams once my time with Fergie Sutherland is up. I'm not aware that it will be up but I say, 'Yes, Mummy, of course.' Two days later I'm catching the train to Newmarket and my mother waves me goodbye at the station. I can see she's tearful and I feel strange too. After all, I'm plunging headlong into the unknown.

At Newmarket station I take a taxi to Fergie Sutherland's racing yard. We drive along a broad road with training establishments running all the way up it. After a while the taxi turns into a gravel drive and I look up at quite a large white-painted house, like a big town house, and I can see the racing yard to one side of it. I'm feeling really shy and frightened now as I knock on the front door. A very pretty dark-haired woman comes to the door. She says her husband is in his office. A few moments later Fergie Sutherland appears. He gives me a grunted hello and I look at him and tell him, 'I'm Simon Blow.'

'I know,' he says. 'Come in.' He wears breeches and he has a peg-leg. He's colourfully dressed, in a hunting waistcoat and a blue shirt. He's about twenty-eight, I guess, and he has a cheeky expression. He reminds me of one of those nineteenth-century coloured prints of boxers – pugilists, weren't they called? I'm not in the house for long when he says, 'I'll take you over to your lodgings.' I pick up my suitcase and we walk down the drive to the wide road I came up from the station. The road is the Bury Road, which goes out of Newmarket to Bury St Edmunds and on to Norfolk. I notice the Heath where the racehorses are exercised and a long range of high beech trees.

Fergie introduces me to the family I'm to stay with. I shake hands. Michael, my landlord, seems about as laid back as could be. I can see at once he's very gentle and laughs easily. Lavender, his wife, welcomes me too. They're very much gentlefolk and I suppose they're taking in lodgers for the same reason as my mother. Fergie seems to know both of them as friends and he stays there chatting for about ten minutes. He doesn't say much to me except, 'Be in the yard at six o'clock,' as he leaves.

Then he pulls on his cap and swaggers out with his stick. The swagger is increased by his peg-top leg. He makes a great play of his missing limb – as if to make a virtue of it.

The next morning I'm in Fergie's yard at six. Apprentices and stable lads are dribbling in too. They look at me, some giving a nod, and carry on. The yard is boxes on four sides with an expanse of grass in the middle. One end leads to Fergie's office and house, and at the other there's an arch which goes to the back road and paddocks. I introduce myself to the head lad and he says there's a horse for me to saddle and get ready. The pace of the lads and apprentices increases. They dart around balancing a saddle and a bridle on one arm. At about 7.20 they start to take the horses out of the boxes. Fergie's now standing at the top of the yard eyeing the scene, his flat cap pulled jauntily to one side. His pugilist's face seems at the ready.

'We're not in the bloody police force!' Fergie yells at me suddenly. I slither to the ground. Everyone's eyes are on me as Fergie's shout brings silence. I've got on hunting-style: that is, foot in the stirrup then swinging my other leg over the saddle. I start again. I vault on. From that day on I mount properly, racing-style.

I don't ride the racehorses, as at eleven and a half stone I'm too heavy. But I ride Fergie's hunters and the odd jumper. I ride out alongside the string and experience the exhilarating expanse of Newmarket Heath. Fergie trains around sixty horses in all, so about twenty-five are exercised each lot. I pick up the language fast and as I get to know the lads I pick up their language, too. There's a lot of talk about 'getting your leg across', which means fucking. It seems harmless to me but when I use the term over lunch with Michael and Lavender, I'm told off at once. Lavender, arching her neck, says, 'Simon, if you want to talk like that you'd better find somewhere else to stay.'

I'm upset now. In the yard I must be on a level with the lads, and at my digs must remember that niceties matter. I show I'm upset, my eyes filling with tears. After lunch Michael comforts me. 'Don't worry. Lavender doesn't mean it. You know we're fond of you.'

My digs are a respite after my day with Fergie. Because whatever I do in the yard, it seems to be wrong. He complains that I've lamed one of his hunters, but it turns out the horse was badly shod. He asks me if I can drive, and I say no. 'God, how useless,' he snaps. What does he expect at sixteen? Then, after I've been there about three weeks, he says, 'You're too comfortable in those digs. You need toughening up.' I'm thinking he doesn't know that I was toughened up long ago in Roehampton. He's looking at this innocent, fragile face and thinking that I've seen nothing. But I don't want to start an argument. I've got a fear of raised voices after my father. So Fergie moves me out of my digs to sleep in the stable loft in the yard where there's bales of hay at one end and thin partitions making four bedrooms at the other. Two of his apprentices sleep there, and one of the lads. From now on I eat my meals with the lads and apprentices.

Most of the apprentices sleep in a house at the end of the back drive, where a couple feeds them. I join them for the morning fry-up with baked beans after first lot. And after evening stables there's a kind of high tea. Slumped in chairs, the apprentices watch television and dawdle through the racing pages of the *Mirror*. They're very easy with me and some evenings I play cards with them. 'All right, Simon, do you want me to explain it?' one of them will say when a particular game confuses me.

The apprentices are half my size and they're called after the towns they come from. There's Stockton and Brummie and Manse, for instance. They're small and thin and all hoping they'll be the next Lester Piggott. They make me think of those pictures of the poor of London's underworld in the novels of Charles Dickens. And like Dickens's poor they're characters, every one. I feel like Oliver Twist in Fagin's den. They dart and dodge and run about as if they're controlled by some invisible wired signal. When no one's looking they light up a cigarette, then quickly stub it out with their fingers.

My only other social activity is when Fergie decides to test me out. One day he says to me, 'Can you play squash?' There's a squash court in the town and he'd rather like a game. I say yes, to avoid another of his sneers. I'm beginning to suspect there's more than a touch of Flashman about Fergie. So in no time he's driving me there, and almost as fast beating me hollow at the game. He hops all over the court on his good leg, sending the ball flying from wall to wall. 'You're not much good at it, are you?' he mutters as he's driving me back to the yard. I think he's pleased. Pleased to make me feel small. That evening I'm glad to be back among the apprentices.

I'm happy being with the lads at Fergie's stables. I find out that most have come from wretched backgrounds in big cities. A lot of them were pushed out because it's one less mouth to feed. They've got cheerful hard faces, used to knocks. The very young ones, who are my age, have baby faces that are vivid with quick movement – faces that have learnt always to be on the alert. There's something that unites me with the lads and it stops me thinking too much about the childhood I've left behind. They've been hurt but they've risen above it. I recognise my hurt in them. That's why we all keep on our cheerful masks.

'Simon, you're real tall,' Stockton says to me. 'Why are you so tall?'

'I couldn't ride on the flat, could I?'

Stockton laughs. 'Even Piggott keeps his bum in the air. Your bum would have to be in the clouds.'

'Don't upset the guv'nor,' says Brummie. 'He can't half lose his temper with you.'

'I think he should behave better with you,' says Stockton, giving me an 'I'd support you if I was bigger' look.

'You're a good lad, Simon,' says Geordie. 'You're one of us.'

So we go into town together, watch a film, or play those card games once evening stables are over. On race days owners in their polished cars choke Newmarket High Street but I don't know that side of racing. Sometimes an owner will come round evening stables and that's when everything has to be ultra-correct. But one of the older lads, Joe, an Irishman, is having an affair with a female owner. He sits on my bed in the loft telling me about his love for her. There are nights when he gets drunk and starts wailing outside. He throws sticks up at the open loft door. I don't like it. He makes my fear return.

After about six weeks in the loft I'm allowed back to my digs. I find it sad not having the lads round me, and I have to readjust myself to being with Michael and Lavender again. Michael was a gentleman farmer and he moved to Newmarket to paint the horses. The walls of the house are full of his paintings. I think this makes them quite hard-up, which is why Lavender is having to let out rooms. They've a small daughter, and from early on they made me one of the family. It happened that Michael was at Stowe with my father and so from the start there was a kind of bond. And I sense Lavender felt for me being on my own. But Michael's a really nice man, not at all stuffy, and mad keen on stories so that he can laugh. He loves laughter. He's started taking me round the pubs in the town, spending hours leaning on the bar with a pint of bitter, followed after stories by another pint, and another. And another.

Lavender doesn't approve of him leading me astray like this. If she's still up when we come in, Michael rather hazy with beer, she gives him one sharp glance, makes a scathing comment, and goes upstairs. But Michael's quite unbothered. 'Shall we have some ham? I'm sure there's some in the larder,' he says to me.

'I think Hugh will join us tonight,' Michael says in his casual, laid-back way. Michael – that name, I think. He's much older than my Michael, so I still see my Michael quite clearly. On his own. It's funny, though, saying the name again. Every time I say it, I wonder about him. A bit of memory flicks up as I'm talking. I see my Michael, then he goes again.

'Who's Hugh?' I ask.

'Hugh Sidebottom. He's tremendous fun,' says Michael as he drives his battered car down the Bury Road, round the red-brick clock tower, and turns off into the yard of the Rutland Arms Hotel. We go to a back bar, frequented in far-off days by race-horse trainers when they were called 'trainer grooms'. There's this big, big man at the bar as we enter. He has a round jovial face and he's tall with it.

Hugh holds a pipe in one hand and a box of matches in the other. The two rarely meet. He lights a match, holds it above the pipe, keeps talking, talking and the match fizzles out. When I know Hugh better I remark on this. 'Absolutely right, old boy. Someone once said to me, "Hugh, you don't smoke a pipe, you smoke matches."'

Hugh, big as he is, isn't at all hearty, not the purple-faced hunting squire type. I like him at once because he makes a cartoon out of the ridiculous in seconds. I don't feel at all nervous with Hugh, whereas I can never relax when I'm with Fergie. Perhaps with Hugh and Michael I'm going to find the family I've never had. Perhaps they'll be like two fathers to me, so then I'll be doing even better than most.

Several nights of the week Hugh, Michael, and this six-foot-three sixteen-year-old are found at this back bar. Of course I'm under age and I've lied to almost everyone about my age. I mumble sort of twenty or twenty-one, then one night Michael and Hugh have a countdown. I settle for seventeen, but they promise not to let on, otherwise I'd be out of the bar straight away.

My mother is coming to see me. She's coming down with

Peter, as there's racing at Newmarket and Peter likes a good bet. But she says he'll go back that evening and that she'll stay on for a few days. So I book her in to the Bedford Lodge Hotel, which lies back off the Bury Road. It's where racing people stay. I want her to meet Michael and Lavender and Hugh; then she should be less worried about me. She'll have to meet Fergie, of course, and I'm rather dreading that.

Once Peter's gone back, I take my mother to meet Michael and Lavender. She charms them quickly. She jokes with them and tells funny stories of her hunting exploits as a girl. How furious she was when a man told her that her false eyelashes were sticking through her veil. 'Now,' she says, 'I think all horses should be doped. I find them absolutely terrifying.'

'Your mother's quite delightful,' Michael says to me afterwards. Next I take Mummy to meet Fergie. Judy, his wife, is there too and Fergie does a lot of swaggering about, giving my mother a drink and all that. He says he'll drive us back to the Bedford Lodge and later he insists on going back yet again to discuss me with my mother. For the first time I see Fergie doing his gallantry act and he's as nice to me as if he'd never been anything else. It doesn't occur to me, however, that he might be interested in my mother. Whatever's happened she's still 'Mummy' to me and not a bit of skirt for others to fancy.

The next day my mother tells me that everything's going to be all right. 'Why?' I ask. 'How did you persuade him? You mean he's not going to be a bully any more?' My mother smiles at me and then turns her head away.

'What happened, Mummy?' I say.

'Look, let's just say you're going to be fine with him from now on.'

Judy always says hello and looks warmly at me – and I think it's rotten that Fergie can't stop winking at every attractive woman. In the winter months he leaves his yard to go to Leicestershire. He takes half a dozen hunters up there and hunts with the crack packs week after week. They say he's fearless on the hunting field, jumping enormous fences and taking his own line across the country. My only riding now is across Newmarket Heath, which is beautiful with its rising and curving expanses of grass and strings of racehorses cantering and galloping on every horizon, but it isn't hunting in the shires. I dream of going there to test my horsemanship.

But I do go somewhere after my mother's effect on Fergie. I haven't been allowed away from Newmarket at all, then suddenly I'm to go with some horses that are to race at Carlisle. It's a three-day outing. We stay in a hostel for stablemen and as I've got a day with nothing to do, I telephone to see if anyone's at Glen, which is only a short train journey away. It's summer and everyone is there and Uncle Christopher says it would be nice to see me.

My cousin, Colin, meets me at the station and my journey from Newmarket to Carlisle in a horsebox is now changed to a ride in Colin's Cadillac. The roads disappear fast and suddenly I'm at Glen with its turrets and pinnacles, and the racecourse hostel seems already to belong to another time. That afternoon I break the news to Uncle Christopher that I'm not at school any more. I'm nervous, as he's paying for my education, but he doesn't seem that surprised. Perhaps after seeing my grand-mother through these marriages and tending her discarded children, he knows there's a genetic tendency to bolt. He sits in the Gothic study looking out to the moors, with a genial smile on his face. I answer his questions about how long I intend to stay at Newmarket, and what I have to do there. At the end of the day Colin drives me back to the station. I haven't seen him since the wedding in Norfolk when my mother asked me to walk past her mother in the hall of that enormous house. 'Do you think I will ever be able to see my grandmother?' I ask Colin. I know he's quite close to her and that when Colin was a very young man my grandmother used to take him to stay in country houses with her. She liked that. They were taken for brother and sister. She liked that better.

'I think it will be possible in a year or two,' he says from the wheel of his smart Cadillac, 'but you mustn't call her Granny or anything like that.'

At last, then, there's going to be a meeting. Or there might be a meeting. I go over in my mind what I will say to her. 'Hello, Clare. It's been a long time.' No, I can't say that, she might smell sarcasm. I can't tell her either that we used to see her from the tops of buses. She'd be furious, just as she was furious when Bill Astor took my mother up to her at a ball and said, 'I thought you might like to meet your daughter.' My mother's told me about her cutting tongue and she might make an unpleasant remark. If she's unpleasant, it would be best not to see her at all.

Time back at Newmarket is passing quickly. Suddenly my three months are up. Fergie calls me into his office. He sits at a desk covered with papers, in his breeches, a riding stock round his neck, and his peg-leg bent under the desk. He looks at me for a moment, not a kind look, and I stand there waiting.

'You're completely useless,' he bellows at me. 'You'll never make a racehorse trainer.' I feel my legs trembling, but am still not quite sure that I'm hearing what he's saying. 'Give it up. Do something else,' he goes on. He stops and then, out of nowhere, I burst into tears. Huge unrelenting tears, my mouth torn apart by them. Fergie is thrown off his guard and he stumbles through to find his wife. He starts trying to say something as Judy takes me through a passage to their house. 'It's not my fault,' he mumbles, his florid face turning to a sulk. 'Bill Astor told me to discourage him.'

Gradually my tears dry as Judy nurses me with a cup of tea. But I'm not that soft, I think as Judy goes on comforting me. No. I'm not. I've an iron will inside me and it's saying, don't leave Newmarket. Stay. Stay there. Go on. Show him he's wrong.

I tell Hugh and Michael about what's happened. Hugh is immediately sympathetic. In minutes he's telling a story about Fergie and I'm laughing. He says, why don't I come and work

for him? But I've promised to return to London and take those
O Levels. That's just what I don't want to do. I'm going to stay
at Newmarket. I've made a family here now – all these new
friends who are taking an interest in my future. It's all so different
to my own flesh and blood. Uncle Tony has written from Rise
telling me to sell my horse because I've no money. That really
hurt.

Hugh says I should do some riding over fences and that he'll
train Moonlight in return for my working and riding out for
him. He's already put Moonlight, who's still in a field with the
farmer at Stowe, on his training list. I'm a registered owner.
Hugh needed her on his list so that he could get his licence. He
says that if you haven't got enough horses they won't let you have
one. 'They' is a bowler-hatted brigadier with a swirl of moustache who controls these matters from Wetherby's, the racing
bigwigs, in Portman Square, London, 'Now look,' Hugh told the
Brigadier. 'You can't shoot a pheasant without a gun and you
can't get a horse to train without a licence.' The bowler-hatted
Brigadier, now listening from his desk without the hat, his silver
hair well-groomed with oil, scratched his head and thought.
After a few moments of this silence he agreed. Hugh should have
a licence.

I tell my mother and Aunt Phyllie that I'm not coming back
to take exams, I'm staying on here. My mother is worried, but
what can she do? She writes saying, 'I don't like you in these bars
so young.' I'm stubborn. I'm not there like my father, I say. I've
told them, too, about the arrangement for Moonlight to go into
training. I'm going to ride with professional jockeys and I'll be
all right. Secretly, Aunt Phyllie's rather pleased and she says in
that case I must have Uncle Philip's racing colours. Quickly I
dash off to the place that puts racing colours together at
Newmarket. Eton blue and black halves, black cap. The knitted
sweater comes out looking very smart, and the silk cap makes me
a real jockey.

'Are you sure my height doesn't matter?' I ask Hugh.

'Not a bit. Anthony Mildmay was well over six foot. You'll be another Mildmay.'

Anthony Mildmay – the top amateur jockey of the years before the war and still a light for every amateur to follow. He would have won the 1936 Grand National if the reins hadn't broken over the second-last fence. Yes, I'll be another Mildmay, I think, ignoring the fact that I don't have his resources. Anthony Mildmay, otherwise Lord Mildmay of Flete, and owner of thousands of acres in Devon.

Hugh says I must buy another horse. Moonlight, he says, could win a race but she needs a professional on her. I'm not experienced enough yet to ride her. I need an old-timer to get some experience on. But I don't have any money to buy a horse. 'Oh, we'll pick one up cheap,' Hugh says, his enthusiasm squashing my anxiety.

Off I go once again to the post office and draw out a hundred and fifty pounds in savings from Godfather Bill's annual present of a hundred pounds. Then Hugh and I set off in pursuit of a suitable mount for me to practise on. We won't get anything special for that money but finally we buy one from two ancient sisters who train horses – a nine-year-old gelding, about seventeen hands in height. 'Absolutely just the thing,' says Hugh, his unlit pipe waving about in one hand. In no time the horse is back at Newmarket and in Hugh's yard.

Within a month I'm leaving the paddock at Doncaster, the horse led out by my trainer, Hugh Sidebottom. It's a new life for me. I know it is. As I canter down to the start I see my name and weight on the board of riders and runners. 'Mr S. Blow – 10 stone 12lbs.'

13

Aunt Phyllie is keeping an eye on my mother. She was really well when she came to Newmarket. But sometimes she's not well and Aunt Phyllie has to put her into a nursing home where she has tests. My mother writes to me at Newmarket about her condition. 'Darling as you know the whole trouble is blood pressure, which I've now had several years. There is no cure and at the moment there's only a vague control with tablets & sometimes by injection. The best control you can get is called *stabilisation* but *this takes time* & means the dosage has to be changed perhaps weekly as the blood pressure fluctuates. (Mine particularly fluctuates.) Those fainting times were a ridge of low pressure where the pills were making it too low – then later it leapt up high again which also makes me ill but in a different way!'

That's what they've finally diagnosed – incurable high blood pressure. I put the letter down and in my mind I'm looking back over the years when all this damage was done. Because of this illness, which now means sudden admittance to a nursing home, those long bad years are never far enough off. They follow me, even if I'm now among different, happier and more stable people.

At night, before sleeping, I hear my father shouting. I see my mother coming up the stairs, her head swollen with bruises and blood pouring. I think of all the years she stood by my father, which led nowhere but to disinheritance, and now this, her illness. The hope that there would be help, the hope that there would be money from her relations. 'The family don't understand,' my mother goes on saying. And all the time the cold indifference of Clare, and the never-ending cruelty of Cicely ... and the battle going on for us to have some security, some safety.

Sometimes safety came from strangers. My mother told us how she stood on Waterloo Station after the divorce, in tears as we went back to school. And the parents of another boy, seeing my mother, went up and asked if they could help. My mother said yes, and they took her home. In her small sitting-room in Burnsall Street they sat with her and listened as she played the songs from *A Star Is Born*. It made her feel better, less lost, as Judy Garland sang out her blues number on 'The Man That Got Away'. And I imagine the two strangers, happily married, sitting there, sharing with my mother for a moment the awfulness of divorce and love ending.

I pick the letter up and read on: 'This is an illness for old people not for me – which is where the tragedy lies – because it *is* a tragedy and far more tricky in a younger person. Particularly me who am emotional & highly strung – the worst possible combination & also now not physically strong.'

How calm she was during those years in Roehampton. How she could make us laugh when there was nothing at all to laugh about. The fairy stories she either read to us or made up. The walks on Barnes Common and the Giant Pond, with the vast, tall trees around it which she made us believe were giants. The fairy ring she found in the woods at Glen ... But she won't die, not now, not at forty-three ... because isn't that what this letter's saying to me? I wouldn't accept her dying. Old people die, like Granny Blow, but not my mother who looks so young and not ill.

I get really sad thinking that perhaps she never will be my dependable mother again. Those days when she came on her own to take us out from Scaitcliffe – so much better when Daddy wasn't there. And we took a boat down the river and she'd brought a picnic. She told us fantastic stories, she made them up, the boat moored to an island. We laughed. That's over – that's gone. So if that's gone, have I got to get used to this? All right, if she's really going under, if . . . and I stop there. How can I go on?

But I can't always control my worrying, and when I worry it opens up the past so fast. That immediate yesterday that's still today. Now I'm at Peanswood with Aunt Phyllie. I'm fourteen and we're going to a ball in a private house. It's a coming-out dance. Aunt Phyllie is giving a dinner party and there are guests staying. After dinner we motor to the dance and all is well until my mother suddenly – half-way through the evening – does her solo bit on the floor again, like the night at the Café de Paris. Aunt Phyllie, in a long old-fashioned dress that suddenly shoots out at the bottom, is talking to other members of the county. Her eyes go to my mother and I see a stricken look on her face, but she keeps talking to Mrs Cooper-Bland and Colonel Loder.

It's well after midnight when we get home. I'm going up to my room when I hear my mother crying at the bottom of the stairs. I pause at the half-landing. I see Aunt Phyllie putting her arms round my mother and she starts to cry too. I sit on the stair ledge watching. I've never seen Aunt Phyllie cry before. I go cold. I tremble. And I'm thinking it's because she's seen so much. She's seen what Clare did to her brother and what happened to my mother. She's seen the nastiness of Cicely to my mother. 'Please can you look after Diana? – Please?' Uncle Tony, a young boy, is saying down the telephone to Aunt Phyllie from Rise. 'My mother's being so unkind to her.' Then she's seen my mother's marriage to my father and all the ghastliness of it. Aunt Phyllie's seen a lot. That's why she's crying, I know. But still I'm caught short, shocked. Aunt Phyllie – so always there and reliable in her tweed suits – is crying. That's what I'm thinking, looking down from the stair ledge, my hands clasped round my knees, looking down, frightened. If Aunt Phyllie's crying, giving way too, we're alone now, David and me, completely alone.

I can still see that night. I'll always see Aunt Phyllie shaking, her arms around my mother, and the dark blue blind half pulled over the door behind them, and beyond the thick dead darkness of the outside. It sticks and sticks. I fight to forget the scene, but these flashes of memory return. I can't kill it. It sticks there, a snapshot selected from a heap of pictures. They're painful. Painful because I've no control over them. They'll pull me back, suddenly, freezing me. Aunt Phyllie, in tears, holding my falling-apart mother. Mummy, so pretty, thin, fragile. And so many other snapshots, awful too, tumble with it.

The pain slips away, vanishes. The screen is blank again. I'm riding my new horse on to the place where we're to practise over hurdles. Bourbon Towers, I've renamed him. That's a monument at Stowe that I used to ride by, and I'm calling him that because I want to keep that picture – me riding across Stowe. I want to build this store of better pictures, happy pictures – like me riding out now to jumping practice.

But I know Bourbon Towers will never win a race; I've bought him to give me a good ride. He's done that already at a racecourse in Lincolnshire that's made up of swift, sharp bends. The excitement of taking him over the hurdles and the shrill voices of the jockeys jostled together and shouting to each other: 'Look out on the left!' 'Steady on the right!' 'Watch that side' – meaning, 'Take care, there's a faller' – and me surging forward among them until I hear the loudspeaker echoing, 'and Bourbon Towers moving into fifth place.' We come in panting, Bourbon's neck slippery like a snake, and we're nowhere near the leaders. But at least I got him into the frame once. And I hear the commentator's voice again.

I envy this friend of mine at Newmarket who's got the money to buy horses that will win. His father buys him horses. Two thousand, three thousand pounds, it doesn't matter. When he tells me of his win at Sandown, Kempton Park or wherever, as he slouches in the chintz armchair in the sitting-room of his house, holding a glass of whisky, I feel envy scald me.

I would like Aunt Phyllie to help but I haven't asked her and I don't dare. She hasn't said anything and it's probably because she would consider it money down the drain. It's not just buying the horses but the training bills, vets' bills, racing bills ... well, really nothing but bills. I say to myself, but if these imaginary horses of mine won races then they'd be even more valuable. Only I know she wants me to be safe, and what I'm dreaming of isn't safe. But perhaps there are some dreams which aren't safe, dreams we shouldn't have but do have. 'You see, Aunt Phyllie,' I start saying to her in my dream, 'if you did this for me it would make all the horrid years go away. When I'm riding over fences nothing's horrid any more.' And then she'd look at me and say, 'You must be sensible, darling, you know my home is your home.'

All right. I won't think about it any more.

My father returns, haunting my thoughts. Alcoholics are selfish, one-track people, and he hasn't given a damn once about the muddle, the no-cash-anywhere despair, he's left. I get sad now as I'm jogging down the road at exercise, expensive stud yards all around. I look at blinding bright green fields, fresh white paint on the fences, boxes like little houses in the corners. Everything so easy, so right. But I'm cut off. Stranded. I'll never have bright green fields for my horses. The bright green fields have gone.

I'm back in the present. Hugh says I'm a natural as a horseman. I can't be a professional steeplechase jockey straight away because of my height and to be a top-flight amateur you have to have good horses to prove yourself on. So I ride on five racecourses in six weeks. My mother comes to see me ride at Birmingham, my brother comes to Doncaster. Will some miracle happen to keep me doing this for ever? But miracles are the stuff of churches. Hugh hopes that Moonlight might still win a race. Hope is vital. But I've no money left at all. Nothing. The post office savings have gone.

Mr S. Blow, owner and amateur rider lasts for months, not years. But in my mind it goes on as if it is happening. Like a dying man still moving after he's shot. I ignore the fact that I've had to sell my horses for tuppence. I go on riding.

Now the family are murmuring about those exams, but I won't go back to London. At last Aunt Phyllie realises that I can't budge. My mother is still puzzled by my determination, but her involvement with Peter distracts her from me. Not Aunt Phyllie. She says she's coming to Newmarket to see her friends Bunty and Petsy: I call them Colonel and Mrs Scrope. Bunty manages Lord Derby's stud and when Aunt Phyllie's there she discusses me with him. I go over to find her smiling as she's always smiled, and with her tweed suit on. Bunty, an old-fashioned type who moves about very fast, has a wicked laugh and sharp eyes that twinkle. Petsy, his wife, offers me a handshake with her left hand, keeping her other arm in a long black glove. She is upright, stiff-backed, and very reserved. I'm shy in front of them. I haven't met many racing bigwigs, and Bunty's one of them. Bunty knows everyone in Newmarket and soon it's settled that he's going to talk to the well-known trainer Sam Armstrong. A few days later Bunty Scrope telephones me. 'Now, Simon, give Sam a call. He'll take you on.'

I call Mr Armstrong and introduce myself. 'Hello, there,' he says in a rather fruity but to-the-point voice. 'Delighted to have you,' he continues. 'My brother, Gerald, trained horses for your aunt, Mrs Hubbersty. Come over and discuss it.' A time is arranged, after evening stables.

I've got a moped, it's half-way between a bicycle and a very weak motorbike. Top speed is about 25 m.p.h. and I've been spluttering down the Bury Road on it for a few months now. Aunt Phyllie bought it for me. Of course, I would have liked a real motorbike, but she wouldn't have considered that. Too expensive, and a sixteen-year-old on a real motorbike – frightfully dangerous. So off I pedal, swinging left at the clock tower into the road that leads to Sam Armstrong's. The stables are painted orange and all the ironwork silver. The house is handsome and showy too.

Sam Armstrong is a stout man who waddles as he walks. I suppose he's in his fifties; he still wears breeches and thick stockings. He takes me into a well-furnished drawing-room and sits me down. Standing by the fireplace and giving the occasional pull to his braces, he tells me the terms. He'll take me on as a pupil trainer and he will pay for my digs. 'You'll find they're a good bunch here,' he says, referring to the lads. I'm to start the following Monday. Within twenty minutes the meeting's over and I chug back up the Bury Road to Michael and Lavender. It'll be difficult, I know. I think how far away I am from my friend who rides in races. I've thirty pounds to live on a month. That's the dregs of my parents' marriage settlement.

On my first day at Sam's I park my moped near the bottom of his three yards and walk up to the first. I go through a small door in a big orange door. Each yard is painted the same orange and silver. It's a showplace, as if Hollywood has hit Newmarket. In the top yard is Sam Armstrong, neatly dressed in a tweed jacket and cap. He's got on the breeches and the thick stockings, and he's strutting like a hurrying peacock. Soon I realise he's a stickler for the smallest thing out of place. And all the time there's a morose, apprehensive twitch in his face. When I tell Hugh about this he says it's because he's terrified some owner's going to say to him, 'Well, how much are you going to rook me for this year, Sam?' Hugh doesn't like Sam. But I do, or perhaps I'm not so strong on his reputation for sharpness. Hugh says if Hitler had won the war Sam would have been the first person down there to greet him with open arms, offering to train his horses.

Sam doesn't talk to me much, except for a nod, and when we're at exercise, 'Simon, tell that damned boy to hold his whip properly.' They're nearly all apprentices in the yard. Sam does it because an apprentice is paid less, but I think, too, he really like making them into jockeys. Quite a few well-known jockeys were apprenticed to Sam. The apprentices look at me suspiciously for the first few weeks. They're not sure whose side I'm on. Discontent breaks into revolt at times. One morning I'm in the middle yard and this mite of an apprentice is swinging on Sam's tie and pummelling him in the tummy. 'Take this boy off me!' Sam shouts, and one of the head lads does. Slowly they begin to talk to me, not a lot though, and I think it would be easier if I didn't have the funny title of 'Assistant Pupil Trainer'. It gives me this sort of on-paper authority. A lot of Sam's apprentices are older than I am, and more experienced. I feel alone. For a while.

At one o'clock I go back to my digs for lunch. There's a girl lodging there who's very much upper class and doing some kind of secretarying for Captain Boyd Rochfort. He trains the Queen's horses and everyone calls him 'the Captain'. He's a big man who wears a grey trilby, and looking at him you'd think that Edward VII was still on the throne. He lives almost next door in the most over-the-top racing mansion of the lot. It could be Brighton and the Hotel Metropole. One lunchtime this girl comes back and as we're all sitting round the table eating she says, 'The Captain's so upset today. Clare Tennyson has died.'

'That's my grandmother,' I say.

'Really,' the girl giggles, 'and you didn't know she'd died.'

'No.'

It's not until the next day that my mother contacts me. She's in Italy with Aunt Phyllie and she rings me from there. 'I've had a telegram from Uncle Christopher. It's from Glen. He says, "Regret your mother died yesterday." My mother's dead,' Mummy says. 'I won't come back for the funeral. It's too far.' She pauses, then says, 'I never knew her.' She's not crying – that's all been done, years ago. So that meeting between me and Clare-the-beauty-that-I-mustn't-call-Granny will never happen now. She'll always be a mystery. The funeral will be in the churchyard near Glen where all the Tennants are buried. I won't go either. It's not the meeting I'd planned.

★

'What did Clare die of?' I ask my mother when I'm next with her.

'Angina. It's a heart disease. The doctor failed to diagnose it in time.'

There's an irony. This woman without a heart died of an undiagnosed heart disease. Did the doctor have a problem finding her heart? Maybe it just gave out with all the burdens it was carrying. Poor Granny. Clare, I mean. She was sixty-four. No age, people say.

We do go to the memorial service. It's held at a 'society' church in Knightsbridge. David and I file into the family pew at Mummy's side. The church is filled with smartly dressed ladies and the smell of expensive scents, and gentlemen in pinstripe suits. I don't know any of them. The service only reminds me of Clare's unending absence as I bend my knees to pray. I think hard of words to say for someone I never knew. I get chilly, and dizzy, and long for it to be over.

I stay behind after evening stables and work out handicaps in Sam's office. I pore over the *Racing Calendar*, a huge broadsheet printed on cream paper, and make additions and subtractions on a pad beside me. I hear footsteps coming from the house. It's Sam, no longer looking morose, his jacket off, still wearing his breeches, with a glass of gin and tonic, slice of lemon floating, held against his belly. 'I'm all for getting money off the rich,' he says, a serious smile on his face. 'All for getting money off them,' he repeats, taking a good sip of his drink.

I'm fascinated by what I'm learning about Sam's career. When I make it as a trainer will I have the same spirit of combat underlying astute charm? He's the first trainer to realise that the old families haven't the cash to play a big part in racing any more. So Sam persuaded the Maharaja of Baroda, who's immensely rich, to put all his thirty horses with him. Baroda was happy with Sam, who won him some classic races. But after a few years he took every horse away, overnight – on a whim. I ask Jack, the box driver, how Sam faced it.

'The Guv'nor was blind drunk for three days. You'd see him drunk in the house. The next season he was back with a string of seventy.'

Hugh tells me that when Sam goes on holiday he puts a notice in the local paper. So when he's in Cape Town, for instance, a notice appears: 'Mr Sam Armstrong will be available for business between 4 p.m. and 6 p.m.', followed by the name and address of his hotel. At Newmarket he writes to his owners every week, telling them how the horse is, and almost what it's eaten that day. The owners love it.

After a while, I'm in a routine. I've lived for a year now with the language of racing stables, and I think in 'lots' and 'strings', and the names of gallops – Warren Hill, Waterfall, Bury Side. Most of the seventy horses go out for daily exercise, in two groups. One string goes out before breakfast, the second string after breakfast. These exercise strings are called 'lots'. Morning stables start at 6.30, then around nine there's an hour's break for breakfast, then it's exercising the second lot. At about one, when the yard's tidy again, we knock off and return for evening stables at 4.30. The day ends at 6.30 p.m.

In the evenings I frequently meet Hugh. He was upset that my career as an amateur never properly took off, and I can't quite gauge whether he's disappointed that I'm with a man he never fails to refer to as 'Slippery Sam' or, in plain short-hand, 'Slippery'. 'I expect at Slippery's,' he'll begin, follow-ing it up with anecdotes and send-ups of Newmarket pretension and skulduggery. Apart from Sam, Hugh loathes Boyd Rochfort and does a pursed-lips mincing take-off of what he's sees as the Captain's precious pomposity. Michael laughs and orders another bitter, then tells a story of Boyd Rochfort. Riding at the end of his string he put his head over a hedge, where children were making a noise in the garden. 'Pray silence, dear children,' the Captain said. 'Her Majesty's horses are passing.'

'Absolutely splendid,' Hugh says, throwing back his head with delight and huge guffaws of laughter. 'He really is the most awful snobbish, vain, pompous shit.'

I don't see much of Fergie's apprentices now because the yards keep themselves to themselves. Sometimes I pass Fergie when I'm riding out and either he ignores me or I get a glare. He failed in his mission with me. I imagine he's peeved about that. I'm glad I'm out of his way.

I'm seventeen and soon I'll be taking my driving test. Sam wants me to drive his van so that I can take the apprentice jockeys to race meetings and report back to him on the race at the same time. I go off to have lessons in Cambridge. David's at Cambridge now, on a grant. I go and visit him in his college. Although we're brothers, we're quite different in temperament. Already he's shutting himself off from everything that's happened, making himself very held-in and distant. I seem to wear my heart on my sleeve wherever I go. People tell me I shouldn't do this as I'll end up getting hurt.

I'm just having lessons to teach me to drive when my mother calls me from London. She wants me to go down there for a night as she's some special news for me. 'What?' I ask. 'Wait, darling. We'll go out for a meal and I'll tell you everything.'

'Can't you tell me now?' I've always hated having to wait, in case it's something wonderful, something that will mean we don't have to worry and be anxious or feel excluded any more.

'It's good news, I promise you,' she says. Now I'm even more anxious. Could there really be good news?

I travel to London and she puts her arms round me as I go through the front door at Burnsall Street. She's put on some weight, which surprises me. What's happening to 'Mrs Matchstick', as one of my prep school masters used to call her? I start worrying, anticipating. We go into the small sitting-room. After the sweep of the Heath at Newmarket I feel confined. 'Is Peter coming round?' I ask. 'No,' she says. She stops, then says suddenly, 'Mark has telephoned me from Washington.' 'Who's Mark?' I ask.

'Mark Blow,' she goes on. 'Don't you remember the man who stayed years ago in Roehampton? You were very small, then.' Now we can't stop talking. I remember this tall, rather white young man. I recall him as nervy. Whether this was because of my father or a built-in part of Mark, I didn't know. Anyway he called my mother out of the blue and he sent some money for my brother and me. Then he sent her a telegram which read, 'Can I make you happy?'

We continue the discussion over a meal in the coffee bar opposite, in the King's Road. Mark is the son of Dick who has the villa. My mother says that he doesn't really get on with his father. I think this is a shame, as staying with Dick in that villa is so nice.

'The point is,' my mother says, looking up from under her red and white spotted headscarf, 'Mark will look after us. I've got to make my life again, and Mark doesn't want any of us to suffer any more. Particularly me, who's been through so much.'

'You don't know him, Mummy,' I murmur.

'He's the sweetest person,' she tells me. 'He's written me many letters already.'

'But why is he suddenly contacting you, now?'

'He fell in love with me in Roehampton. He saw some of Daddy's behaviour and he didn't think the marriage would last. But he had to wait until he was certain.'

'So once he knew we were at a different address, he called,' I mumble, still working it out.

'He got me through the telephone book.' She smiles a little. 'He looked me up, "Blow, Diana."'

I put my arm round my mother and hug her. 'I'm really happy for you, Mummy,' I say.

'Mark is quite rich,' she continues. 'He inherited a lot of money through his mother. I can hand back the family covenants.'

'That'll be a relief. But what does he do in Washington?' I ask, trying to get a picture of this man.

'He's studying sociology. He's thirty-three now, but as he doesn't need to earn a living he wants to go on studying.'

'He won't like horse-racing.' I try to visualise my bookish stepfather-to-be on a racecourse.

'He only wants our happiness, darling. You mustn't worry. I'm going to Washington very soon. And if everything works out – the sex, that is – then I'll marry him.'

'It will be all right, won't it?'

'Of course it will. He's in love with me. Mark's never been out with anyone before.'

'Thirty-three, Mummy, and no sex with anyone?'

'He was waiting for me.'

'And what about Peter?'

'Furious,' my mother says, 'but the relationship isn't good for me.'

Later I'm running it through my mind in bed. It's my mother's chance. It really is. She's always saying there's no place for a divorced woman. As she gets older it'll be more difficult. I'm pleased that it's the end of Peter. I can understand his anger at being replaced like this. But he's got other women, I bet he has. He doesn't exactly shout 'Monogamy' as often as he shouts 'Dostoevsky'. So that's good: it's good my mother being with a man who's not bitter, who's open. Who's really going to give himself to her. Mark will look after her, I know that. And I can carry on at Newmarket without having to worry.

I sleep. At last there's someone for my mother and there's a home for us.

It's not long before I've been with Sam a year. I get a car – a Mini Minor – bought with money sent by Mark. My mother's in Washington now. She's married Mark, but I haven't seen my stepfather – that's what he is, only it sounds strange saying, 'stepfather' – although my mother says I will like him. 'He's a darling person,' she writes to me. She says, too that he's made a settlement of money on her. She talks with great excitement about the Bankers' Trust, a firm that looks after it, and Wall Street, where she now has investments. I think she's all right at last. And it's true what she said: this security will be good for David and me too.

But I'm thinking hard in my high-up bedroom that looks over the strings of horses that clatter up the Bury Road. Do I really want to be a racehorse trainer? It's riding I like, and now that I've mixed with the racing crowd for nearly two years, I'm not sure. I like the open air and the Heath, riding across it and thinking of King Charles II watching his horses at exercise from his revolving hut at the top of Warren Hill, but nobody except me thinks of it like that. I'm happy with the lads and the apprentices, but once I'm a trainer they'd be on a different level. There wouldn't be any time for humming pop songs with them or playing cards. I'd have to talk serious racing – form, handicaps and breeding – and all the fun might go out of it. And I don't see myself being able to butter up owners the way Sam can. That's because Hugh brought my laughter back, and I keep seeing the funny side of everything. Like the telegram Sam sent to an owner: 'Horse ran beautifully – last.' I've enjoyed the laughter and I've got an instinct that becoming a fully fledged trainer could be a dismal disappointment.

Of course the gilded racing young I've met here don't read much and that's a disadvantage too. Nor do the trainers. Not at all. Volumes on horse-breeding, Tattersall's yearling sales, and *Horses in Training* is all I ever see on their shelves. I complain to Michael and Lavender. 'But what did you expect?' Michael says to me with an amused smile. 'You've come to the headquarters of racing.'

True. It would have been too much to expect to discuss the characters in *Martin Chuzzlewit* with a fellow cloth-capped trainer while waiting for our horses to strike the gallops.

'Perhaps I'll go back to London. It might be sensible to have some qualifications behind me.' Sensible, I say – that's because of my father; I've always got to remember to be sensible. The word echoes in my head. I carry the guilt of what he's done.

'Oh no. Newmarket's so nice,' says Michael. 'You'll miss the fresh air and the bars.' Meaning he, Michael, would miss all that. Michael's hooked on his evening wander to the bars.

I'll miss you and Lavender and Hugh and the mad talk in the yards.

'Do us a favour Simon,' says Bolton, a tousle-haired boy with black rims under his fingernails from constantly holding saddle-soaped reins. 'Lend us two quid till Monday.'

'I haven't got two quid.'

'I'll pay you back. My dad's sending me ten. It'll be all right.'

'Your dad's dead.'

'No, he's alive. It's my mum what's dead. You remember, I told you. She hanged herself on the washing line.'

'OK. Here you are.'

Bolton scampers off, hair slicked back with cream, through the orange door of the bottom yard.

I keep at it. I do two more months of riding out, going round with my bucket of clay to put on horses' tendons after the lots, driving to race meetings, collecting Sam's son-in-law jockey, Piggott, for doing work on the gallops – then as quickly as I left Stowe, I make up my mind. I tell Sam I'm going back to London. I'm going back to take the exams I should have taken at Stowe. It's evening, and he's got the gin and tonic clasped to his belly. His eyebrows dart up, the expression he has when he's on the alert for a new owner. He looks at me, and takes a swallow of gin. 'Oh, I wouldn't bother about those things. You'll do much better staying here.'

But I've made up my mind. I've said that I'll come back later, when I've got the exams, and Sam says I'm to come down and keep riding out when I can. We leave it like that.

Tugging at me somewhere is regret at what I'm doing. It really will mean no more riding over the Heath each morning. Or winding in and out of the belt of beech trees, the sunlight cutting shadows across horses and lads. Or going up the gallop where King Charles II had his revolving hut. No more strings of horses restlessly bouncing their stunted jockeys as they've been bouncing them here for hundreds of years. No more living always a little in history. I'd built up a background for myself here at Newmarket, where I feel safe, cosy. Now I'm letting it go.

And that's why I say goodbye to everyone slowly. The lads, Michael and Lavender, Hugh, and Hugh's gentle wife, the rich boy I envy, Lester and his wife, Sam's daughter Susan. I remember the hunt ball I went to with Lester and Susan and Lester pouring champagne over a tail-coated splutterer with a purple face who'd spoken too loudly about us keeping low company – by which he meant Piggott. Farewell to my apprentices and all the mad, mad talk. And more, the so much more that I'm going to miss when it's no longer there. Goodbye.

14

SOMEBODY'S SHOT PRESIDENT Kennedy and my mother's marriage to Mark is over. It ended while I was at Newmarket. She'd come over to England with him and they'd rented a maisonette apartment in Ebury Street. I went there and met him – tall, wiry, sallow-faced and in one of those American suits that looks as if it lives in a pressing machine. We went round crammers together because Mark had told my mother that I must have qualifications. My mother said, 'Mark really wants to live in France. But I don't want to leave you and David alone here. I think we'll live there eventually.'

I thought how nice for my mother to be able to choose countries. But I wondered why they couldn't go straight away. Apparently my mother told Mark that she must be near 'the boys' because we're not old enough yet to be left on our own. I didn't argue with her because it might look as if I want her out of the way, but I've managed on my own for two years now and I'd quite enjoy going to France. Another thing that's tricky is that Mark doesn't like my mother talking at all about the past. If she walks down a pavement in Chelsea, say, and mentions something that's happened there, he goes cold.

'The sex is working perfectly,' my mother says to me. It's true that Mark had never had sex before. She said he had the apartment in Washington soundproofed in case it made a frightful noise. It sounds shocking, my mother talking so freely about sex, but it's been a great help, too. It's made it all quite natural to me, so I'll never be one of those Englishmen who makes sudden conversational leaps because he doesn't know what to say.

But after six months in London, Mark goes. He sends my mother a telegram while she's in Cambridge visiting David, who's playing Hotspur in a production of *Henry IV*. My mother's just fastening his sword belt for him when she's given a telegram. It reads: 'Please return London at once, Mark.'

The 'Can I make you happy?' telegram is still in her mind.

When she gets out of the taxi, and opens the front door, Mark's waiting in the hall with everything packed. 'I can't go on with the marriage,' he says and exits to the Cadogan Hotel in Sloane Street. I feel nauseous. Sloane Street. Where we watched my mother's mother from the tops of buses. And it's the same hotel where Oscar Wilde was arrested. Mark's fled to a hotel in the street that's made my mother so unhappy looking at her mother, a misery in turn transmitted to me.

There's something bad about that street.

My mother tells me all this in the deserted sitting-room in Ebury Street, her eyes brimming with tears. There's no Burnsall Street because that's let and when the tenants have gone it will be sold. The past is past, my mother says, and Burnsall Street's the past. She says, 'I must start again. Remake my life. I will.' She's worn out, she's clutching at hope. As she stirs her tea, the tears fall. Yes, if she can, if she can, I'm thinking. The worst has happened, is happening... I walk round the room, from chair to chair. I go to the long window and she says that's where she stood the night he left; tears pour down her face. My mother can't think clearly. I don't think she has for days. Mark leaving is like a death where you go over and over events to see how it all could have been avoided.

'I wanted to make it work,' she says.

'What went wrong?' I ask. I don't know if I should, but I do.

'He must have discovered that I'm not well. He knew about the nurse who came round to give me the energy injection.'

'He shouldn't go because of that. If anything, he should stay.'

But now she's crying again and I say I'll go to the Cadogan Hotel and talk to him. She says, 'Oh darling, do.' Then I put my arm round her and she holds me close. 'I've always got you and David,' she says. She looks up and tries to smile. 'We must stand together.'

Mark's in his large bedroom at the Cadogan Hotel. He says I'm to sit down, which I do. And he sits near me dressed in one of those pressing-machine suits. He really does look quite Italian, I'm thinking, as he starts to speak. Yet in everything, he's one hundred per cent American. He never mentions his mother – Eleanor, Dick's first wife. My mother says Mark was very knocked by her death. She was Italian-Greek by origin and her family were very rich. One of the most elegant women in Florence, she was a wealthy, chic divorceé with a great apartment. Her lover was Polish and a cripple. It was Mark who told his mother that she ought to return to New York; give up Florence. Eleanor had everything packed and the lover knew that she was going. So that evening he came round and shot her, and afterwards shot himself.

My mother says Mark blamed himself for telling her to return to New York. It wasn't his fault, or anyone's, but I do see that's difficult to accept. My mother says Mark can't forgive himself.

The Eleanor story is in my mind as I sit there fighting for my mother. I tell Mark that he can't do this – he can't just leave my mother without any reason. I've got strong ideals and I believe in doing what you set out to do: no swerving, no ducking. But we start going round in circles, with Mark repeating and repeating that it isn't going to work and he can't go on with it. He doesn't bring up the subject of my brother. I say this because

David's been having an affair with Dick's third wife. It started before Mark's 'Can I make you happy?' telegram. When he found out, Mark went a bit wild with David. But he doesn't mention this today. He's cold, to the point, and nice to me. He's always been nice to me, only today it's awkward because he's being nice and leaving my mother at the same time.

'Can I give Diana something?' he says to me. 'Can I buy her some chocolates?' This throws me. I don't mind him calling her Diana to me. But to give her something now? When he's taking himself away. And chocolates?

''I don't think this is the moment for chocolates,' I say.

'Oh,' he says. 'Oh.'

There isn't much more I can do. Nothing, really. He's made up his mind. I tell him that it will finish my mother, but this has no effect. I've been with him for over an hour and I say I'd better go. I have to get back to my mother. So he gets up with a half-smile on his face, because at least he realises there's nothing to smile properly about. I leave him closing the door of his Cadogan hotel suite on me.

After that my stepfather of one year asks my mother for a divorce. It's a depressing time, hardly relieved by my mother having some money at last. None of this is over by the time I return to London. It's not long before I'm looking back on my two years at Newmarket with nostalgia, regret, and an urgent desire to get in my car and drive straight back there. But I don't. I must do these exams because my mother's got the idea that we've got to have steady, tremendously normal lives. I have a feeling that it won't be possible, at least not for me.

Can I have seen too much of the abnormal? I don't know. There's no one to ask. I couldn't ask Aunt Phyllie. It would worry her. I've got to keep up a front.

At least the money is making my mother independent. No more begging from relatives. She's told Uncle Tony that there's no need for his covenant any more. This wasn't well received. He said the covenants would have to run for seven years or it would mess up his tax position. So the covenants continue, except my education one, which ran out after I'd been at Newmarket for a year. Uncle Christopher didn't renew it when my mother finally came into a small sum of money on the death of Clare. No, not a bequest. She left her nothing, just this marriage settlement which was arranged when my mother was born.

There's a wait now until I go to a crammer. A whole summer. My brother's busy at Cambridge, so my mother asks if I can go to Sicily with her, to a hotel right on the sea. I say, all right I'll come. If she goes away somewhere she might recover from Mark. And it'll stop me thinking about Newmarket. I've been going back there to ride out, but it's not helping. I don't belong to the place any more and it's upsetting being there, and then not there. It'll be good for me to go to Sicily. Although I'm not into a mother-son relationship – no Granny Blow and Uncle Jonathan, thank you – Mummy's got to have one of us with her. She's not too pleased with David just now as she thinks his affair with Mark's stepmother might have put Mark off the marriage. She thinks David's let her down. But he hasn't, I tell her. After all, Mark was old enough to take it on the chin.

Days after Mark left, Aunt Elizabeth telephoned to ask Mark and my mother to dinner. Uncle Christopher is so pleased my mother's got a secure life at last. But no sooner had Aunt Elizabeth spoken than my mother had to tell her, 'He's gone.'

'What did Aunt Elizabeth say?' I asked her.

'She gasped several times,' my mother said. Once Aunt Elizabeth had recovered from the shock, she said, 'Well, you'd better come on your own and tell us.'

At dinner my mother threw a very emotional scene. Any hope that Uncle Christopher and Aunt Elizabeth might have had for a peaceful evening were dashed. My mother gave me a hair-raising description of her behaviour that night. She'd blamed David very dramatically for the end of her marriage, and as she did so kept swallowing more wine. 'David's wrecked my life,'

she said. Now Uncle Christopher has asked to see David, to
question him, but David doesn't want to be interviewed in this
way. He won't go.

We have to be very careful with Mummy now as she so easily
knocks people to pieces with a few words. I know it's the result of
all the suffering she's had, and after what Mark's done she's ultra-
quick to feel a wound. That's why more than ever now she wants
our lives to revolve around her – yet we're both getting older. And
that's why she's angry with David. It's difficult, very difficult. I
only hope she'll get over some of the Mark disaster in Sicily.

We arrive at our hotel on the sea. There aren't that many people
– it's a kind of individual hotel, no buses letting out hundreds of
tourists. A few people on the terrace and it's early evening when
we arrive so the beach is empty. A whitewashed bar off the
terrace is decorated with bamboo. At the bar is a fifty-year-old
blonde woman, dark brown from the beach.

I'm sitting at the bar with my mother. The blonde-haired
woman is talking loudly to the barman. Behind the bar coloured
lights twinkle like lit-up vines.

'There's only one hotel in Sicily. At Taormina, anyway. This
is it. It's so private. It's special. Marie-Louisa is a wonderful
person.' Marie-Louisa is the owner. A large woman, whom we
soon get to know. She sits for hours in an armchair looking at
the sea and smiling.

The blonde speaks with an accent that isn't Italian. She begins
to ask us questions and it's not long before my mother's telling her
that she's not well and that she's here to feel better. '*Sono stanco,
molto stanco,*' my mother says, giving the words a punch because
that's how Italians say it. She has an exhausted look. Sometimes I
wish my mother was on the stage. The woman tells us her name
is Lena and that her husband, Roberto, is an excellent doctor.

'You must talk to Roberto. You must absolutely talk to
Roberto,' Lena says. 'He will know.'

She talks of her life with her husband, a wonderful man who has never been unfaithful to her. She repeats this several times as she sweeps back her bleached hair with a large pink comb.

I sit there listening. I think, so marriage can work, then. But I wonder what Roberto has to say about it. Lena can't stop talking. I wonder if he ever talks. Four men come into the bar. They wear jewellery and make a lot of gestures with their arms. As they walk their bottoms swing and lilt, rise and fall.

'Italian pansies,' my mother says. I stare, unable to associate them with anything I know.

I lie on the beach sunbathing. At one o'clock we have lunch on the terrace. My mother's not drinking at the moment. She's getting calmer too. It's the sun that's the strongest drug for my mother. In the sun she doesn't need any other.

We have long lunches. We've met a very smart in-the-news fashion designer and her husband. Mary has a shop on the King's Road and her husband, Alexander, owns a restaurant. I think they're tremendously sophisticated. He smokes lots of French cigarettes and tells funny stories. My mother returns to the beach but I sit on the terrace talking. Alexander orders more wine and tells me about the con men and cads who hang about Chelsea. They're all his friends, too. I listen and laugh.

Alexander has seen my father. Mary's shop is below the office of Mr Whelan, who sells my father's houses. He thinks of my father as a Regency character. Some days he seems flush with money, and the next day not a bean. I don't tell him any more. I don't want to stop laughing.

The Italian pansies come into the bar and start dancing the cha-cha, twisting their bodies, exaggerating every gesture. I watch them out of a corner of my eye. I'm intrigued.

Two days later my mother tells me about her visit from Roberto. 'Did he prescribe any medicine?' I ask. My mother laughs. 'No. He sat by my bed and said did I want him as a doctor or as a man.'

'And what was your answer?'

'I told him I liked him as a man.'

My mother has fallen for Roberto. They're having an affair. My mother doesn't seem to care about Lena: she's less important to her than her own needs. Mummy reminds me of the story of Mrs Stone. It's a film, *The Roman Spring of Mrs Stone*, from a story by Tennessee Williams about a woman of fifty looking for love. My mother sees herself as one of his heroines. I hear again her fear that time is running out. 'How old is Rome?' she says, quoting the scathing remark of the gigolo to Mrs Stone. 'Three thousand years. And what are you? Fifty?' My mother makes a joke out of it. I pretend it's a joke too. But the more I hear these stories, the more I'm trapped inside my mother's life. I'm beginning to see life as she sees it. The claustrophobic searching and impatient waiting. I'm not nineteen yet, and already I'm anxious about love never happening.

Three weeks later we're back in London. Now we're living in Donne Place, a cul-de-sac not far from Burnsall Street. Still in Chelsea, but closer to Knightsbridge. I don't like the house. It's a box with ugly inside doors that have plastic handles. My mother says it's got a garden but it's no more than a backyard with a surround of concrete borders. A little further up are four houses designed by my father. They're much nicer. But my mother doesn't care what sort of house she lives in: everything's temporary until the right man comes along. She tells herself he will. Roberto wasn't him. He gave her a moment of affection until Lena caught him out, then he went back like a whipped dog.

Aunt Phyllie's been taken ill in Italy. Uncle Tony's flown out with her doctor from Harley Street. They've brought her back in a special plane for just the three of them, and we go to see her in the London Clinic. It's hepatitis and we think she may not pull through. In the winter she had shingles and she's over seventy now. She doesn't know that Mark has left Mummy. My mother's kept it from her. If she does die, we want her to die believing that everything's all right for us now, that Mummy's difficulties are over. I've not seen anyone near to dying, and looking at Aunt Phyllie propped in her hospital bed I notice that her skin is like yellow parchment.

She smiles, the dimples breaking out, as we go in, each of us giving her a kiss on the cheek. Her hair pokes out from under a bonnet. Next time the bonnet's gone and there are just a few red-coloured strands rolled into little curls. Otherwise Aunt Phyllie's quite bald. She talks quite clearly, but her arms shake a little when she lifts them. When she says 'if I ever get over this' a chill, a prickle on my skin, goes through me. My brother's filling her in on what's going on in politics. She listens and then looks at him, and says, 'What's happening in Europe?'

I think of her not being here any more. Aunt Phyllie's life is tumbling about in my head. Aunt Phyllie is walking in the garden at Hesse talking to a German baron. The year is 1912, and he is keen on her. 'You want to fight us,' Aunt Phyllie tells him. 'Zat is not so, Miss Bettell, not so,' he replies. 'Oh, yes it is,' she answers. I'm snapped out of it by David saying as we leave the clinic, 'You know once Aunt Phyllie would have said, "What's happening in the Empire?"' He's impressed that Aunt Phyllie can accept the end of her England quite naturally.

When I see Aunt Phyllie two days later she's losing consciousness. My mother, David and I stand at the end of her bed. I notice she's got shiny, waxy skin. I notice, too, that she's plucking at the sheets and coming out with sentences in fluent French. She's never spoken French before. What part of her memory can Aunt Phyllie be wandering in? We try to talk to her but she only stares and doesn't answer. I know she's sinking, and she knows it too. Her maid, Edith, suddenly bursts into the room with a freshly killed chicken from Peanswood: 'I thought Madam would like this.' Then Edith screws up her eyes as she realises that Aunt Phyllie is unlikely to want a chicken right now.

Two more days pass and then Aunt Phyllie's gone. That sitting up and talking and seeming all right often happens, the nurse tells us, but usually death follows. Once the plucking starts, that's it. Aunt Phyllie's gone. I'm glad I wasn't with her when she died. I don't want to think of her as waxen and shiny; I want to remember Aunt Phyllie at Ragdale, sitting on her sofa, all dimples and smiles, with her collection of silver cows by her elbow on the table.

Everything happens so fast after her death. Those visits to the clinic slip away fast into a vanished world. A day later there's the announcement in *The Times* and, within days, her funeral. Luigi's come at once from Italy and he drives us as we follow behind the hearse that's taking Aunt Phyllie's body back to Ragdale. Luigi doesn't talk a lot; he was too fond of Aunt Phyllie. I'm thinking of how she made England a home for him and now that's ended. And the home she made for Mummy, David and me is over too. I've got to adjust to Aunt Phyllie not being there, and that won't be easy.

The funeral's to be in Ragdale parish church. The old church that stands like a crumbling sandcastle of ancient ironstone above the hamlet of Ragdale village. The church, too, where we went on Sundays with Aunt Phyllie and where we giggled into our hands as Aunt Phyllie's singing went higher and higher in a spiral of tuneless descant.

We're to have lunch at Ragdale, which is now a country club. As our car goes through the Iron Gates, I see the little boy I was. As we go down the drive and pass Pat the cowman's house, I see myself crouched in the back of the red Royal Mail van and feel my excitement as the postman drove me to the Iron Gates, dropping me off so that I could walk back over the furrowed fields. The stableyard stands just as it was but there are no horses now and the tack room where I swung my legs is empty and abandoned. The yard seems forgotten; is forgotten. Inside the house the familiar smell of Ragdale hits me, but none of Aunt Phyllie is here. Aunt Phyllie's drawing-room is now the club's dining-room. There are dark, circular hotel dining tables everywhere.

That doesn't make sense to me. It's Aunt Phyllie's home – our home – I say, just as I insist she's still alive.

'We' is my mother, my brother, me, Uncle Tony and Aunt Jane, then my mother's other Bethell half-brother with his wife. My mother doesn't see this other half-brother a lot. After lunch we drive to the church. As we near the church I see for the first time that the Old Hall that looked over Ragdale church really has gone. The Old Hall where we shouted down the well is a rough field. Aunt Phyllie sold it to a tennis court firm. The bricks were ground down to make floors for courts.

Luigi, wearing a suit, shoulders the coffin. He's wearing dark glasses and I know that's because he's upset.

The small country church is filled but I don't notice the other people because I'm sitting in the front pew staring at the coffin. That's where she is now, Aunt Phyllie. I wonder about the dimples on her cheeks. I keep imagining her back alive. Five days ago she died, that's all. I can hear her laughter. I can see Luigi standing by her armchair at Peanswood telling her how much the pigs fetched at Battle market. 'Oh, that is good,' says Aunt Phyllie. 'We'll come and see the little baby ones tomorrow.' I'm sitting opposite her, watching her talk to Luigi.

The service ends and we file out behind the coffin. My mother goes first, and then David and me. At the side of the church just by the door, Uncle Philip's sundial has been lifted off and moved to one side. There are the graveside prayers, the noise of earth hitting the coffin and Aunt Phyllie is committed to her last resting place. After that everybody drifts away.

But I go on thinking about Aunt Phyllie and pretending she's still here.

Now I'm back at school. Or a kind of school. It's a tutorial place in Fulham and every morning I walk there from Donne Place. Coming home, I'm walking down the King's Road and I see this tall man coming towards me. He stops and stares into the skies, then, making jerky flinging movements, carries on. I realise at once it's my father. What am I to do? He mustn't see me. I'm nervous at avoiding him and nervous that he'll see me. Trembling inside, I dart into the first shop and hide.

I wait until he's gone past. It's strange cutting one's own father. And that's another, a new way in which I'm isolated. My friends at the crammer's have all got fathers. They talk about them, and their mothers, too. They all live together. I listen but I can't be part of it: they've got a home life and I don't have that. I can't explain my kind of home life either, I can only keep quiet.

But that day in the King's Road doesn't end there. I see my father again, and again I dart and dodge. He's got a house now at the end of the King's Road. That's why I keep seeing him. Then one afternoon I see him and I say to myself, 'Go and say hello to him. You can't keep avoiding him.' Then I think, well, he's not really been a father at all. But suddenly I'm telling myself, 'Do it. Say hello.'

'Hello, Daddy,' I say. And my father throws himself backwards. 'It's me. It's Simon.'

Then he makes a leap forwards. He clutches at me and smothers me in a bear hug. 'My darling boy,' he says into my ear.

I free myself. I don't want him kissing me. Now I'm regretting what I've done but I'm trapped.

'Come and see us. Very soon. Tonight,' he says. 'I will,' I say. 'I'll phone you, but I've got to get home now.' The word 'home' makes him ask, 'How's Mummy?'

'She's all right. She's well.'

'How splendid!' he says. And I wince. 'Come and see us,' he says again. 'Come and see the baby. We've a little daughter. She's two. A sister for you.'

So they've had a child. But there can't be any money. And I think back to my mother's abortion long ago. 'That's nice for you, Daddy,' I reply. 'Yes, of course I'll come and see you,' and I smile, but not much, and walk away, then walk faster towards Donne Place.

I turn back and see my father in the distance, stopping, staring, his legs flinging about – out of control, but somehow each foot making the pavement, a St Vitus's dance.

I arrive back at Donne Place and tell my mother what I've done. She's worried: 'Now you've brought him into our lives again.' But I tell her that he has his new wife, Catherine, and a baby of two years old. I say I feel sorry for him – a bit, that is – as I don't think he's well. And that it was getting difficult as every time I go down the King's Road there he is, and I'm tired, embarrassed at hiding from him in shops.

David's angry too. He doesn't understand why I said hello. He gets quite hysterical about it. So I should have gone on ignoring him: but it's too late.

I'm depressed and cut-off by their refusal to sympathise. David won't come and see Daddy. He gives me a hard, stony-faced look and says, 'He's a dreadful man. What he's done is unforgivable.' I'll have to go on my own.

Perhaps any news of my father or Uncle Jonathan can only be bad. I've run into Uncle Jonathan too. I'd set off for the horse trials at Badminton and wandering across the fields I saw this man coming towards me. I could see by the swagger it was Uncle Jonathan. He was with a girl, his brown trilby hat tilted over his forehead.

'Uncle Jonathan,' I said, and he drew back as if he'd never seen me before in his life. So I said, 'I'm Simon ... Simon Blow ... your nephew.'

At this he breaks into an enormous welcome. The girl teeters and says, 'What a strange family you are, you don't even know your own nephew.' Uncle Jonathan beams and spits through his teeth, 'My dear Simon, how simply tremendous to see you.'

Like my father, everything's over the top.

'You must come to Hilles. Come at once.' He turns back to the girl. I can see that he doesn't want her attention to stray but he wants to impress her by showing how genuinely pleased he is to see his nephew. So he says to me, emphatically, by way of a parting remark: '*Any* time. Just telephone.'

A few weeks, or a month goes by, and I telephone Hilles. I've never telephoned the family home before. I haven't even been there since Granny Blow's funeral. That was eight years ago, and seems like two hundred. But it couldn't feel like a home to me, even though it was built by my grandfather. I know he loved my father and was so proud he wanted to be an architect. But he died when my father was twenty-three. Perhaps that was the trouble.

Now Uncle Jonathan's speaking.

'It'll be very nice indeed to see you. And bring a girl if you want.'

I'm to bring a girl if I want to. But there was a tone in the voice that said 'I might want the girl you bring.' Well, I'm not pimping for Uncle Jonathan.

It takes me back to when I was little. Uncle Jonathan strides up and down, round in circles, and up and down again. After I've been there for a few hours he says, 'What do you think your father would have done with this place?' I can't answer. Uncle Jonathan's bullying is still inside me. I'm eighteen now but that person I was, the person I often look at in those long-ago photographs, is here. Always here inside me. How am I to know, if I say what I want to say, that he won't take me by the arm and throw me across the room? What I *want* to say is, 'Why did you take everything? And where has it got you?'

Instead of which I say nothing. This allows Uncle Jonathan to go on talking as if nothing ghastly has ever happened between us. He asks me whether I think he should concentrate on running the estate or go into Parliament. 'Pretty easy, really, getting into Parliament,' he says, taking another stride. 'Oh, yes, of course,' is all I can manage. But I should say: 'You bungled it last time. You got up on the rostrum, the Tory candidate for

Stroud, and fainted. One heckle and you were down. When you staggered up and tried to start again, they heckled you some more, and you couldn't take it so you fainted again.'

I know I should stand up to a bully, because a bully is really a coward. But a bit of me is thinking that it would be cruel to make him face the truth. He's lived in his delusions ever since Granny Blow told him he was a genius. He knows the whole thing is rubbish, really. Later that day he swings back to the ancestors, Granny Blow's Tollemache forebears. Throwing his arm across the table, as if inviting me to stare at his veins, he intones: 'Better blood than most of the dukes in England when you've got ancestors who touched swords at Crécy.'

A young Italian looks after Uncle Jonathan. Francesco cooks our meals, otherwise there's no one in the house. I look at the life-size portraits of the Stuart monarchs, portraits I've not seen since Granny Blow's death, and wonder now what help they've been. Hilles has mystery and romance but it stops there. Hilles connects with nothing beyond its fantasy. Is this why Uncle Jonathan doesn't believe anything matters but ancestors?

Just as I'm thinking this he comes into the room. 'Shall we go and feed some beasts?' Off I go behind what I now think must be Uncle Jonathan's mock-confident swagger, his hands pushed deep into his jacket pockets. We leap into a car, stop to collect some bales of hay, and drive on up the hillside to a large grass field. We leap out and he tells me to scatter the hay about, which I do, and he does the same. As we drive through the valley he tells me I must go and shoot some pigeons with Francesco.

We pass Holcombe, a fairy-tale manor house nestling in a valley. This is the house that the gypsy architect – a landed squire by now – bought and extended, perhaps to be a home for his younger son. It's a place that is as enchanted as Hilles and Uncle Jonathan has just sold it. He's glad he's sold it to an outsider because he'd been worried that he would feel obliged to 'sell' it to my father.

'I didn't want my brother living on my doorstep,' he says. I feel a stab inside me. What about us? Has my uncle no morality?

I spend hours at dusk, crouched down, letting off cartridges. Pigeons have razor-sharp eyes. I miss, and so does Francesco. That's about it for my experience of farming life with Uncle Jonathan. Back at Hilles Uncle Jonathan is striding about again: he says we must all bind together as a family. I say that's a good idea, but I don't think there's a chance he means it.

Next day I leave and he tells me to come down whenever I like. 'Bring a girl,' he repeats. After that he waves me off on the drive, then he's gone.

David's been to see him too. He went down with a friend, just for a day, and got a lecture from Uncle Jonathan about looking after Daddy. He told David he must do more for 'Purcell' as he doesn't have much money. Coming away from Hilles David was white with fury, his hands clenched tight round the steering wheel.

I think, as I'm walking to the crammer's, what lies ahead for Uncle Jonathan? Will somebody want him as a husband one day? Is the big wide world ever going to proclaim his genius? Granny Blow told us that the world never recognises a genius. What talk. All she's done is destroy her family. Isn't she the cause of Uncle Jonathan's awful behaviour? And maybe it's she who's really answerable for my father's smashed-up life. I've got to work out this damage that's struck me too; I'm struggling to find answers.

I want to free myself and get back to something normal. At the crammer's I've made new friends – Charles and his older brother Piers. They're Roman Catholic boys who were at Downside. Charles's parents live on a farm in Hertfordshire and his mother remembers my mother when she was a débutante. When I go there for the first time she exclaims, ' I know exactly who you are. Diana Bethell's son.'

I'm often told I look like my mother, but coming from

Charles's mother it makes me feel less on the outside. At Hilles
I don't think anyone would know who I am.

Charles and his brother are ace skiers. Every year they go to a
ski resort for several weeks. I've never been to a skiing place – I
was always staying with relations. In Hertfordshire Charles and I
go out rough shooting. They have the kind of family life I've
always wanted but that disinheritance and my father's drinking
put an end to. I try not to think about it, because every time I
do I'm pitched into this awful isolation.

One day Charles asks me where the Blows come from and I
tell him about Hilles. 'It's really beautiful,' I say. I show him some
photographs.

'Who lives there?' he asks me.

'My uncle. He inherited, not my father. My uncle wanted it,
and he got it.'

'That's odd. I thought your father was the eldest.'

'Yes. He is.'

'So no Schloss Blow for you.'

I make a joke out of it. I say it makes you stand on your own
feet. But I don't feel that. It's just that I'm learning to wear a
mask. So when, a few hours later, we go to have drinks with
their neighbour, the exiled Prince Frederick of Prussia, who's
now a farmer, I've got to make it appear that everything's been
easy. 'Fritzy', as they call him, is tall and handsome, with exqui-
site manners. He talks to me with that earnest, 'I'm interested in
everything you say' face. I gather he married a very rich heiress.
Is that what I should do?

I often wish that I'd been born differently. I know there are
people for whom things are terrible most of the time, but they
seem more united than my lot. They have singsongs in pubs,
look after each other, get a laugh out of their troubles – like in
the melodies of the music hall stars, Bud Flanagan and Chesney
Allen. I know all their songs by heart. I don't think any of my
relations have heard of them, though. When, years later, I asked
my cousin John Tollemache's wife why nobody could see the

stress on our faces, she said, 'It was difficult to know what to do. These things just didn't happen.'

The day comes when I feel guilt at not calling my father, so I phone. His wife – my stepmother – answers.

'Oh, he'll be so pleased. Hold on. I'll get him.'

'My darling boy. Do come over. Come for dinner. It'll be splendid to see you. How wonderful.'

A week later I'm having dinner with them at 35 Park Walk. The house stands on a corner and there are several floors. It's the last of four terraced houses, all restored by my father. The others have been sold but he's kept this one for himself. That doesn't mean he's got some money because I soon realise that he hasn't. We have dinner in the semi-basement, but my father can't keep still. He gets up in the middle of eating, starts to go up the stairs, and comes down again.

'He worries a lot,' Catherine tells me when he's out of the room. I want to say that he's always been like that, but don't feel I should. My father tells me there's a big scheme about to come off, and of course he's anxious in case something goes wrong. When he's back in the room for a moment I ask about the two-year-old child asleep upstairs. That's my half-sister. They've called her Catherine, too, which strikes me as confusing. So I think of her as Baby Catherine. My father took me to see her when I arrived. He made loving noises at her and I looked on, aghast. Loving noises, fine, but how will he pay for her?

'Isn't she wonderful?' my father says, throwing up his head like horses do.

My stepmother says, 'He's so fond of her.'

My father sips wine over dinner. He's not drunk, but he's had enough to start him off arguing. After dinner, we're sitting upstairs. Suddenly my father's out of his chair and walking up and down the small room. And out of it on to the landing, up to the floor above, then back into the room again.

'I know I'm right,' he says out of the blue. 'It's important he wears a good suit for the meeting.'

'Well if you want to throw your money away, that's your lookout,' says my stepmother.

I don't follow the argument, except there's some middle man who's fixing up my father's newest scheme. When he goes out of the room Catherine explains.

'I've said to your father, "That man's a crook." Does he listen? No. Your father's already bought him a car. I don't believe all this talk about the garages. Not a word of it.'

Apparently this man, Hugo Kent, has promised my father that he can be the architect for all the Agip garages in England. My father insists that this contract is going to earn him millions. Hugo needs my father's financial support – it's a matter of giving the right appearance at endless meetings while the negotiations are going on. Already it's cost my father several thousand pounds.

Catherine stops talking suddenly because my father's in the room again. He darts in, his movements jerky, a cigarette between his fingers. 'I want Simon to meet Kent. I know he'll like him.' My stepmother says nothing. She sits there, very neat in her lime-coloured suit. I notice how carefully she dresses. Her red hair is immaculately permed. From upstairs comes the sound of a child crying.

'There now, all your moving around, going up and down those stairs, you've woken the baby.'

My father stands there, glaring at my stepmother with blood-shot, angry eyes. His upper lip is pulled like a visor over the lower. Then he's staring into nowhere. He inhales his cigarette. Now he's up the stairs again. 'I'll give her a hug,' he says.

My stepmother tuts. She lowers her head and shakes it. 'I'm so sorry you should see this,' she says to me. 'Your father can be difficult.' I smile. I want to show her that it doesn't matter. But I'm sad, because I see there's nothing ahead for my father. There's nothing ahead for my stepmother either and nothing for the little girl, my half-sister. I try to hide this feeling of oppression which is like a weight inside me. It's the weight of trying to find something to say when silence is all there really is.

'Perhaps ... perhaps the garages will work,' I say to my step-mother. She sighs. Her delicate long hands smooth out her skirt, adjusting it.

In a short while I'm kissing my stepmother good-night. My father gives me one of his gripping hugs. The smell of cigarettes and drink makes me nauseous. I promise that I'll meet Hugo soon. 'Splendid, darling boy,' he says.

I walk home down the deserted streets. There are no stars in the sky, only a muffled, cloud-covered moon. I keep on walking trying to push my father, the whole evening, out of my mind. But after twenty-five minutes it's still lodged there even more firmly. I'm in a tunnel with no way out, and I feel the happy friendships I'm making at the crammer's receding further and further. Friendships which are bringing hope of a normal life, wiped out by this evening I've spent with my father.

'You shouldn't have gone to see him,' my mother says to me the next day. 'I don't think he's well now,' I say. But she's right.

Since Mark left, Peter's started coming round again. He's spiteful because Mark gave my mother money. Even more cross that she's won a divorce settlement. He says she should give the money away – to the Labour Party – and that after that they should find a country pub and run it together. I know she's seeing him because now she'll do anything for someone's atten-tion. Anyone could come into her life, anyone. But at least she said no straight away to this suggestion.

I want him to go. He bullies my mother. He talks as if he knows everything. What he really knows about is dodging tax. He's hardly paid a penny in his life.

David and I thought things would be better now my mother's got some money, but it's not making her any steadier. I wish she could have had it earlier, at the time of the divorce. But now she's exhausted. She's like a hunted animal running from one hiding place to the next, hoping that God in the form of an eternal lover will rescue her.

She's starting to take heavier and heavier doses of barbiturates. 'It'll calm my nerves,' she says as she swallows three or four. Within hours she's wavering on her feet and words come out slowly as if it's hard to control them. Sometimes she swallows pills quickly in case she's seen, like a naughty child. I've been to see her doctor, as one weekend she took twenty-seven Nembutal pills. I asked him not to prescribe such large doses. 'Well,' the doctor said, 'your mother's a difficult case to deal with. One just has to jog along as best one may.' He shook his head.

She gets angry if he doesn't make out her prescriptions, so he gives her what she wants to keep the peace. Just as she's got to have her 'energy' injection. That's Largactyl. She takes the sleeping pills during the day too and balances them with Dexedrine. When I come through the front door, I never know how she's going to be. Passing out, or passing out and trying to cook me a meal. She says that David and I are going to be all right. It's her life that's been ruined, not ours. I don't say anything, but I'm relieved when I go off to stay with friends.

I'm on my own with her because David's at Cambridge and it often frightens me. What if she did take an overdose accidentally? I can't solve her emotional difficulties. At eighteen it's too hard. Far too hard. I want to leave the crammer's. I should leave home. My own life's slipping away from me.

On a bad visit to Rise she pretty well overdosed then spent all day in her room, sleeping it off. That night Aunt Jane and Uncle Tony had a dinner party for other local landowners and their wives. 'Surely Diana won't be well enough,' I heard my aunt say to my uncle. But by a quarter to eight I found Mummy sitting at her dressing table, carefully applying eye-shadow. She was concentrating hard. I knew she was intending to make it.

Cicely haunts her when she's at Rise. But no one knows that. And I think my mother's haunted, too, by the sort of man she should have married. Well, they're all here tonight. I'm sitting at the dining table, the running silver fox in the centre of the table. Men in dinner jackets and women in evening dresses are bending forward over the first course. My mother's not come down yet. A few moments later the door is pushed open and my mother stands in the doorway, dressed to the full. She stares at everyone, not moving.

'I think you should sit down, Diana,' Uncle Tony says. My mother moves slowly across the room, head held high, mascara ringed round her eyes, and slowly takes her seat.

Dinner is fine. My mother eats quietly, not raising her voice. But after dinner she starts demanding glasses of gin – on top of the barbiturates which haven't yet worn off.

'Don't give her any more bloody gin,' says Uncle Tony following me, one leg swinging, to the drinks cupboard.

'It will be worse if we don't,' I answer.

I give my mother the gin. She's on the sofa in the drawing-room talking to a rather shy county Englishman. After some sips of her drink I hear my mother say, throwing him a dramatic stare, 'If you feel like *changer la vie* why don't you look me up in London?'

Everybody hears – at least I think they do. The mild county Englishman shifts uncomfortably on the sofa. Leans sideways, as if looking at his shiny patent leather shoe. Looks back at my mother with a weak smile and mumbles, 'Yes, of course.' Then he stands up and says he must be going.

This starts the rest of the dinner party drifting off. My mother stays on the sofa, the mascara noticeably dramatising her, and sips her drink, leaving a rim of red lipstick on the glass.

Six months later I sit my exams. I don't like classrooms. I sit there with the clock ticking, and the days of exams tick like the clock. I'm nervous, worried. But it's all over nothing, I tell myself. I must stop worrying. It's the worrying that started years ago as I lay in bed with Fuzziepeg. Weeks later the results come through. I've passed. It's over.

Just before the exams I got a letter from Michael. He's in his final year at university and he's applying for a teaching job abroad. He says he may live in Nairobi. I wonder how he looks now. Is he still – yes – is he still as he was? Once there was no one for me but Michael, and Mr and Mrs Ivens – the parents I might have had. 'Come to Africa and join me,' Michael says. I wish I could.

My stepmother telephones. 'I don't know what to do about your father,' she says. 'I have to dress him now and tie his shoe-laces for him. His movements are all over the place. And as for that man Kent – I don't know, I don't. Oh, Simon, he's taking so much off your father.'

I wish I could fly out of windows. Second to the right and straight on till morning.

15

'He does so want to give you dinner at the Savoy,' Catherine says to me. I wonder where on earth my father's finding the money. Why wonder? It's nothing to do with me – not my affair. What I can do is to try and take some of the weight off her. She had no idea when she met my father in the drinking club that they'd soon be in this mess. 'He was such a gentleman,' she keeps saying to me. That's where she's gone wrong, this innocent redhead from Inverness, who thought it was all so simple if you married a gentleman. Because if any proof is needed that being a gentleman is no guarantee of reliable, I-can-handle-it behaviour, then take a look at my father.

I've met Hugo Kent now. We all met in a pub in the Strand. My father kept turning to me whenever Hugo Kent went to the bar to order the drinks, or went to the Gents. 'What do you think?' he'd say. 'Agip garages all over the country.' Or, 'He's all right, don't you think?' Or, 'Hugo says we'll have the contract any day now.' Or just leaning over me and saying 'Agip', as if the word alone meant millions.

The truth is that Hugo Kent isn't all right. He's annoyingly smooth and wears an expensively cut suit. There's a lot of bluster in his talk which my father can't see through. But my father is telling himself that it's all going to happen. I make out that I believe it, too. I smile and join in Hugo's nonsense because I know it's my father's last hope. And what if it turned out not to be nonsense? I have doubts, big doubts, but I can't be one hundred per cent sure.

My stepmother appears in the most extravagant gown for the evening at the Savoy. My father's put on tails, or she's put them on for him, because I know he really can't dress himself any more. We're sitting at a table in the darkened dining-room, with the orchestra playing and people dancing, but I'm hardly comfortable. I make polite remarks to my father and stepmother, but everything to do with my father now is sour for me.

My father keeps throwing his head up, dropping it, and giving twitches as if he's having electric shocks. He sits back again. Then his whole body jumps again. People pretend not to notice.

My father's delighted I'm with them. When he's sitting still for a second, he puts his hand over mine and says, 'My darling boy.' My stepmother wants to be seen, wants to have fun, so I take her to the floor and we dance for about ten minutes. When we come back to the table my father is wiping his eyes.

'What is it?' my stepmother asks once we've sat down. My father shakes his head: 'It's nothing,' but his eyes are wet. He takes my stepmother's hand. 'This is the last time I'll be with you,' he says. Tears run down his face. I'm upset, too, but I look away. I tell myself it's between them.

At home I tell my mother about my father crying at the Savoy. She doesn't seem to care. I don't understand yet about love dying, and I'm shocked. Once she would have said, 'What a terrible man', but now she just sits down on the sofa and says 'Oh, really.' My brother doesn't want to know, either. He doesn't want to hear. I'm alone with the problem.

My stepmother leans on me. I'm all she's got. She says my father must go into a hospital; she can't be at home with him any longer. He's quite young still, though he does look older than forty-seven. Haggard. Cigarettes and drink, I suppose. But that's all he is. Forty-seven. It's going round the family that he may not be well. Uncle Jonathan has called: he wants me to take my father to Hilles.

Being sucked into my father's self-destruction bothers me, because other things are beginning to happen. Better things. I won't be pulled down. I'm not trapped. Not any more. Aunt Phyllie left me some money: not a fortune, but enough to free me. So far I've been to Vienna with Piers, my friend from the crammer, and his girlfriend Arabella. Arabella's parents own a Schloss in a small skiing village, Zell-am-Zee, and we stop there on the way. It's the first time I've seen snow in a foreign country. I'm really impressed by her parents' house – it's white with little turrets at the corners.

Arabella's mother is a 'society' beauty. The first time I meet her she's wearing a kind of afternoon dressing-gown and arranging roses in a small white vase. I can't take my eyes off her white arms, white like china. She has a circle of literary and generally arty friends and Arabella's father, who's Austrian, earns the money to keep her living this way. At least, I think that's how it goes. They live in a big house on the north side of Hyde Park – the kind of house we might have lived in if...

But I don't want to talk about my father beating my mother, and the debts and the disinheritance. These things have made me an outsider to my own sort. I've got dreams about how life should be. Dreams that I will have friends who aren't cold and ungiving; who will tell me everything's all right and give me plenty of hugs, because that means safety. 'Tread softly,' Yeats wrote, 'because you tread on my dreams.' If we all could learn to tread softly, how different it could be.

'He's very eccentric, your friend Simon,' I overhear Arabella's mother say to her one day, as their maid is opening the door to let me in. Why should she say that? Are all my efforts to be normal and ordinary not working? Now I'm wondering what normal means. Am I an oddball because I talk a lot with my new friends and get very excited as if on a high? It's just that I'm on the run from the past, trying for a new life, so I'm like an actor auditioning for a new play.

But the past comes back all the time. I'm like King Canute impossibly holding back the tide. But the sea rushes over me. The hospital has diagnosed my father as incurably ill. They say he'll never regain control of his movements again. He doesn't know this. He's still trying to do architectural drawings, but his hand, which once was so firm, shoots everywhere. I feel sorry for him: this is how he's paying for his terrible behaviour.

Uncle Jonathan's just rung from Hilles. 'I want you to bring Purcell down here as soon as you can,' he says. 'I want to see for myself how he is.'

Uncle Jonathan's got a wife now. She's eighteen to his well over forty years, and she comes from Sri Lanka. I saw her at his wedding but I didn't talk to her. She's skinny as can be, but beautiful, with full lips. What will she think when she sees my father? I wonder what Uncle Jonathan's told her about him. I start wishing I'd come from a loyal, supportive family. I'm nervous, edgy.

I'm driving my father down to Hilles. He sits in the car talking. He doesn't really want to see his brother, so he keeps on talking about Hugo Kent and the Agip garages. I ask him about my grandfather. He says that when the crisis happened, when my grandfather fell out with his major patron, the Duke of Westminster, 'I had to sleep in Daddy's bed to stop him throwing himself out of the window.'

Our talk is disjointed. My father moves from one topic to another. He doesn't talk about my mother, he doesn't ask about David. He says that his illness will soon go. I think back to the night at the Savoy.

I'm going down the steep drive that leads to Hilles and as the house comes into view my father gazes at his boyhood home, as if it's a place he has no connection with. We get out of the car in the courtyard and my father goes on staring vacantly as if he's lost. Then Uncle Jonathan strides through a door under the arch and greets us.

'My dear Purcell – Simon – tremendous to see you both.' He turns and leads us inside.

My father hovers in the hall, still looking at the house like a stranger. Soon we're having supper and Uncle Jonathan's wife sits at one end of the table, dressed like a mannequin, giving unsure smiles. She doesn't say much. Behind us is the hall with its Stuart monarchs. Uncle Jonathan, his plate piled high with spaghetti, asks my father questions, endless questions. About his work, about my stepmother, about his little daughter. I sit there, pretty silent, watching the brothers.

At bedtime Uncle Jonathan says to my father, 'You mustn't smoke in the bedroom, Purcell. It's forbidden.'

'Why shouldn't I?'

'Do you want your father's house to burn down a second time?' At this they start arguing. My father moves round the long, wide, vividly patterned Morris carpet while Uncle Jonathan follows him. They circle and circle until at last my father, defeated, moves out of the room. Uncle Jonathan swings round to me and says, 'Simon, I think you should sleep with your father tonight.'

'No,' I say, 'that's not a good idea.'

'I do think you should keep your father company,' he insists.

'I'll sleep on my own in the room next to my father,' I answer. What kind of a scary night is he planning for me?

From downstairs we hear my father moving around his room – his shoes scuffing the floor – or rather, the room which was Granny Blow's. Uncle Jonathan, tense and ruffled, takes a bottle of whisky from behind a tapestry and pours himself a quarter-tumbler. He swigs it back, his face tight.

I'm not long in bed before I hear my father getting up. Every move can be heard at Hilles, every footfall. The wall that separates my room from his is wooden panelling. I hear him go along the passage and down the big oak staircase that his father made: it's like an echoing bell of wood, so thick and wide are the treads. My father goes half-way down it, then comes up again. He wavers on the landing outside my door. He's coming in, I think, and he's going to stand at my bed with those mad eyes of his, no longer in touch, staring down at me. But I hear the noise of his shoes on the wooden floor as he turns to his room, the room where his mother died and where Botticelli's spring goddess woven into tapestry by his father's friend William Morris hangs on the wall.

My father goes on moving. Lying for twenty minutes on the bed, turning over, turning back, then going to the staircase where his uneven steps twist on the oak treads. Halting, continuing, then halting again; stopping at my door, going on, back to his bedroom. All night I lie in my bed shivering, waiting for it to end. But the pattern repeats and repeats until the new day breaks.

'I'll keep your father down here for a few days,' Uncle Jonathan announces. 'He'll soon be all right.'

My father winces. He doesn't confront Uncle Jonathan. He sits silent in the leather chair at the oak table. He just says he'd like to call Catherine and I hear him on the phone telling her he'll be home soon. My father leaning over the phone in his dark double-breasted suit, his face long and sad. And this was the man who was once a brave cross-country rider, a winner of races, the heart-throb of many girls.

'Purcell, I'll put you in a guest-house down the road and collect you in the morning.'

Uncle Jonathan doesn't want to handle my father on his own.

Feeling drained, I go home to London to find my mother in the sitting-room at Donne Place. She's not interested in Hilles or my father but says she must go abroad soon. She breaks into a song: 'Nice work if you can get it, and you can get it if you try.' One of her Soho friends is with her. One of the 'real people' that Peter yapped about.

★

'And so Diana, I said to la Principessa, "Too much for the seaside, but all right for entertaining shits!"'

It's John Deakin, perched in an armchair, a goblet of gin and tonic in one hand, a cigarette in the other. Deakin's a photographer, once up there with Cecil Beaton, but now claimed by drink and Soho. He looks like a stretched-out gnome and he wears a shabby drink-stained suit over a black polo-neck sweater. My mother sits listening to the story. He pauses suddenly as if the words have got lost, drowned in their emotions. Deakin delights in his stories, which are often about his pick-ups and in particular the Italian male prostitute who refused his money: 'You're too good for money, Signor Deakin.' And Deakin throws his hands out like octopus tentacles.

My mother doesn't know much about homosexuality. It wasn't on the agenda at Rise Park, but she does know about her Uncle Stephen – Clare's youngest brother – who lies in bed at Wilsford, his face powdered and treated. Wilsford, a manor-house built by my architect grandfather for Pamela Wilsford, a dream in stone nestling in Wiltshire's Avon valley, where my mother grew to love Pamela – her 'sensitive' grandmother. Wilsford, now lived in by Uncle Stephen, his eyelids closed in a cocoon of thoughts – thoughts of his own beauty, all mixed up with the names of scents, a heartfelt poem, and the allure of soldiers and sailors.

'He's a pansy,' my mother has said to me of her uncle.

For someone who's been through so much, my mother's attitude to those who sleep with their own sex is unadvanced. Deakin's stories are helping to bring her up to date.

'Did you sleep with Prince Miko?' my mother asks, trying to be there.

'Diana,' says Deakin, gulping his gin, 'he was only six.'

Deakin has two great Soho sparring partners. Their friendship is welded together by catty remarks. 'And do you know Francis Bacon?' Deakin says, turning to me. He doesn't wait for an answer. 'I told Francis last night,' Deakin plunges on, 'that his paintings will end up in an ashcan on the Portobello Road.'

We take Deakin out for a meal. He's fairly drunk by now and his face disappears and reappears in a succession of different contortions. My mother is intrigued by him. He's been with Daniel Farson to visit Uncle Stephen. Dan Farson, Deakin's other sparring partner and a well-known television personality, wants to make a programme about Uncle Stephen. Deakin seized the opportunity to put Farson down.

'I know whose room this is,' said Deakin on seeing Uncle Stephen's drawing-room – a room drenched in silk, make-up and beads. 'It's Léa's.'

'How clever of you, Mr Deakin,' cooed Uncle Stephen.

'Who's Léa?' asked Farson.

'*Chéri* – Colette, you idiot!' said Deakin loudly.

Now Deakin's face gets closer and closer to his food. He raises it occasionally to give me some advice on life. 'Go in digger! Go in at the deep end!' He becomes incomprehensible, looking at my mother, then at me, his face like a tragic clown.

My mother isn't fazed by Deakin. She enjoys him. Soho and the bohemians have shown her that there's a life outside her background. 'Is it really all bottoms up?' she now says, bewildered and still a touch innocent about homosexuality. She laughs a little, then turns dramatic and says she's failed with the country houses. That's a reference to my father.

Well, she certainly wouldn't be able to play it calm and conventional at Blenheim as Clare did. I tell her she's moving on, and I see that I'm moving on too. I'm definitely happier going to pubs in the East End – sailors' pubs, pubs with drag shows – than I am making 'talk' in some stately house about the problems of inheritance tax.

Soho and the East End are a relief, too, after my father. Other people getting drunk, merry, doesn't bother me. I'm not involved. With my father it goes back too far, to the terror I wish I'd never been caught in. I keep thinking about what will happen. Park Walk's an illusion, I know, it's mortgaged. Hugo Kent's drifted off the scene: my father doesn't realise that he'll never be back. Nor will the money my father's given him, or the Agip garages. My stepmother is calling me now, desperately worried.

'I can't go on,' she says. 'Something's got to be done. Your father's up all night long – lighting cigarettes, dropping the matches anywhere. You've got to put him into a home. He'll burn this house down, and us too.'

I register no shock, simply fatigue. 'All right, I'll talk to the hospital,' I tell her.

I go to see the specialist at the National Hospital for Nervous Diseases.

'To be frank, it would be for his own good if you were to agree to a committal. You see,' the specialist says, looking towards the ceiling, 'he'll never be normal again. In six months or a year from now, he'll be a vegetable. And that's the way he'll stay.'

'Until?' I venture.

'Well, yes ... until the end.'

'Then he'd better be committed. At least he'll be looked after.'

I'm at Park Walk waiting for the nurses to arrive. I've been warned that the patient often puts up a fight but they're used to that. It will be a help, I'm told, if I can be there, as it's difficult for Catherine to go through with it on her own. It's about nine in the morning and my father's so pleased to see me.

'How wonderful,' he exclaims. 'Wonderful to see you, Simon darling. Isn't it thrilling about Agip?'

'Yes,' I say, the gorge rising in my throat. 'Yes.' I put on an excited smile.

'I do want to get rid of these mortgages – Agip will do that.'

'Yes, Daddy, that'll be terrific,' I tell him. He's walking about in corduroy trousers and socks, with his shirt-sleeves undone. We're in the sitting-room, the windows hung with dark velvet curtains – my stepmother's choice – but I recognise some things from Roehampton. There's a photograph of my grandfather and a watercolour copy of a painting by Gainsborough of a Tollemache ancestress: a woman in a silk gown in a windy landscape. My father walks round, stops, stares, oblivious to everything but the Agip deal.

'Let me put your shoes on,' my stepmother shouts from upstairs.

The doorbell goes and my stepmother comes down to answer it. 'Yes, he's in there,' I hear her say, but my father picks nothing up. Suddenly three men in hospital white come in and quickly unfold a stretcher. Before my father knows it two of them have taken him from behind, holding him in half-nelsons. 'What are you doing? Leave me alone!' he shouts as he kicks and throws his head around. I look away for a moment. I hear one of the nurses say, 'Steady now. Steady.' When I turn round he's on the stretcher and they're tying him down with canvas straps. But he goes on trying to shout and as they lift the stretcher I see that his face is red, the veins swelling on his neck. As they carry him through to the small hall Catherine sits on the stairs, and I can see she's in a state of shock. Only my father's head can move a little now and he shouts, 'Let me go! Let me go!'

In the street the nurses turn the stretcher towards the open doors of the ambulance and I watch my father sideways. There's defeat on his face, defeat and indignation, like a man taken prisoner. I stand in the doorway feeling dizzy, sick and dazed. I'm feeling guilt where no guilt should be. At the same time I think that no father should let a son go through this. Then my head's empty and I hear nothing but the ticking of tired thoughts. I watch the stretcher until the last sight of my father – his head, his hair tousled and sticking out, his neck veins still pulsing, as the men slide him into the ambulance. A hospital man darts round and the doors are shut.

The ambulance glides away, taking my father to Friern Barnet

Mental Hospital, which in former days was Colney Hatch Asylum.

My mother doesn't react when I tell her. She's numb over anything to do with my father – she's got herself to pull through. But she asks how my stepmother and my father's little girl are going to live. I say I don't know. She's exhausted, too, my mother, and I've noticed that she's putting on an unhealthy amount of weight. There are times when she's funny, sending herself up. 'I'm a slow puncture,' she says and she laughs. 'A slow puncture.' And when she's keeping her control she quotes the last words of her heroine, Nurse Edith Cavell: 'I must have no hatred or bitterness towards anyone.'

I've told Uncle Jonathan that my father's gone to this 'place' – a looney bin. Uncle Jonathan's written to me saying he's horrified. He thought my father seemed completely balanced, and that when he discussed the situation in the Middle East with him, 'your father made absolute sense'. He had hoped that nothing would be done in a hurry. Well, I think, you moved him to a guest-house in a hurry, all right.

Two weeks later I make the long journey from Donne Place to Friern Barnet. It's a vast overbearing yellowish-brick mansion set in parkland with tall conifers. At reception I tell them I've come to see Mr Blow. I wait and after some minutes I see my father coming down a long, never-ending coved-ceilinged passage with white tiled walls. He's wearing his suit as if he's in Bond Street, but his head is lolling on one side. He gives me a hug and says 'Splendid.'

We walk out of the building, cross the grass and sit on a bench.

'I'll be out of here in no time,' my father says.

'That's terrific,' I say, keeping up the pretence.

'They all call me "the Captain",' he says.

'You've told them about the war?'

'No. The others say I look like a captain.'

We talk about his stay with the Blücher family in Czechoslovakia before the war. He's talking about days when he was a great success, in demand everywhere. The Blüchers adored him. I'm sad that I did not know my father then. I'm sad that I'm hearing about it now, staring at the old Colney Hatch asylum.

'The Blüchers had the coat Napoleon wore at Waterloo,' he tells me. 'I sketched it one day. Count Blücher would hunt deer in the forests and some days I stayed behind and drew.'

'What did you do with the sketch?'

'It was burnt in the fire at Hilles.' He looks away, as if distracted. As he gazes into the distance, my mind drifts to that conversation with the doctor. How he said that my father can never come out because within a year he won't even be able to talk. He'll be a vegetable. I hate that description. The doctor said his brain cells are disintegrating: already half have gone. That's why he can't dress himself and why his limbs have been packing up for the last six years. The cells that tell him when to move his arms and legs have gone. It's part of dementia. Soon his mind will go. It all makes me feel pretty dreadful. He's paid the price now, and I don't want to judge him, I don't want to condemn him. There's no point. He's forty-seven with nothing ever to look forward to.

'I want to do some sketching while I'm here,' he says, suddenly swinging his head back to me.

'What an excellent plan, Daddy.'

Soon we're walking back towards the ugly building with its bland plate-glass windows and mock Italian towers and cupolas. 'I'm so pleased you came,' he says, throwing his head up. 'Tell Catherine I'll be home in ten days.'

Near the long passage, I say 'Goodbye, Daddy. I'll come and see you soon.' And he says, 'Absolutely no need. I'll be home in no time.' He hugs me, his unshaven face scratching my cheek. 'Goodbye, my darling boy,' he says.

I watch him walking away from me down the passage. He

hangs his head to one side again and his legs kick out this way and that.

Two weeks later my father's solicitor telephones me: 'I've got some bad news for you, I'm afraid. Your father died this morning. He had a heart attack.'

I'm numb – it's like a paralysis of thinking. Within seconds, though, I feel the calm, the quiet fatigue of immense relief. Dry eyed, I say, 'He can't do anyone harm now, or harm himself any more. He had to die.'

I go on seeing friends in between making arrangements for my father's funeral. I've never said much to them about my father and I don't now. It's as if I'm going to the funeral of someone I once knew, far away in another country. Uncle Jonathan arranges for the service to be in Gloucester Cathedral. This tradition, which started with the funeral of my grandfather, has to be kept. I wonder why. Granny Blow's pride? Family pride? A matter of covering it all up. Because there are so few who come, so few. My father had passed out of life long before he died. And as I join in the hymns – 'He who would valiant be' and 'For all the saints, who from their labours rest' – and stumble over words that don't apply, I'm hollow with awareness of the unreality of this burying. Only the choir in their starched ruffs, red cassocks and white surplices, their fluted voices rising to the high vaulted roof, bring back to me some innocence my father once had. The day when he wrote in his boyhood diary, 'Try to be a brick.'

After the cathedral service the big black cars drive out of Gloucester to the hilltop on the Hilles estate where my grandfather and Granny Blow are. An isolated windswept hilltop, but on this summer day it's still and windless. In the distance a grass and gorse-covered hill and, in the valley, the Cathedral and lines of houses and streets. We stand round my father's grave, Uncle Jonathan in a crumpled grey suit, white-faced but emotionless, my stepmother dabbing her eyes and wobbling on black high heels, and David and myself. Neither of us cries.

My mother's come too. Because we're here, she is. She has no need to say goodbye to the man she once loved because for her he died long ago. 'I'm food for destroyers,' she said after the years with my father. She's said it often. Perhaps the words have worn themselves out. Today she's detached, unhearing, as if locked away somewhere else.

I watch my father's coffin lowered deep into the moist brown earth. I see a worm ease itself out of the soil. The sun shines down on us as a cloud moves away.

After the burial no one speaks. We're to go back to Hilles for tea. Quite a few old countrymen who lived on the estate in my grandfather's day have come. One of them comes up to me. 'So you're Purcell's boy,' he says, his face creased and veined. He starts to talk about my father as a boy. Confiding and leaning closer: 'He was pretty free with the whisky on his twenty-first,' he says. I want to say, if you can't do that on your twenty-first, when can you? But I go on listening because he wants to show me how close he's been to my family. After a while, he looks across at Uncle Jonathan. 'You might have thought he'd have put on something better for his brother's funeral,' he says.

I look at Uncle Jonathan, too. I can see that beneath that severe mask he's troubled. I overhear him telling my father's lawyer that he intends to help my stepmother and my little half-sister. I hope he means it, because if my father had lived my step-mother says he would have been declared bankrupt within weeks. There was no money left, only debts, and he would never have got on his feet again. My father died in time. Just in time.

It's over. There's nothing more to say. We move over the Morris carpet like shadows. I want to get back to London. I want to find some happiness. It's possible, isn't it?

16

I'VE GOT A job in Paris in a French publishing house. Now I can shake off the past.

But what I really wanted was to write a film. I did a script and then rang up Diane Cilento, who's in a play at the Royal Court Theatre, because I thought she'd be right for the main female lead. She was really nice and asked me to come and see her. In her dressing-room after the show we chatted and I gave her the script. I don't really know how these things are done but a few days later she said she'd read it and invited me to the house in Acton where she lives with her husband, Sean Connery. I went over there and she told me I ought to see a film being made: one that she was in was going to be shot in Australia. She said she'd arrange for me to work on the set and be paid. I was very excited and I started having a whole new lot of dreams. Much better ones.

But the film was cancelled. My mother was relieved, because she wants me to lead a very steady life without risks. I know all her relations are watching me too, to see if I go off the rails. 'Well you know what his father was like,' they're waiting to say with supercilious nods. At least if I tuck myself away in Paris they can't get at me. Who knows – one day perhaps I will make a film, or write a play, or do something which the relations would disapprove of as being 'far too risky'. But how can my mother expect my life to be safe?

★

Uncle Jonathan's been to visit my stepmother. He went round not long after my father's funeral to see if there was anything he should take out of the house. 'Should' – the cheek of it. Catherine's afraid of him, or unable to stand up to him, and so he cleared out everything to do with my grandfather, and handed her a cheque for a hundred pounds. He's taken a watercolour by John Ruskin. I'm upset about that. It was a wedding present from my grandfather to my parents. Now it's gone. So I say I'm going to stand up to Uncle Jonathan, like my mother did after we were disinherited. I telephone him at Hilles from Park Walk, my stepmother sitting beside me. I ask him why he took this picture.

'I'm not prepared to discuss my nature,' Uncle Jonathan says in that clipped 'I'm so important' voice, and hangs up. I'm seething. Then I think it's better not to get involved with any of this. I'm glad I'm going to Paris. Whatever I've heard about the French, I bet they're not as bad as Uncle Jonathan. Perhaps he's done these things to us because he's terribly insecure. I'm beginning to see that. Nothing removes the pain, though. The years of his cruelty flash and burn inside me, like candles unable to gutter.

I'm sitting in a café on the Boulevard Saint-Germain, just round the corner from my lodgings. I've got a room in the apartment of an elderly French lady who's very keen on music and obviously annoyed because I don't play an instrument. But she's pleased I'm not German. '*Étes-vous bosch?*' she said as she opened the front door for the first time. I said no, I'm English. 'The bosch came twice to Paris, and me, I refused to move.' And she pushed her wheelchair back down the dark, cold passage. Madame Hammasser doesn't believe in heating, it's too expensive. My room smells of cats. Madame Hammasser has three. Cats and music are her life.

The doors of the café swing rapidly to and fro and a young French boy comes in. He sits next to me. He keeps throwing me glances. I sort of know what it's about but tell myself I don't. He gives a brief smile and I return it. Soon he asks me where I'm from. I tell him. My French isn't fluent but when he speaks I understand most of what he says. He tells me his name is Jean-Pierre and that he lives in a studio near to the Luxembourg. He's only been to England once, for a summer. 'I was in Brighton,' he says, over-stressing the 'on'. As we go on talking his eyes keep wandering over me. I feel good, as if a warmth is coming towards me. In a pause in the conversation he turns to me and says, 'I'll show you where I live. OK? Let's go.'

It's dark outside, lights everywhere, and the streets spread out ahead of us like fans dotted with diamonds. We walk nearly to the Luxembourg Gardens. Tall thin trees and statues make it a garden of shadows, silhouettes, ghosts. Jean-Pierre turns off down a narrow road with almost no kerb. The buildings seem to be swaying, leaning to one side and then to another. He stops, opens a door, and there's a loud click as he switches the light on. We climb four flights of stairs. He looks back, gives that smile again, and says, 'Paris is a city of staircases.' I smile, too. Laugh.

The room isn't small. There's a large bed made into a day-bed and further off in the room a table and armchairs. Because we're near the roof the windows are smaller; the view is over silvery roof-tops. I'm standing looking out when Jean-Pierre comes up to me. He has almost black hair and a slim pale face. His eyebrows are arched, pronounced. He reminds me of portraits I've seen in the Louvre of men in armour, their hands on plumed helmets.

His eyes look into mine and he takes my hand. 'You're nervous?' he asks. I shake my head. 'You look frightened,' he tells me. 'No I'm not,' I lie. 'I'm twenty, that's all.' He puts his arm round my waist and his face comes nearer, his lips nearer. He kisses me on the face and I close my arm round him. For the first time since Michael, peace surrounds me. The churning of my stomach isn't there any more. Jean-Pierre goes on kissing, finding my mouth, my tongue. He leads me across the room.

In bed he kisses me everywhere. And I kiss him back. As I kiss his arms, his face, his body, my lips striking places that bring out sighs, moans, all the nastiness of the years, all the uncertainty slips away. He reaches down towards my waist, his hand covers my erect cock, he takes it, caresses, rubs it. His head goes down, his mouth closing over it. And all the time, so much pain, hurt, vanishing.

Now I'm lost, lost, outside time, barriers, conventions. I want to get away, be free, not running any more like the silver fox on the Rise dining-table. Not running from all those gruff voices saying 'Simon should do this' or 'Simon should do that.' I'm going somewhere far away and I look back on what I've left behind and it's small, so small. I give to Jean-Pierre, give completely and he smiles as he takes me and I smile inwardly, quietly, knowing that nothing matters at all.

Jean-Pierre and I meet again. We drift through the city and he tells me that one day he will be a doctor. Just now he's preparing for exams and in a few weeks he has to concentrate hard so it's going to be difficult. I don't talk much about my life in England. It's better not to, I think. But I tell him that my father has just died and that my mother lives on her own in London. He says he's sorry that my father died; he must have been 'not old'. He asks what my father died of. 'A heart attack,' I say. Then, 'Shall we go to Versailles?' Talking of my father makes me anxious, starts me worrying again.

All the time I'm working in the publishing house. I'm like an apprentice doing odd jobs here and there. After a few months I'm sent to assist one of the managers. François is really nice to me. He's married for the second time. He knows a lot about French literature and when there's nothing for me to do he lets me sit at my desk reading. He approves of my reading French novels and sometimes we have lunch together. One night we go to Les Halles. We stay up until the early hours and he buys huge bunches of flowers for his wife. We joke about some of the directors. One is from an old aristocratic family and François says that when he sighs '*Merde*' he can get away with it. There's another who's full of airs. When he's left the room, François says, 'He thinks he's Napoleon.'

I'm learning French, as no one speaks English in the office. My mother rings me up from London and says she'll come soon to visit me. She hopes I'm meeting lots of nice French girls. I say of course, naturally. But I don't know many people in Paris. I know the family in the place I have lunch every day, where I get a really good meal for only fifteen francs. I know François, Jean-Pierre, and my American friend, Fred.

Fred is three years older than me and he's here working on a magazine. He's also writing a novel and chasing girls. I tell him that I've gone the other way, and he doesn't mind at all but says I should get to know girls. He gives me vivid descriptions of the girls he sleeps with. By the time he's finished I feel I've slept with them all too. Quite quickly he's become a very good friend and we see each other several times a week.

One day Fred looks at me and says, 'There's so much loneliness in you, Simon. You've got the loneliness of six people.'

I say, 'Have I?' and turn away.

Going back to my lodging that night I think about this. It's disturbed me. Is it because I've never known what it's like to be welcomed? Staying with relations over the years isn't the same as being welcomed. Aunt Phyllie was the nearest I came to having a home, and I hear her saying, 'My home is your home.' But Aunt Phyllie's gone. Jean-Pierre says to me sometimes, '*Vous avez tellement peur, mon petit Simon.*'

My mother's been over to Paris now. I introduced her to François and she spoke fluent French with him. She says it comes from her French ancestress, Madame de Genlis, the royal governess and belletrist who had a child by Philippe Égalité. This child, known as La Belle Pamela, married an Irishman, Lord Edward Fitzgerald, and their daughter, another Pamela, was my mother's great-great-grandmother. This makes my mother's fluency very romantic to me. I see myself in the court of Versailles talking intimately with my cousin, the Sun King. It makes the grimness of Roehampton days disappear fast.

I've one relation in Paris – Uncle Harold, who lives in an apartment off the Champs-Elysées. When my mother's here we have lunch with him. Uncle Harold reminds me of Tweedledum without Tweedledee. He's terribly friendly. We sit at the table in his sitting-room. On the wall is a painting of Clare, her hands enfolded in a muff, a little winter hat on her head, and smiling a real posed smile. My mother glances at it. 'What a woman!' she exclaims. Uncle Harold chokes. 'A woman more sinned against,' he splutters. It takes a while for things to calm down. After lunch my mother stops in Uncle Harold's bedroom on her way back from the bathroom. Uncle Harold is showing me a photograph of his father Lionel Tennyson, Captain of England, wielding a cricket bat. My mother goes to the mantelpiece and sees one of the many photographs of Clare that are dotted about the room. Poor Uncle Harold. The story of Beauty and the Beast swims in my head. Then my mother plucks up the photograph, faces the mirror with it and demands, 'And how do we compare?'

Uncle Harold stutters, fumbles with the ends of his waistcoat, and says nothing.

My mother can't let what Clare's done to her rest. Any reminder takes her back to the love she longed for as a child. She holds up the photograph to tell us that she is as beautiful as her mother, that her mother didn't discard her because she lacked beauty, but because her mother had no heart.

That night I sleep with Jean-Pierre. I don't tell my mother.

Susan, a girl I know from the crammer's, has come to Paris. She phones me from the hotel where she's staying. She's a tall elegant redhead – attractive, oh, yes, definitely attractive. We go out for dinner and afterwards sit in a café. Susan suggests I walk back to her hotel with her. When we reach the hotel she suggests I see her to her room. She opens the door and puts her face into mine. Next I'm kissing her and she shuts the door so that I'm safely inside. In no time she's kissing me, then leading me to the bed.

On the bed she's fondling me, putting her hand to where she feels my excitement. But I keep thinking, I want to get away. I'm excited but I still want to get away. It's wrong, I know. I could go through with it, but there's something not there. I don't know what it is. As I'm kissing her I've got that terrible churning feeling again. I tell her that if we're going any further I'd better get some protection. She nods eagerly and whispers softly in my ear, 'Yes.' I get up off the bed, straighten my clothes, and looking back at her leave the room.

I'm walking down the street now and I decide in a few moments I'll go back and not really look for that kind of shop. Instead I stop at a shop filled with antiques. There's a pair of golden chairs with swans' heads for arms. And a tapestry with animals – leopards and big birds like turkeys – wandering out of tropical trees. I move on down the street asking myself, how long can I give it? I stop by a shop filled with rare books. I think that one day I'll have a library and shelves of ancient leather books so that I can pull them down and read writers' thoughts from a first edition. What's wrong with me? I meet girls at dances and I tell myself I fancy quite a few of them. One or two come on strong, pressing themselves against me. And yet after an hour or so of this with their waving tongues going for my mouth, I start running off, thinking I'd like a rest ... or something different ... something quite different. Is it that I've had so much of this to deal with – women's demands, women's emotions, women's feelings? I don't know.

Slowly I turn and slowly walk back up the street towards the hotel. I go up in the lift, my hands wet with nerves, tension.

I knock on Susan's door. She opens it, naked with a towel round her. 'I'm sorry, Susan,' I say. 'I can't find any.' I can see she's hurt now, but I don't try to kiss her. It wouldn't help. 'I'd better go,' I say. 'It was a great evening.' 'Great,' she says very quietly. 'Yes. Thank you.'

I'm back in London, alone with my mother. David's doing post-graduate work in Iran and Peter's out now, out of her life. He'd been carrying on with another woman, twenty years younger than my mother, and so she kicked him out. But she's upset and that isn't helping her health. She needs someone. And she's still putting on so much weight. Bags of fat now on her arms. As for the tiny waist that I remember, it's only a memory. There are ripples of loose flesh across her stomach. She'll never again be as she is in the drawing that Stephen Ward, Godfather Bill's osteopath friend, did of her one evening at Cliveden. She pushes the drawing into her handbag when she goes to the hairdresser. 'Here, Jean Seberg style,' she says. That's the last image of my mother in her beauty. She must have been forty-three then but looked no more than twenty-five.

Now she's forty-eight. She carries on as if nothing's changed in her. As if her body's going makes no difference. It wouldn't matter if she wanted to spend her time gossiping with old friends about the past. But she won't do that. She wants a lover, a big-time lover. When someone said to her, 'But Diana you have so many friends,' she swung her head round dramatically and said, 'Friends! Who wants friends?' I know it's her hunger for love that's making her knock herself out with drugs or come down from her bedroom at night to devour anything sweet in the fridge.

A few months back David went with her to a clinic in Switzerland. It was filled with people fighting addiction. They made my mother do pottery. David spoke with the doctor and he seriously suggested: 'Your mother should take up a hobby. How about stamp collecting?' That didn't appeal to her any more than the pottery. Stamp collecting isn't a lover. She didn't even find it funny. There are days, though, when she sees the comedy, black comedy, of a woman who's past forty-five looking for love. It's when she's in a laugh-at-myself mood that she repeats the gigolo's remark to Mrs Stone: 'Rome. How old is Rome? Three thousand years. And what are you? Fifty?'

I do understand what she's going through. My father destroyed her faith in herself. When he was twelve, Michael said to me, 'Your mum needs telling how great she is.' I've learnt now that rejection is real and a killer, that there's only so much rejection a person can deal with. My mother's had too much – my father, Clare and Cicely – and it's cracked her. Watching her is unbearable, and I'm feeling my own life flash by in seconds. But I want my life. I'm twenty and being moved on fast, too fast.

With the divorce settlement from Mark my mother's bought a villa in Le Lavendou. It's a new village with groups of houses built in the style of Provence. My mother's is on one level, but with a view towards the sea from the terrace. She had the idea that she was more suited to living in France. Cicely's words are always with her, 'No Englishman will ever want you. You're far too emotional.' But the little villa isn't used. My mother can't drive and it's up in the hills. She's been there a few times, but last time she had a crack-up and a neighbour friend took her to the hospital in Nice. I travelled down from Paris to see her. I met the doctor and talked with him. He believes in tough treatment to bring his patients round: '*Avec mes patients, moi, je fais le boxe,*' he said to me.

The tactics of the doctor didn't work. What will happen to my mother? Can she be made better? I'm frightened by the questions.

My boss, François, is coming to London for a weekend away from his family. I'm in London for two weeks' holiday and he wants me to show him round. I've told him about the pubs in the East End and he would very much like to see them. He wants me to book him a hotel.

When François met my mother in London he saw her in a bad way. So that he wouldn't see too much I took him to the sailors' pubs in the East End, the pubs on the docks where there are jukeboxes and lads dancing with lads. He liked them. There's nothing like that in Paris. It gave him a break from married routine as well. He says it's important to break away. He forgets that I'm twenty and in spite of what I've seen I want to believe that people can go on loving for ever. I like to think that what happened to my mother and father isn't the everyday. If it is, I may as well stop living now. I fill my head with dreams to make sure it's all going to be different.

Late one evening François tells me that his first marriage came unstuck because his wife found out that he'd been homosexual. 'Can you stop being homosexual, then?' I ask. He looks a little worried and says, 'I've learnt to hide it.'

I'm surprised. 'Are there thousands of married men hiding their real selves?' I ask.

'Many more than you would think,' François tells me.

I'm driving him back to his hotel after an evening of pubs. I'm going down the Embankment with the black water of the Thames, dark but shining, on one side of me when suddenly François announces, 'That night we spent in Les Halles, I should have told you what I felt. The bunches of flowers I bought for my wife, I should have given them to you.'

I don't know what to say now. I'm silent. I had no idea, and I'm embarrassed. Advances that I don't want to reciprocate I find hell. Fortunately, after a few moments, François saves the situation. Perhaps he's picked something up from my reaction.

'I should have kissed you, not her,' he carries on, then pauses and smiles. 'But it's all right, dear Simon, because now we're friends.'

I'm thinking of Mike at Burnsall Street, playing *The Dam Busters* march and saying that nothing is black and white.

François sees my mother taking pills, mixing them with alcohol, and all the dramatic turns that follow. She tells him about life being like a boxing match and it's a matter of how many times you can stand up again. Later, back in Paris, he says to me, 'Your mother is a brave woman, but she's someone who no longer has anything to cling to. It's tragic.'

But she does. She clings to David and me. More to me, because David's moved out of Donne Place to live in Hampstead. If he's with us and she starts to be difficult he leaves the house and I'm left there trying to manage Mummy and fight for a life of my own.

There's a life in Paris for me. I've got my friend Fred, and he's working on a novel. I'm wondering if I shouldn't do the same but there are too many young men writing novels, and I think I'd better find out what this grown-up world I'm entering is really like. Already Jean-Pierre has drifted away and I'm learning for myself that maybe people aren't constant, are not reliable. In one café I go to there's always a group of wise old queens. They know me and when I pass they beckon me to sit with them – flattering me and looking at me because I'm young. One of them, Austen, lives in a cheap hotel off the Boulevard Saint-Germain and has teeming, mad ideas. He holds his hotel room key up when he talks as if he's conducting life. He can't stop quoting Francis Thompson's poem 'The Hound of Heaven', about finding God. Everything's in this poem, he says, and off he goes – 'I fled Him, down the nights and down the days; I fled Him, down the arches of the years' – his key waving. Another of these old queens, Richard, wears a well-cut suit, highly polished shoes, and a genuine Cartier watch. There's a story that he once picked up a male prostitute who attempted to rob him after he'd been paid. He was about to take the Cartier watch when he noticed the enamel face with Roman numerals, and threw it down again saying, 'That's too old-fashioned. It's worthless.'

I sit with them for a bit, until I find their own loss, dressed up in manic laughter, hard to bear.

Often at night I walk the boulevards alone. I look up at the apartments and wonder if I will ever live in one and think how nice it would be to have a fine apartment here and sit staring for hours at the Seine. During the days I have no time to dream. I must be in the office by nine o'clock. The office day ends at 5.30 and then, but not always, I dream.

Soon my time in Paris will end. Austen, who also tells fortunes, foresaw a long involvement for me here. Waving his hotel key in my face he said, 'You will be running one of the largest publishing organisations in Paris.' I don't know where he got his psychic information from because so far I've been given no real responsibility beyond being in on time. *'Monsieur Blow, les horaires!'* one of the directors rebukes me. It's ten past nine. So I've lost ten minutes of reading Proust, I say to myself, as I climb the stairs to the office I share with François.

England is far, so far, and then all at once it's close. Reading of the narrator's childhood in Proust for the first time, I think of Hilles again. The narrator's bite into the little cake, the madeleine, takes me back too. I'm watching Granny Blow as she makes scones in the kitchen at Hilles, adjusting and poking her curl of white plaited hair with floury hands. I see Uncle Jonathan stride with swaggering steps through the house, and I see and hear Aunt Luty, Granny Blow's handmaiden, hovering round her mother. 'Oh, Mummy. Oh, Mummy,' she bleats. Now Uncle Jonathan forces my six-year-old arm down a sick calf's throat. 'You little coward,' he shouts. 'Put your arm there!' and he pulls my arm. I stand shaking in the dark shed, believing that the calf will bite my arm off. Will swallow it.

François, sitting at the other end of the room, notices my eyes drifting away from the page. 'Is that the effect of Proust on you?' he asks.

Later that day I ask myself, 'Will these people ever lie down? Be quiet?'

I'm in my familiar café. It's early evening, and I'm sitting there pensively. The wise old queens arrive and I half concentrate as they say hello. A man with them starts talking to me. He's much younger than they are, about twenty-six. He has dark curly hair and bronze brown eyes. He asks me why I'm looking worried, as if the world will end. I look up. 'But I'm not worried,' I protest. 'It's just how I look when I'm thinking.'

'And how do you look when you're not thinking?'

'I don't know,' I say. 'If I look in a mirror I start thinking.'

'You come from the North. I come from the South,' he goes on and as he talks his dark eyes glitter like a deep well in sunlight. 'In the South we smile. The sun smiles and we smile.'

Why's he taking this interest in me? I'm sitting there thinking other thoughts – his dark eyes, Susan whom I let down – and he starts to talk about French writers.

'You must read Gide,' he says, *'Les Nourritures terrestres*. You need to free yourself.'

'I've read that one,' I tell him. 'I've got the message.'

'Now all you need is courage,' he goes on. 'Forget the North. You must smile.'

He's very civilised, very nice. All through that evening he talks to me. He tells me he's half-French, half-Spanish but that he was educated in France. He says he wants to meet me again. I say it's possible but soon I'm going back to England. He's on a month's holiday from the Embassy in Copenhagen where he works, and while he's on holiday he would like to see England.

'You must visit us in London then,' I say.

'Let's discuss that.' He puts out his hand for me to shake. 'Xavier. I'm Xavier.' I shake his hand and say, 'Simon.' His dark eyes stare into mine.

It's late and the café is emptying. The old queens have gone and Xavier says, 'Why not walk back to my hotel with me? We can continue our conversation in my room.'

'No. I couldn't do that. I hardly know you,' I tell him.

'You won't know me any better by staying here.' I look again at his eyes, his light tanned skin, and the black curls of his hair. I feel an isolation growing. That same isolation I felt long ago when my father was beating my mother and there was no one else in the house...

'OK. I'll walk with you.'

We walk together down the street, turning into narrower streets, the old buildings, greyish white and scarred, leaning above us. Xavier stops at a sign that's lit in yellow neon and starts to turn into a hotel. He glances at me and says, 'Come upstairs for a moment.'

'But it's half-past one,' I tell him.

'Yes. And soon it will be three o'clock,' he says, his dark eyes, glittering wells, smiling at me, talking to me.

I follow him upstairs because I can think of no reason not to. No reason that isn't cold and unfeeling. And I mustn't be silly, priggish, and cold – Xavier's right, I must fight the North.

Next morning I leave at 8.30. 'You are an angel,' Xavier says, 'but angels have to be careful not to get their wings damaged. You need protecting.'

In a few months I leave Paris. I shut the door on my apartment in the rue Saint-Rustique, a street tucked in behind the Place du Tertre in Montmartre, where Renoir painted. I've had the apartment for a year, and I've been in Paris for a year and a half. Every day except Saturdays and Sundays I've taken the Métro across Paris to the 19th arrondissement. I've sat at my desk reading novels when not ordering paper or running through a proof. François has been a good friend, far more a friend than a boss. My French is fluent now; there's been no one here apart from Fred to speak English with. I've had the occasional dinner with Uncle Harold. But when I'm with him I always have to act as someone I'm not. I couldn't talk about my feelings or my life.

So I play conventional, or have a stab at it. And then there's been walking the streets, the boulevards, drifting from café to café, the meals in my little restaurants, the Sundays wandering in art galleries, watching the leaves change colour in the Tuileries gardens. Yes, the long, long days, and often the long, long nights of being alone.

Xavier's gone on ahead to London, where he's staying with my mother. He's so polite that I thought she would be pleased. She is, and when I arrive they seem to have become friends. She doesn't appear to know anything of what's going on between us and I'm certain he won't have told her.

'I want David and Simon to choose sensible girls who will make them both happy,' she says to Xavier. Then she tells him that her life is over, a ruin, but that we will be all right. She's made sure of that.

I go along with it, but I'm thinking, how does Mummy know? She can't know we're going to be all right.

I give Xavier a tour of England. I take him to Cambridge and we walk round the colleges. Later that evening he says, 'Simon, can you do me a great kindness and lend me some money. My money is delayed, but it will arrive soon. I'll pay you straight back.'

I've already lent Xavier a small sum in London and I say, 'You really will pay me back, won't you?' Suddenly he rounds on me and says, 'What are you suggesting?' I retreat, tell him he's being absurd, ridiculous. That I'm not suggesting anything.

Xavier and I are back in London, living in Donne Place. He's very gentle and thoughtful with me as my mother is having a breakdown. I can't make out what's brought it on, but the signs are always the same. She cries a lot, is up eating throughout the night, and knocking herself out with pills in the day. Her doctor is sending her to the Priory, a nursing home a few streets away from Roehampton Lane. Once she's gone I'm alone in the house with Xavier and we pass the days going to galleries and museums. I'm starting to relax, too, and Xavier says that in the

summer, when he has two weeks' holiday, we're to go to Tunisia.
After three days or so, I say I'm going to visit my mother and we
make a plan to go to the cinema that evening when I return. I
leave Xavier at the underground station and he says that he will
see me back at the house later.

But the house is double-locked when I get back. Strange, I
think, it's never double-locked unless we're all away. I manage to
lever open a window at street level. I climb in. The sitting-room
is quiet; the whole house is quiet. I shout, 'Xavier! Xavier!'
There's no response. No sound: a terrifying stillness. Everything's
as it was, nothing missing, nothing that I see. Then I notice that
several French paperbacks are missing from the shelf in the
sitting-room. I'm puzzled, suspicious. Why take books? That is,
if I'm right. I go upstairs to my bedroom and open my cupboard.
Two suits have gone. Now I'm in a panic. I know what's happened but I can't accept it. *Be careful your wings don't get damaged.*
You're an angel. You need so much affection. Yes. Yes. I go into my
mother's bedroom and open a drawer in her writing desk where
I keep a brooch Aunt Phyllie left me – a diamond and enamel
racehorse. Not there. My gold wristwatch. Not there.

Xavier is a thief. He tricked me. Oh, well, I say. But I feel a
fool – and that's the worst bit: a fool for having believed in him.
But how could I have known? What is it Pascal says? 'All the
unhappiness of men comes from one single thing, which is their
inability to be at ease in a room.' But we've got to leave our
rooms. I let myself go adrift: I left my room. Now I'm utterly
dejected.

I don't tell anyone because I'll just appear a complete fool. I
let someone into my heart, a person who coldly saw the fool in
me. And so tricked me. No fun this, at twenty-one, or any age.
I hear the cackling of the wise old queens.

My mother's out of the nursing home now. She's better, but
how long will it last? Questions again. David comes over and

discovers that Xavier took some of his clothes too. I tell them what happened, but I don't mention the nature of the relationship. Except my brother says that Xavier told my mother about it when he was alone in the house with her. She's never said a word to me. David thinks it might have partly caused her breakdown, that she knew something she'd rather not know. He said she had hallucinations that she saw me coming down the stairs covered in blood.

I don't know what to do. I apply myself to finding a job. I don't want to sleep with any more men, I'm going to sleep with girls from now on. If I get a sensible job then everything will go back to normal. Hang on. How am I to know what normal is?

In Soho I meet John Deakin. 'Dig in digger,' he keeps telling me. 'Go in at the deep end.' Apparently Dan Farson is giving up his house on the Isle of Dogs and I think I might take it. It's a river bargeman's house fronting the Thames and the rent is cheap. It would get me away from home and I could pay for it out of the small amount of money Aunt Phyllie left me. I'd be spending capital, but that advice from old buffers about 'never touch capital' is fine only if you've got enough not to touch. It doesn't apply to me. It never will. So I tell Dan I'm interested and he takes me over the place.

Dan's amused. West End boy goes East is how he sees it. Is that what I am? So many categories and divisions. Deakin upsets the plan by telling Dan I don't want to buy any of Dan's mother's 'awful furniture'. I never said that, in fact, but it's too late. There's a scene in the French – one of Dan's Soho haunts – when Dan, fairly plastered, turns on me. In the background Deakin is grinning, gin and tonic clasped in one hand.

So I stay on at home – by which I mean Donne Place. Neither Burnsall Street nor Donne Place is home as other boys that I know have homes. It's not like staying with Charles in Hertfordshire. There's no skirting of woods, rough shooting or dining with jovial neighbours. Some evenings my mother goes down the street to a pub where there's a piano. Sometimes I go with her. She taps the pianist on the shoulder and says, 'I would like you to play "Stranger in Paradise" for me.' My mother stands there swaying to the tune, her face in a dream as if she's holding the eternal lover in her arms.

There is no one in her life now. Not a word from Mark since he vanished. A year after he'd gone he rang Uncle Tony to tell him that the money he gave my mother was pure charity. That was another hurt for my mother to sustain. I don't think he'll ever contact her again. My mother's stopped thinking about him. The barbiturates help.

There's so much my mother doesn't want to face any more. 'The winds grow colder, and suddenly you're older,' she keeps quoting. That, and 'How many times can a person stand up again?' But the French doctor's boxing treatment isn't right for her. I've got to keep her dreaming. She knows the reality too well.

She cries so easily, dabbing the flow with a handkerchief that gradually blackens from running mascara. Then she'll say, 'I must pull myself together. No more doing a Wyndham.' That's a reference to her grandmother Pamela, who cried a lot too. Pamela partly brought her up and my mother loved her. But Pamela's life was cushioned. Are tears hereditary? I believe my mother would cry less if things had been different.

17

I'M TWENTY-TWO and ghosts are all around me. Ghosts. Places of childhood that never come again. People gone. Places gone. Every place and every person leaving something. I can't make anything disappear without a trace. We don't go to Scotland, to Glen now. Uncle Christopher has given the house and estate to Colin, his heir, and built a house for himself and his wife, solid dependable Aunt Elizabeth, in Corfu. We don't go much to the Tollemache cousins either. Once we were always with them. The four boy cousins, children of my father's first cousin John, who shoot and fish and sail and live at Helmingham Hall in Suffolk, the house with a moat and a drawbridge that goes up every night.

We went to Helmingham together a few years back, my mother and I. My mother, her life so different, forgot to leave a tip for the staff. So in her thank-you letter she put some notes and lots of loose change. The letter burst open and was resealed by the Post Office. My mother forgot, too, that with the loose change it would weigh more than a normal letter. So the resealed envelope was presented to Cousin John by the butler with, 'There'll be extra postage to pay, my lord.' John's wife, Dinah, wrote to my mother, 'John still hasn't recovered from the shock.'

That's why Mummy can't pick up the past. She's gone beyond it into a place where country houses and all the niceties – good behaviour, what you say and what you don't say – aren't recognised. Then suddenly Bill Astor will ring up. He'll ask how she is, they'll have a brief conversation, and that will be it. No plans to see him. None. Someone who's been her friend since she was eighteen. But that doesn't matter to her.

My godfather's had a stroke. There's been a scandal at Cliveden. Stephen Ward, the artist and bone doctor who drew my mother, has been up on a charge of living off immoral earnings. Godfather Bill had given him a cottage on the estate and Ward was taking 'his girls' to Bill Astor's swimming pool where they and my godfather and all played around. A government minister was involved and the whole thing blew right up in my godfather's face. 'Poor Bill,' my mother says. She rocks with laughter, finding the scandal very funny.

Anything that goes beyond the normal boundaries appeals to my mother. She likes to see convention turned on its head. Except, that is, where my sexuality is concerned. She says that David and I are going to find wonderful wives and be wonderfully happy. Meanwhile we have to watch her going under emotionally. I wish so much she could find some strength again. There's a nosy neighbour who lifts her white curtain every time she spots my mother going by. 'I saw Diana Blow. She looked a little odd,' I overheard this woman gossiping one day. 'I see very strange people going to her house,' she went on. 'Yes,' I wanted to butt in. 'My mother collects damaged people. She's the Pied Piper of damage.'

Deakin's been round to photograph her. When she sees the pictures, she's thrilled. Pleased by how tragic she looks, pleased that her life is in her face. She wants everyone to know that in her face is life in all its tragedy. She's playing the main character in her own drama. When she goes to a night-club with my brother and two of his Cambridge friends, she interrupts the singer, Tom Jones, in the middle of a song. He's crooning a line that goes, 'If you haven't got love, you haven't got anything ...' when my mother shouts from her table, 'It's true! It's true!' The manager comes over and asks if she could be a little quieter.

Today we're anxious. My brother and I have to get her through a family wedding. Uncle Tony's daughter, my first cousin Camilla, is getting married in Wiltshire, on the estate of my aunt's family. After the church service there's a reception in the house, Longford Castle. There are so many guests, so many relations. For some time I lose my mother because I'm going round talking, as people do at weddings. I say to a Tennant cousin of hers, 'You must talk to my mother', then turn round and see my mother about to keel over. I leave the cousin mouthing to no one, and quickly put my arm around her. Her eyes are glazed and she doesn't speak. Holding her upright, I catch David's attention. He comes over quickly and I say, 'We've got to get Mummy out of here. Now. At once.' David takes her other arm and we carry her through the big ancestor-hung rooms, lifting her two inches off the ground to make it look as if she's still walking. We get her out of the house and on to the bus that's taking guests to the station for the return journey to London. Fortunately we don't have to wait long because the reception is nearly over. Other guests soon fill the bus, and we let my mother sleep.

We get her into an empty compartment on the train, put her in a corner and rest her head against the window. It's embarrassing, but when other people come into the compartment they just think, poor woman, she's tired. Then a man comes down the corridor, peers in and recognises my mother. 'Good God! Diana! I haven't seen you for an age.' He's a Bethell relation – rather a wild one, which is rare – and the only response he gets from my mother is the opening of two bleary eyes; her mouth is unable to utter words. The wild relation seems to grasp the picture, and very quickly. He smiles cheerily and says, 'I always told you, Diana, you should have been on the boards.' He gives us a smile, too, and an understanding wink, then moves on down the corridor.

On the platform in London David is furious. 'Why couldn't she control herself?' he says. 'Why did she have to do this today in front of everyone – all those people – her own family.' My mother hasn't come round yet from the handful of barbiturates she took earlier in the day, so she doesn't fully take in what David has said. I look at her face and there's a wall around it. The wall of her own unending sadness.

Later that evening I say to David, 'It's fear of Cicely that made her do it.' Cicely was there. The beak nose, the chilly spectacles that sent my mother back to her room at Rise all those years ago.

That past won't leave my mother, but she brings comfort to others in their suffering. Uncle Jonathan's promise to help my father's second wife came to nothing. So my mother steps in. She makes out a covenant for my stepmother. I find a frightening irony here. Alarming. Very alarming.

I have my mother's uncertainty in me. I move from one job to another, and while I'm working I dream that I will be this or I will be that. Then I think that I must be safe, do nothing risky. Nothing that ends in bouncing cheques and bankruptcy, like my father. I move to a big publishing house in Grosvenor Street. I hate it. I work at a printing plant in Crawley New Town. I hate that too. There is sex. It brings moments of security. But I've discovered this security has to be constantly renewed.

If I didn't stay with my mother, would it be different? Should I move out? There's a young man who visits her, and she's making do with this. She met him in the pub where she goes to listen to her old songs. In the streets they're singing 'Lucy in the Sky with Diamonds' and my mother's swaying to 'Blue Moon'. The young man doesn't have any money. I think my mother gives him some. He sleeps in her bed some nights.

I drift from straight-laced trips to the country, port after dinner and all that, to the raw talk of Soho. My mother's been on her own to the French Pub. She tells me a handsome man came up to her and said, 'You look interesting.'

'And what did you say?'

'I just said, "Perhaps."'

I'm going off to stay with Charles in Hertfordshire. It's a relief going to his family. I'm learning to be young, learning to play around, learning to be my age. At Donne Place it's something I have to forget about. I'm sitting opposite my mother at Donne Place just before I leave and we're talking about her childhood at Rise. She looks towards me and says, 'I don't blame Clare for anything. I never knew her. I blame Cicely. Cicely did the damage.'

I'm thinking it's about equal, but I don't carry on the conversation as I have to leave. My mother stands up as I do and I notice as I'm facing her in the small doorway that her face is drained of colour. She puts her arms round me and hugs me, and as I draw away, the front door open, I say, 'Are you all right, Mummy? You look rather pale.' She says, 'I'm fine, darling. Don't worry. I'm fine.' So I shut the front door behind me, leaving her on her own.

For a few days I push everything to the back of my mind. When I get back I find David at Donne Place. He tells me that Mummy's having a nervous breakdown and the doctor's trying to find a hospital bed for her. David says there's a nurse upstairs with her. I put my head round her bedroom door. She's not conscious, but she's turning round and round in her bed. I hope the doctor can find somewhere to help her soon. David tells me the doctor says we're not to be concerned.

With the nurse upstairs, and nothing for David and me to do but wait, I feel the boxed-in smallness of Donne Place. There's nothing to worry about so I fix up to have a drink with a friend, not far away in Chelsea. Two hours later I come back. As I walk towards our house, I see David standing outside on the pavement. 'Mummy died an hour ago,' he says.

It's so sudden, so shocking, I begin to cry and I can't stop. David walks me up and down the pavement. Up and down Donne Place. He remains very controlled. That's because he knows I'm going to take it hard. My mother's not in the house any more. Already she's on her way to the mortuary.

'How did she die?' I ask David. 'A cerebral haemorrhage,' he tells me. 'So it wasn't a nervous breakdown, it was a haemorrhage coming on.' 'Yes,' he says. 'The doctor misdiagnosed. But if she had recovered it would have been worse. She would have been paralysed, unable to move, even unable to speak, and she might have lived on like that for years.' Instead, it's over. Fifty-one, she was. By a few weeks.

I'm still crying and slowly realising – but most of me not realising – what it means. Neither of us sleeps in Donne Place that night. We go to stay with friends. David in one direction, me in another.

I think of my mother saying, 'Don't put me under those yews.' She didn't want to be buried at Rise. She never did say where, I tell David the next day. And a London cemetery isn't right: too cold, too impersonal, a place where she has no contacts. So I say to David, 'Let's bury Mummy at Wilsford, near to her grandmother. Wilsford was the place where she knew love.'

We've got to tell the family. 'You should have kept more in touch,' says Uncle Tony at Rise. But we did keep in touch. Uncle Tony's life as a squire was too far from what my mother had become. He couldn't handle her. He knew that, but death brings memories, guilt, embarrassment. David writes to Uncle Christopher in Corfu. We get his letter after the funeral, but he's replied quickly all the same. He's distressed. He thought she might have lived far longer with modern medicine. 'Fifty-one is very young to die,' he writes. He's pleased that she's to be buried at Wilsford and says it's quite true that his mother was particularly fond of her. He goes on to say that our mother had a lot of suffering that she had done nothing to deserve. And ends: 'I wonder what will become of you now.'

I can answer that one. I will go on, because one has to. The years have taught me that. There are no options, no alternatives. You go on. That's all. That's it.

Within days David and I are at St Michael's Church, Wilsford. The church and Wilsford Manor, where Great-granny Pamela lived, are separated by only a stretch of lawn; the house, built by my architect grandfather of chequered flint-and-stone in the old Wiltshire style, says, 'I wasn't built yesterday, I've been here for ever.' And below the house, the church, the lawn, the River Avon twisting like shimmering mercury through the marsh.

David and I stand in the church. Two young men alone in black tail-coats. It's July, and a warm day. Wilsford Manor sleeps; Great-uncle Stephen inside it sleeps too. I think of Uncle Stephen, dressed in chiffon, reading my mother fairy stories. Gradually, the relations arrive. Uncle Tony on his own, looking the squire, very solemn. My mother's first cousin, Colin Tennant, not on his island in the West Indies, not entertaining Princess Margaret today. Uncle Harold, dear Uncle Harold, always kept sensitive by my mother to the coldness of Clare. My father's secretary, the highly-strung Ann, whom I used to hear banging at the upright typewriter in Roehampton, with a cigarette hanging from her mouth, and her worried look, coping with my father. Ann, who saw so much in those terrible, unforgotten days.

The local vicar enters, utterly identifiable Church of England: tall, stooped, weathered face and watery eyes. He speaks those lines about taking nothing out of this world – grim lines that offer no comfort. I stand in the front pew next to my brother, a few yards away from the coffin, a box of new wood with my mother inside, inside until she crumbles away. Then come the hymns: 'Dear Lord and Father of Mankind,' the choir from nearby Amesbury sings, '. . . The silence of eternity interpreted by love.' The funeral sentences sung to the music of Purcell: 'Man that is born of Woman has but a short time to live.' And then something not at all Church of England but chosen by David and me: 'Ithaca', a poem by the Greek poet Constantine Cavafy. We think of my mother's journey into knowledge, knowledge of life, and like the poet's journey to Ithaca, one where there was always a dream, a dream not fulfilled.

'It's rather outside the Anglican canon,' the vicar said as he read through the poem before the service. 'But I'll make an exception,' and he smiled gently, through his watery eyes.

David and I stand on either side as the coffin is lowered into the grave. I think of my mother saying, when she thought of her end and its finality, 'What am I going to do down there? What? Six feet under.' I don't know what you're going to do, Mummy. I only hope that it's better there than it's been up here for you.

I cried for five days. In the mornings when I woke the tears started. I had no control over them. All sorts of things in my head going back over the years. Perhaps I won't cry much again. I'm going to make myself tough. I've seen people doing this. I'm not crying now.

A cousin of my mother's has lent us her cottage, which is next to Wilsford, and we go there after the burial. I'm just going in when I hear loud heavy footsteps. I turn, and see Uncle Jonathan bearing down on me with his mannequin wife by his side. 'My dear Simon,' he says. Just that. He's really large now and he's wearing tails. He's missed the service, but he offers no apology. Anxious to get to the gathering, he steams past me and in no time I see him talking to my mother's cousin, Colin. I don't know what they're talking about. Eton, perhaps. Or Uncle Jonathan's on about the problems of running an estate. He's very keen on discussing that. He makes Hilles sound like twenty thousand acres, not nine hundred.

What would my mother say if she knew he was at her funeral? She'd laugh. A Bethell cousin, whom we call Cousin Enid, is here, pushing her daughter, Felicity, in a wheelchair. Felicity, who caught polio at the age of eighteen. Cousin Enid, bright and sparky, is now in her seventies. She grabs me affectionately. 'What a moving service. Poor Diana. I have such memories of her at Rise. Tony was in tears throughout. Couldn't stop sobbing.'

Memories, feelings, surface at funerals. Funny, that. As if you can't have them any other time. Uncle Tony in tears. Funny that, too.

'There was a thing to do. And it is done now. The high song is over.' That line my mother often quoted towards the end. She'd found it in something she was reading by Humbert Wolfe, a poet long forgotten. I go back to the grave and think on it.

But that song. I heard it. I hear it. It's still there.

18

I'm ALONE IN Donne Place. David's gone back to work in Iran and the house is being sold to pay the death duties. The bungalow in Le Lavendou is being sold too. After that there's a bit for David and me. Mark's money, that is. The money he said was pure charity. Nothing's changed in the house since my mother died six months ago. But I'm starting to clear stuff out. A friend is helping. She's clearing my mother's bedroom. 'It's amazing, Simon,' she says, 'I've found your mother's comb. There's hair in it, as if she's still alive.' 'She isn't alive,' I say. 'She'll never be alive again.'

I turn the pages of the wedding book, and read the captions. 'Society girl's romance.' 'Her mother is a beauty.' 'For her it's wedding bells.' 'Hunting beauty and chic.' And so they go on, talking of a time I never knew. Then I think, where is that hamper in the attic? Lost. Gone. Where's Fuzziepeg, the koala bear who caught my tears? Lost. Gone. Where's Michael, who held me close when things were bad? Lost. Gone. Aunt Phyllie. Ragdale. Mr Ward, polishing the leather. Jean, Aunt Phyllie's maid, reading to me in bed. The rooks in the park at Ragdale, circling the high trees, cawing, cawing. The list won't end. Tears start – but no. No more tears. Remember. Remember. There is tomorrow. That's what she said.

ACKNOWLEDGEMENTS

The author and publishers wish to thank the following for permission to reproduce copyright material: 'The Man That Got Away', pp. 94 and 262, words and music by Harold Arlen and Ira Gershwin © 1954 Harwin Music Corp. and Chappell Morris Ltd, Warner Chappell Music Publishing Ltd, London W6 8BS; 'Blue Moon', p. 123, words and music by Richard Rodgers and Lorenz Hart © 1934 EMI Catalogue Partnership, EMI Robbins Catalog Inc. and EMI United Partnership. Worldwide Print Rights Controlled by Warner Bros. INC, USA/IMP Ltd; 'Cool Water', p. 132, words and music by Bob Nolan © 1936 American Music Inc. and B. Feldman & Co. Ltd, EMI Music Publishing Ltd, London WC2H 0EA. All lyrics reproduced by permission of International Music Publications Limited.